I. Kirsch

INSTRUCTIONAL THEORIES IN ACTION

INSTRUCTIONAL THEORIES IN ACTION

Lessons Illustrating Selected Theories and Models

edited by

Charles M. Reigeluth

 LAWRENCE ERLBAUM ASSOCIATES, PUBLISHERS

1987   Hillsdale, New Jersey   Hove and London

Lawrence Erlbaum Associates, Inc., Publishers
365 Broadway
Hillsdale, New Jersey 07642

Library of Congress Cataloging-in-Publication Data

Instructional theories in action.

    Bibliography: p.
    Includes index.
    1. Lesson planning.   2. Teaching.   I. Reigeluth,
Charles M.

LB1027.4.I57   1987   371.3   86-24215
ISBN 0-89859-825-7

Printed in the United States of America
10 9 8 7 6 5 4 3 2

This book is dedicated to all students of the instructional process, in the hope that it will help them do a better job at one of the noblest pursuits of humankind—helping others to learn.

Contents

List of Contributors

ALLAN COLLINS • Bolt, Beranek & Newman, Inc., 50 Moulton Street, Cambridge, MA 2138

GEORGE GROPPER • Apt. 1005, 4 Longfellow Place., Boston, MA 02114

JOHN KELLER • College of Education-ERDF, 305B Stone Building, Florida State University, Tallahassee, FL 32306

TOM KOPP • Miami University, Oxford, OH 45056

LEV LANDA • 41-57 76th Street, Elmhurst, NY 11373

M. DAVID MERRILL • Instructional Technology Dept., Utah State University, Logan, UT 84322

HARRY MOUTON • School of Education, 330 Huntington Hall, Syracuse University, Syracuse, NY 13244.

BARBARA PETRY • 2122 Lakeshore Avenue, Apt. 303, Oakland, CA 94606

CHARLES M. REIGELUTH • School of Education, 330 Huntington Hall, Syracuse University, Syracuse, NY 13244

Joseph M. Scandura • Learning, Instructional Systems Design
and Computer-Based Instruction, 3700 Walnut Street, University of
Pennsylvania, Philadelphia, PA 19104

Glenn Snelbecker • Temple University, 217 Ritter Annex, T.U.
004–00, Philadelphia, PA 19122

George Stevens • American College of Healthcare Executives, 840
North Lakeshore Drive, Chicago, IL 60611

Preface

This book provides an introduction to instructional strategies for prospective instructional designers, teachers, trainers in business and industry, and educational psychologists. It is designed as a companion to *Instructional Design Theories and Models: An Overview of their Current Status,* published in 1983. Although this book comes later, it is a simpler, more concrete introduction to the same eight theories that the earlier book describes in considerably greater detail. It is simpler because it describes only the most important prescriptions of each theory and because it describes them in less detail. It is more concrete because each theory is illustrated by a lesson. Furthermore, comments identify which prescriptions from the theory are being implemented at each point in the lesson. Chapter forewords and editor's footnotes help to compare and contrast the theories, and study questions are also provided. After reading this book, you may wish to seek a deeper understanding of the theories by referring to the more detailed "green book," as it is (affectionately) called.

It is my hope that this book will serve a variety of purposes:

1. that it will *excite* you about the power and utility of our growing knowledge regarding what instructional techniques to use when in order to make your instruction more effective and appealing,
2. that it will introduce you to a broad range of *techniques* to use to make your instruction more effective and appealing,
3. that it will facilitate *comparison* of the various techniques prescribed by the different theories, so you will gain greater insight as to
   - when the theories are prescribing the same techniques for the same

situation, only with different terminology (in which case they duplicate each other),

- when they are prescribing different techniques for the same situation (in which case they contradict, or compete with, each other), and
- when they are prescribing different techniques for different situations (in which case they are compatible with each other and can be integrated into a single, more comprehensive theory of instruction), and finally

4. that it will facilitate *integration* of the various theories, so that we will have a more powerful knowledge base for making our instruction more effective and appealing.

We are now working on the next step beyond these two books: integrating all useful prescriptions into a common knowledge base, with a consistent set of terminology. Our intention is to put it into a form that is easy for practitioners to use,

- to *produce* instructional systems or resources,
- to *improve* existing instructional systems or resources, and
- to *select* the best available instructional systems or resources.

If you have any suggestions, please write! We would appreciate all the input we can get.

C.M.R.

INSTRUCTIONAL
THEORIES
IN ACTION

1 Introduction

Charles M. Reigeluth
Syracuse University

WHAT IS INSTRUCTIONAL THEORY?

The purpose of the field of instruction is to provide educators and trainers with prescriptions for making their instruction more effective and appealing. Over the past 20 years, methods of instruction (such as expository and discovery) have been analyzed to identify fairly elementary components that comprise them, such as examples, feedback, visual representations, and mnemonics. Many prescriptions for the use of such strategy components have been generated and validated since the mid 1960s. However, those prescriptions are mostly piecemeal—isolated bits and pieces that do not take into consideration the full range of components that a given unit of instruction should have.

Clearly, what teachers, textbook writers, and other instructional developers need are prescriptions that are more integrated and more comprehensive. This is what *prescriptive instructional theories* are meant to offer: They prescribe optimal combinations of strategy components for different situations. The few efforts that have been undertaken to achieve a measure of comprehensiveness have mostly produced independent and relatively incomplete knowledge bases, and most use inconsistent terminology. Hence, this book and its more advanced companion, *Instructional-Design Theories and Models: An Overview of Their Current Status* (Reigeluth, 1983), represent but a small step forward in a sorely needed integrative effort. The companion volume provides a thorough description of each of the theories illustrated in this volume, whereas each chapter in this volume provides a summary of the prescriptions for a theory, followed by a lesson and commentary that illustrate and explain each prescription.

Instructional theory addresses two questions: What methods should be used in

1

the design of instruction? and when should each be used? These two concerns can be labeled as *methods* and *situations*. Statements that link situations and methods are called "principles" or "theories."

Methods of Instruction.   Methods may be individual *strategy components*, the elementary building blocks from which methods are created. Or they may be *models* of instruction: sets of strategy components that have been combined to optimize the quality of the instruction.

Situations of Instruction.   How do you know when a certain method of instruction should be used? One way is to examine the instructional *outcomes:* the effects of each method. However, it has been found that the same method can have different effects under different *conditions*. Conditions include such variables as the nature of the content or learning task, the nature of the learners, and the nature of the institutional setting. Together, the desired outcomes and the conditions constitute the situations, or the bases for prescribing when to use each strategy component or each model of instruction.

Principles of Instruction.   A *descriptive* principle of instruction describes the effects of a single strategy component. It identifies the likely outcome(s) for a given strategy component under given condition(s). A *prescriptive* principle of instruction, on the other hand, prescribes when the strategy component should be used. It identifies the strategy component that should be used for a given desired outcome and condition(s).

Theories of Instruction.   A *descriptive* theory of instruction describes the effects of a whole model of instruction (integrated set of strategy components), instead of just the effects of a single strategy component. A *prescriptive* theory of instruction prescribes when a given model or set of models should be used. It identifies the instructional model that should be used for a given desired outcome and condition(s). The more comprehensive an instructional theory is, the more models it prescribes for different kinds of desired outcomes and conditions.

HISTORICAL TRENDS

The field of instruction, like most disciplines, began with an emphasis on *philosophical* concerns, which entailed the expression of opinions and conjecture (see, e.g., Dewey, 1916). With the advent of Skinner's focus on programmed instruction in the 1950s, this phase finally (considering that education is one of the oldest professions) gave way to a focus on *validated prescriptions,* which require the scientific testing of opinions and conjecture through research. As with other disciplines, initial research on instruction tended to focus on very general, vague variables, such as discovery versus expository methods and lecture versus discussion formats. However, in that research two different discovery methods often differed more than an expository and a discovery method differed, making it impossible to identify reliable causes of superior outcomes.

Therefore, the discipline soon entered an *analysis* phase, during which phenomena were broken down into manageable components upon which research was conducted (see, e.g., Evans, Homme, & Glaser, 1964). Today much piecemeal knowledge about the effects of different instructional strategy components has been generated and validated. However, it is also common for the analysis phase in a discipline to be followed by a *synthesis* phase, during which that piecemeal knowledge is integrated into progressively more comprehensive models and theories. Although there are signs that such a synthesis phase has begun in the field of instruction, our educational and training problems today are such that we cannot afford to drag our feet in this endeavor. There is a strong need for much more work to integrate our current knowledge into optimal models of instruction, each of which is prescribed for different kinds of instructional situations.

In response to this need, the editor and authors of this book wrote *Instructional Design Theories and Models: An Overview of Their Current Status* (1983). Its primary purpose was to contribute to an integration of instructional prescriptions. That book assembled and described the most comprehensive and thorough of those instructional theories that are still undergoing some further development, to the best knowledge of the editor. (Other notable instructional theories include the various instructional prescriptions of Ausubel, 1968; Bruner, 1960, 1966; and Skinner, 1954, 1965; all of which are no longer under development; and the more recent prescriptions of Bloom, 1976, 1981; Case, 1978a, 1978b; Lawson & Lawson, 1980; Markle, 1978; and Rothkopf, 1981; all of which are, in the editor's opinion, of narrower scope of detailed instructional prescriptions than those included here.) That book went beyond assembling and describing the theories illustrated in this volume; it also attempted to facilitate integration into a common knowledge base through chapter forewords and extensive editor's notes that compared and contrasted individual prescriptions and that assessed overall strengths (unique contributions) and weaknesses (omissions) of each theory.

WHY THIS BOOK?

Understanding.   The primary purpose of this book is to help educators and trainers to create more effective and appealing instruction by making it easier to understand the various methods of instruction that are prescribed by these prominent instructional theories. Each of the original theorists (with one exception) has developed a lesson that illustrates most of the methods that his theory prescribes. Therefore, this book provides a more *concrete understanding* of the instructional theories than does the companion volume. In addition, each author has written numbered comments that identify the specific prescription from his theory that is being implemented at each point in the lesson. These comments have been written in such a way that they are understandable to a reader who has not read the earlier book. Because this book is a more concrete description of the instructional theories, we recommend that someone new to these theories read this book before the earlier book.

Comparison.   Another important purpose of this book is to facilitate comparison and contrast of these instructional theories. As one author has put it (Gropper, 1983), most of the theories represented here were developed as "independent knowledge bases" with entirely different terminologies. By having all authors develop their lessons for the *same* set of objectives and test items (see p. 5), it is easier for the reader to cut through the terminology differences and make direct comparisons among the instructional theories. Editor's Notes have been added to further facilitate such comparisons.

Integration.   A third important purpose in producing this book is to contribute to the integration of our existing knowledge about instruction. It is our hope that this book will show that, rather than competing with each other, these theories complement each other. There are many commonalities among these theories: that is, many theories prescribe the same methods for the same situations (all in different terminology, though!). Most of the differences in methods prescribed by the theories are due to differences in the situations for which they are prescribed. For example, a discovery approach may be appropriate in some cases but not in others. It would hardly be appropriate for teaching a group of surgeons the latest technique in their field. This book can help draw attention to the need to view instructional theories not as competing with each other but as making *unique contributions* to a truly integrated, comprehensive set of prescriptions for creating effective and appealing instruction. An educator or trainer will benefit by having *all* of these various methods of instruction in his or her repertoire.

Chapter Format

Each chapter has three main sections: an introduction, a lesson, and a set of comments. The *introduction* presents a summary of the theory's major prescriptions. Occasionally, some general information about the overall design of the lesson is also included here. The *lesson* may take a variety of forms. The authors were advised that the lesson "may be in the form of written materials, a sample dialogue between teacher and student(s), a 'map' showing how the topics might be sequenced within a complete course, a description (including drawings, etc.) of any nonprint media that would be used, or any combination of the above." In the lesson, a bracketed number appears in the margin opposite each characteristic of the lesson for which the author has written a comment. All *comments* appear in the third section of the chapter, and they explain what prescription is being implemented at that particular point in the lesson. Occasional reference is made to pages in the earlier book where more detailed descriptions of the prescriptions can be found.

Each chapter's lesson covers the same set of objectives and test items, both of which are listed in the next section. Although the objectives were selected to provide a broad sample of types of learning, the authors were all encouraged to include additional objectives if such were necessary to adequately illustrate important aspects of their theories. If any of the standard objectives (listed below) were inappropriate for a given theory, the author was instructed to indicate so and to not include it in the lesson.

Objectives and Test Items

Our desire was to choose a set of objectives that are broadly representative of real-world learning tasks. In particular, we wanted to include some objectives that require remembering information and others that require skill application, and within the domain of skill application we wanted to include a variety of types of skills or content. The following are the objectives that were decided upon:

1. Students will be able to classify previously unencountered lenses as to whether or not they are convex lenses.
2. Students will be able to define focal length.
3. Students will be able to explain or predict what effect different convex lenses will have on light rays.
4. Students will be able to explain the way in which the curvature of a lens influences both the magnification and the focal length of different lenses.
5. Students will be able to state from memory the three significant events in the history of the microscope.
6. Students will be able to use a previously unencountered optical microscope properly.

Using *Gagné's* (1977) terminology, these objectives are of two domains: verbal information (Objectives 2, 4, and 5) and intellectual skills (Objectives 1, 3, and 6). Within the intellectual skills domain, the desired behaviors include concept classification (Objective 1) and rule using (Objectives 3 and 6). Using *Merrill's* (Merrill, 1983) terminology, these objectives are of two levels: remember (Objectives 2, 4, and 5) and use (Objectives 1, 3, and 6). Within the use level, the content types include concept (Objective 1), principle (Objective 3), and procedure (Objective 6). Notably absent are any objectives for Gagné's "cognitive strategies" domain, or Merrill's "find" level, largely because the amount or length of instruction that is required to teach such objectives is prohibitively large for an undertaking such as this book.

Just as examples serve as concrete illustrations of a rule or generality, so test items serve as concrete illustrations of an objective. The following test items were supplied to the authors of the lessons in this book.

Objective 1. Students will be able to classify previously unencountered lenses as to whether or not they are convex lenses.

5. In the following picture (Fig. 1.1), place a check mark beside the lenses that are convex.

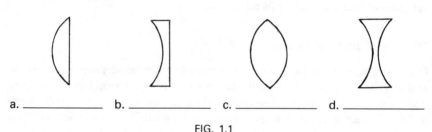

a. _____   b. _____   c. _____   d. _____

FIG. 1.1

12. Examine the lenses on the table and write down the letter of each one that is convex. (Eight samples are given.)

Objective 2. Students will be able to define focal length.

6. What does the term "focal length" mean?

Objective 3. Students will be able to explain or predict what effect different convex lenses will have on light rays.

7. Explain what will happen to the light rays in Fig. 1.2 by drawing their path through and beyond the lens:

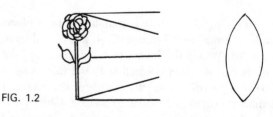

FIG. 1.2

13. (a) Rank the lenses on the table according to the degree to which they bend light rays, that is, the lens that bends light rays the most would be

number 1, and the one that bends light rays the least would be number 6, with the others falling in between. Place the letter of each lens next to its appropriate rank. (Six samples are given.)

(1)   (4)
(2)   (5)
(3)   (6)

(b) Explain why number 1 should bend light rays the most and why number 6 should bend them the least.

Objective 4.   Students will be able to explain the way in which the curvature of a lens influences both the magnification and the focal length of different lenses.

8. In the picture in Fig. 1.3, place a check mark by the lens that has the *shortest* focal length.

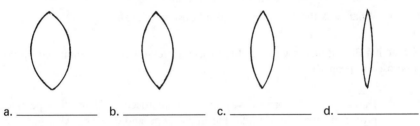

a. _____   b. _____   c. _____   d. _____

FIG. 1.3

9. In the picture in Fig. 1.4, place a check mark by the lens that has the greatest degree of magnification.

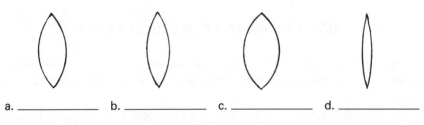

a. _____   b. _____   c. _____   d. _____

FIG. 1.4

14. (a) Rank the lenses on the table according to the height they must be held in order to make the rays converge to a point on the table top. Thus, the lens that should be nearest the table top will be number 1, while the

one that should be furthest will be number 4. Place the letter of each lens next to its appropriate rank. (Four samples are given.)

(1)   (3)
(2)   (4)

(b) Explain why number 1 should be nearest the table and why number 4 should be furthest.

Objective 5.   Students will be able to state from memory the three significant events in the history of the microscope.

1. What was the first type of magnifying glass used, and when was it first used?
2. When were glass lenses (of the type now used) first introduced?
3. Who developed the first compound microscope?
4. When was the first compound microscope developed?

Objective 6.   Students will be able to use a previously unencountered optical microscope properly.

10. Demonstrate the proper way to use a microscope: Using the specimen provided, examine it under the microscope and describe what you see
    (a) using the low-power objective
    (b) using the intermediate-power objective, and
    (c) using the high-power objective.
11. (Same as 10 but use different microscope and specimen.)

SUGGESTIONS FOR READING THIS BOOK

Discovery Approach.   To facilitate deeper understanding of and greater ability to use the prescriptions contained in this book, we suggest the following:

1. Read the portion of the lesson that corresponds to the first numbered comment.
2. Try to guess what the comment says, based on the chapter introduction or your own intuition.
3. Look at the numbered comment to see how close you were.
4. Continue this process for each remaining numbered comment.

Expository Approach.   If you want to take the easier (but less fruitful) route, we suggest the following:

1. Read the portion of the lesson that corresponds to the first numbered comment. While reading, keep a finger in the comments section so that you can easily flip to the numbered comment as the number is encountered in the lesson.
2. Read the numbered comment, while keeping a finger in the lesson section so that you can easily flip back to it.
3. Return to the lesson to see each aspect of it that the comment identified.
4. Continue this process for each remaining numbered comment.

If you prefer an abstract rather than concrete approach, you could skip step 1.

You ought to keep in mind the objectives and test items in any attempt to evaluate the lessons that follow. However, please also consider that the authors were encouraged to supplement these objectives with any others that they felt were necessary to illustrate important aspects of their respective theories.

Try to concentrate on comparing the theories to find ways that they duplicate each other and ways that they complement each other. Try also to identify how these theories might be integrated into a single comprehensive knowledge base— that is, what prescriptions each theory would contribute to such a knowledge base—and what form might best depict such a comprehensive knowledge base. Then publish your conclusions and share them with us! We would be delighted to see them. Together we can push back the frontiers of instructional design and build a truly useful knowledge base for designers.

REFERENCES

Ausubel, D. P. (1968). *Educational psychology: A cognitive view.* New York: Holt, Rinehart & Winston.

Bloom, B. S. (1976). *Human characteristics and school learning.* New York: McGraw-Hill.

Bloom, B. S. (1981). *All our children learning.* New York: McGraw-Hill.

Bruner, J. S. (1960). *The process of education.* New York: Random House.

Bruner, J. S. (1966). *Toward a theory of instruction.* New York: W. W. Norton.

Case, R. (1978a). Piaget and beyond: Toward a developmentally based theory and technology of instruction. In R. Glaser (Ed.), *Advances in instructional psychology* (Vol. 1). Hillsdale, NJ: Lawrence Erlbaum Associates.

Case, R. (1978b). A developmentally based theory and technology of instruction. *Review of Educational Research, 48,* 439–463.

Dewey, J. (1916). *Democracy and education.* New York: Macmillan.

Evans, J. L., Homme, L. E., & Glaser, R. (1962). The RulEg system for the construction of programmed verbal learning sequences. *Journal of Educational Research, 55,* 573–578.

Gagné, R. M. (1977). *The conditions of learning and theory of instruction* (3rd ed.). New York: Holt, Rinehart & Winston.

Gropper, G. L. (1983). A behavioral approach to instructional prescription. In C. M. Reigeluth (Ed.), *Instructional-design theories and models: An overview of their current status*. Hillsdale, NJ: Lawrence Erlbaum Associates.

Lawson, A. E., & Lawson, C. A. (1980). A theory of teaching for conceptual understanding, rational thought, and creativity. *The psychology of teaching for thinking and creativity* (1980 AETS Yearbook, pp. 104–149). Columbus, OH: Ohio State University.

Markle, S. M. (1978). *Designs for instructional designers*. Champaign, IL: Stipes Publishing.

Merrill, M. D. (1983). Component display theory. In C. M. Reigeluth (Ed.), *Instructional-design theories and models: An overview of their current status*. Hillsdale, NJ: Lawrence Erlbaum Associates.

Reigeluth, C. M. (Ed.) (1983). *Instructional-design theories and models: An overview of their current status*. Hillsdale, NJ: Lawrence Erlbaum Associates.

Rothkopf, E. Z. (1981). A macroscopic model of instruction and purposive learning: An overview. *Instructional Science, 10*, 105–122.

Skinner, B. F. (1954). The science of learning and the art of teaching. *Harvard Educational Review, 24*(2), 86–97.

Skinner, B. F. (1965). Reflections on a decade of teaching machines. In R. Glaser (Ed.), *Teaching machines and programmed learning*, II. Washington, D.C.: National Education Association.

2 A Lesson Based on the Gagné-Briggs Theory of Instruction

Barbara Petry, Harry Mouton,
Charles M. Reigeluth
Syracuse University

FOREWORD

History

The Gagné-Briggs theory of instruction was first developed in the 1960s, although its development has continued to date. It is affectionately known by many as the granddaddy of instructional theories. It was the first major attempt to integrate a wide range of knowledge about learning and instruction (from many theoretical perspectives) into a comprehensive theory of instruction. Its impact on the field has been immense.

Unique Contributions

One of the most outstanding features of the Gagné-Briggs instructional theory is that it is so comprehensive. It prescribes the nature of instruction for all three of Bloom's domains of knowledge: cognitive, affective, and psychomotor; and within the cognitive domain it prescribes methods for teaching verbal information (remember-level knowledge), intellectual skills (application of generalizable knowledge), and cognitive strategies (the higher thought processes).

This instructional theory is also comprehensive in the breadth of instructional strategies that it prescribes. The nine events of instruction include gaining the learners' attention, presenting objectives, and stimulating recall of relevant prior knowledge, all of which have tended to be overlooked by more recent instructional theories. In fairness, however, it should be pointed out that many of the more recent theorists have opted to sacrifice breadth in order to achieve greater depth, that is, to provide more detailed guidance for instructional designers and teachers. The net result is that the Gagné-Briggs theory provides a comprehensive framework within which much of the more recent work can be subsumed.

In addition to the nine events of instruction, this theory provides unique prescriptions for the selection and sequencing of content. Once a terminal objective has been identified within the intellectual skills category, the designer/instructor should identify its learning prerequisites (simpler component skills) that the learners have not yet mastered, and those prerequisites should be taught. With respect to sequencing, Gagné-Briggs proposes a hierarchical sequence in which the simpler component skills are taught before the more complex skills of which they are a part.

Similarities

The Gagné-Briggs theory of instruction has a number of prescriptions in common with other instructional theories, such as presenting the stimulus material, providing learning guidance of various kinds, requiring overt responses (practice) from the learners, and providing feedback about those responses. These and other similarities are identified in the chapter with Editor's Notes.

Issues to Think About

One important issue is how to operationalize the prescriptions provided by this instructional theory. Because of its breadth, this theory offers few specific instructions for implementation. For example, how should one go about providing learning guidance? To what extent do the other instructional theories in this book provide such operationalization? And to what extent does this theory provide a vehicle for integrating all the diverse prescriptions of the theories in this book into a common knowledge base about instruction?

STUDY QUESTIONS

1. What are the five categories of human learned capabilities?
2. Why is it useful to distinguish the five categories?
3. What are the five types of intellectual skills?
4. What relationship exists among those five types of intellectual skills?
5. What prescriptions do Gagné-Briggs make with respect to the sequence in which instructional content should be presented to the learners?
6. What are the nine events of instruction?
7. For what situations does each event differ?
8. How does each of the nine events of instruction differ for each such situation?

C.M.R.

INTRODUCTION TO THE THEORY

Over the years, Robert Gagné and Leslie Briggs developed a wide variety of instructional prescriptions (Briggs, 1977; Briggs & Wager, 1981; Gagné, 1974, 1985; Gagné & Briggs, 1979). Taken together, these prescriptions constitute a theory of instruction, because different methods of instruction are prescribed for different situations. Gagné also developed a theory about how learning occurs, and Briggs developed many instructional development procedures; but neither of these two important contributions is the focus of this chapter. This chapter describes the Gagné-Briggs prescriptions about what instruction should be like for any given situation, and it illustrates those prescriptions in a lesson, along with commentary about which prescription is being implemented at each point in the lesson.

The Gagné-Briggs theory of instruction is comprised of three major sets of prescriptions: It prescribes different methods of instruction for each of five categories of **learned capabilities:** it identifies nine **events of instruction,** which should usually comprise the instruction intended to develop any desired capability; and it prescribes a way to **sequence** instruction based on intellectual skills. These three sets of prescriptions are described next, followed by the lesson and then by the commentary on the prescriptions used in the design of the lesson.

The Categories of Learned Capabilities

For the purposes of designing instruction, Gagné (1984, 1985) describes five categories of human learned capabilities, each of which requires different instructional prescriptions.* These are:

1. Verbal information.
2. Intellectual skills, which have five subcategories
   A. discriminations
   B. concrete concepts
   C. defined concepts
   D. rules
   E. higher-order rules (problem solving).
3. Cognitive strategies.
4. Attitudes.
5. Motor skills.

Before instruction can be designed and developed, it is necessary to identify the category into which the desired learned capability fits. This is because the

---

*The use of types of objectives as the basis for prescribing methods of instruction is also an important part of the theories of Merrill (p. 204) and Gropper (p. 52).

instruction differs for each category. The critical attributes of each category are described below.

Verbal Information.   Individuals have learned verbal information when they are able to recall it. They may write, type, s.ate, or recite such information as names, labels, sentences, arguments, single propositions, or groups of related propositions.*

Intellectual Skills.   Individuals use an intellectual skill when they show competence or interact with the environment using symbols or language. They show they know how to do something of an intellectual sort. Details of Gagné's five intellectual skills follow.†

> *Discriminations.* Learners discriminate when they state whether things are the same or different. The may discriminate along one or more physical dimensions. They may discriminate, for example, sizes, colors, shapes, and sounds. This is a very basic intellectual skill.
>
> *Concrete concepts.* Learners have acquired a concrete concept when they can identify previously unencountered instances of a class of objects, class of object properties, or class of events by instant recognition. Concepts of this type are identified by pointing at them or marking them in some manner— they do not have to be, and usually cannot be, identified by means of a definition. "Ball," "wheel," "penny," "triangle," and "rectangle" are examples of concrete concepts.
>
> *Defined concepts.* Learners have acquired a defined concept when they use a definition to put something they have not previously encountered into a class (or some things into classes). Their behavior shows that they know the parameters of the class or classes. Concepts such as "family," "alien," "nucleus," "igneous rock," and "electrical resistance" are defined concepts.‡
>
> *Rules.* Learners have acquired a rule when they can demonstrate its application to previously unencountered instances. A rule is a relation between two or more concepts. An example is the use of "Ohm's law," represented by $V = IR$, to solve electrical circuit problems.§
>
> *Higher-order rules (problem solving).* When learners use two or more pre-

---

*Verbal information is similar to Merrill's "remember-instance" and "remember-generality" (p. 203) and Gropper's "recall or apply facts" (p. 51).

†Intellectual skills are similar to Merrill's "use" level of performance (p. 203).

‡Concrete and defined concepts (and perhaps discriminations as well) are equivalent to Merrill's "use concepts" (p. 203) and Gropper's "apply definitions to examples or illustrate them with examples" (p. 51).

§Rules correspond to Merrill's "use procedures" and "use principles" (p. 203) and Gropper's "follow procedural rules" (p. 51).

viously learned rules to answer a question about an unfamiliar situation, they are attaining a higher-order rule by problem solving. Success with a problem-solving exercise involves mastery of a set of concepts and rules that must then be combined to solve the problem. In addition, because the situation itself is unfamiliar, the learners must search out and choose which rules to use. In physics, different "projectile motion" problems require the use of different combinations and sequences among the various "laws of motion" for their solution.*

Cognitive Strategies. Learners have acquired cognitive strategies when they have developed ways to improve the effectiveness and efficiency of their own intellectual and learning processes; when they can learn independently; when they can propose and solve original problems. Breaking a problem into parts, working backwards from the solution, summarizing text, and using mnemonics are examples of cognitive strategies.† Although Gagné (1985) describes cognitive strategies applicable to attending, learning, and remembering, the examples used in this section include only problem-solving strategies, following Gagné and Briggs (1979).

Attitudes. Attitudes are complex mental states of human beings that affect their choices of personal action towards people, things, and events. Learners have an attitude when they choose to make consistent choices in repeated situations. Behavior in a single situation is not an indication of an attitude. Rather, consistent behavior in a variety of similar situations indicates that the attitude exists. Consistent choices of personal action such as preferring rock music to classical, driving within the speed limit, being honest, and being afraid of snakes reflect attitudes that have been learned.‡

Motor Skills. Learners have developed a motor skill when they perform a physical task utilizing equipment or materials according to a routinized procedure. Their behavior says nothing of their ability to recognize a need to apply the procedure to a specific problem; they can merely carry out the procedure correctly, with appropriate speed, accuracy, force, and smoothness. Driving a

---

*Problem solving is the same as Merrill's "find" (p. 203) and Gropper's "solving problems" (p. 51).

†Cognitive strategies are the same as Landa's "general, content-independent abilities" (p. 123) and Scandura's "higher-order rules" (p. 165) and are somewhat similar to Merrill's "find" level of performance (p. 203).

‡This theory is unique among the ones in this book in addressing methods for teaching attitudes and outcomes. Even Keller's prescriptions, which deal exclusively with affective considerations, address attitudes and motives only insofar as they are means for achieving cognitive ends rather than as ends in themselves for which optimal means need to be prescribed.

car, throwing a ball, climbing a rope, driving a golf ball, and correctly using a woodturning machine are examples of motor skills.*

Identifying the category of learned capability into which the desired learning fits is important because Gagné and Briggs prescribe different methods of instruction for each category of learned capabili.y. For further descriptions of the learned capabilities, see Gagné (1984, 1985) and Gagné and Briggs (1979).

The Events of Instruction

Once the desired learning outcomes have been identified and classified as previously described, the instructional methods most appropriate for the desired outcomes can be prescribed. In learning theory, the information-processing model describes the act of learning as an internal process that has several stages. Gagné (1985) proposes that those stages are enhanced by means of a specific order of instructional methods he calls "the events of instruction." The events of instruction establish the internal and external "conditions of learning" essential for the various types of learned capability to be learned. More extensive accounts of the relationship between the learning theory, the internal and external conditions of learning, and the events of instruction can be found in Gagné (1985) and Gagné and Briggs (1979).

Gagné (1985) has identified nine events of instruction for any desired learning (see Fig. 2.1). He argues that these nine different events must always be considered as potential ways of providing external support for the internal act of learning. Furthermore, he proposes that the nature of the instruction in an event should differ depending on the category of learned capability expected as the outcome of the instruction. "Learning intellectual skills requires a different design of instructional events from those required for learning verbal information or those required for learning motor skills, and so on" (p. 245). The next section describes the different events in light of the various learned capabilities (adapted from Gagné, 1985; Gagné & Briggs, 1979; and Gagné, Wager, & Rojas, 1981).

1. Gaining Attention

For *all* learned capability outcomes the attention of the students is gained by introducing rapid stimulus changes. For group instruction, gesturing, raising the voice, and providing a highly visual demonstration may gain the students' attention. Use of words such as "Look!" or "Watch!" can help. For computer-assisted instruction, rapidly changing visual displays are useful. For individualized instruction, provide a variety of novel situations designed to appeal to the students' interest and curiosity. For all presentation forms, matching the

---

*The only other theories in this book that address motor skills at all are Landa's and Gropper's. Neither addresses them to the extent that Gagné and Briggs do.

1. Gaining attention
2. Informing the learner of the lesson objective
3. Stimulating recall of prior learning
4. Presenting the stimulus material with distinctive features
5. Providing learning guidance
6. Eliciting performance
7. Providing informative feedback
8. Assessing performance
9. Enhancing retention and learning transfer

FIG. 2.1   The nine events of instruction.

stimulus to the content is also advantageous. For *problem solving,* raise the learners' curiosity by presenting a hypothetical situation or by asking a rhetorical question.*

2. Informing the Learner of the Lesson Objective(s)

"When learners comprehend the objective of instruction, they will acquire an expectancy that normally persists throughout the time learning is taking place and that will be confirmed by the feedback given when learning is complete" (Gagné, 1985, p. 247). Providing learners with the objective of the instruction helps them answer that very important question, "How will I know when I have learned?" Following is a summary of the different instructional techniques that inform the learner of the objective for each of the learning capabilities:†

Verbal information. State in simple terms what the learner will be able to say or do after he or she has learned.

Intellectual skill. Describe and demonstrate the activity to which the concept, rule, or procedure applies.

Cognitive strategy. Clarify the nature of the solution expected and describe or demonstrate the strategy. A verbal communication may be very effective.

Attitude. As providing the objective would defeat the purpose of the instruction, the learner should be informed later, after he or she has chosen to behave in the appropriate manner (see Event 5).

Motor skill. Demonstrate the expected performance.

---

*This strategy component is not directly addressed by any of the other theories in this book except for Keller's (p. 293), and there are even important differences there (see p. 293 for details).

†This strategy is similarly not directly addressed by any of the other theories in this book except for Keller's (p. 294).

17

3. Stimulating Recall of Prior Learning

Before engaging in the instruction, the learner is asked to recall some things previously learned. What is to be recalled should be naturally related to the new learning. The kinds of things recalled are different for each of the different learned capabilities desired as outcomes.*

Verbal information. Stimulate recall of well-organized and previously learned bodies of knowledge. This could be done by an "advance organizer" (Ausubel, 1960), by "adjunct questions" (Rothkopf, 1970), or by summaries and outlines.

Intellectual skill. Stimulate recall of prerequisite rules and concepts that are components of the problem, rule, or concept to be learned.

Cognitive strategy. Stimulate recall of similar task strategies and task-relevant rules and concepts.

Attitude. Stimulate recall of the situation and action involved in personal choice as well as relevant information and skills. Remind learner of the human model and the model's characteristics.

Motor skill. Stimulate recall of the "executive subroutine" and part skills, if appropriate.

4. Presenting the Stimulus Material with Distinctive Features

Any stimulus must have its distinctive features clearly delineated. Highlight important features of diagrams or charts; use headings or bold or italic print in printed text; use variety of tone, pitch, and volume in speech.†

Verbal information. Display printed or auditorially delivered verbal statements in an organized, systematic fashion. Present in propositional form and emphasize distinctive features.‡

Intellectual skill. Delineate distinctive features of objects and symbols to be formed into the concept or rule or problem to be solved. Present varied examples of the concept, rule, or problem.§

---

*This prescription has been integrated into Merrill's theory (p. 207) but without the level of guidance provided by Gagné-Briggs.

†This is very similar to Gropper's "eliciting stimuli" (p. 47).

‡Merrill provides a number of more detailed prescriptions about this (see Fig. 7.3).

§This appears to include primarily Merrill's "examples" (p. 204), Gropper's "examples" (p. 54), Landa's "demonstrations" (p. 121, footnote 12), and Collins' "positive exemplars" (p. 183). However, the nature of the examples is not prescribed to the level of guidance that characterizes Merrill's theory.

Cognitive strategy. Describe the novel problem; then describe and show what the strategy accomplishes.

Attitude. Have the human model describe and demonstrate the general nature of the choice of personal action to be presented.*

Motor skill. Display the situation in existence at initiation of skill performance; demonstrate executive subroutine; provide tools or implements.†

5. Providing Learning Guidance

This involves making the stimulus as meaningful as possible. In general, use concrete examples of abstract terms and concepts, and elaborate each idea by relating it to others already in memory.‡

Verbal information. Elaborate content by relating it to larger bodies of knowledge in memory;§ emphasize verbal links and provide concrete examples; use images, spatial arrays,‖ and mnemonics.

Intellectual skill. Give divergent concrete instances and noninstances of a concept or applications of a rule; provide verbal cues to the proper combining sequence.

Cognitive strategy. Provide verbal description of the strategy, followed by one or more concrete examples; provide prompts and hints to the novel solution.

Attitude. Have the human model describe or demonstrate the action choice; students observe positive reinforcement of model's behavior.¶

Motor skill. Require direct and continued practice; provide feedback of performance achievement.

---

*This prescription is unique among the theories in this book.

†This is also unique among the theories in this book.

‡This would include Merrill's "help," "alternative representation," "mnemonic" (p. 207), and perhaps even "generality" (p. 204), and it would include Gropper's "cues" (pp. 47 and 55). Gagné-Briggs provide somewhat less detailed guidance here than do Merrill and especially Gropper (pp. 54–56), although it should also be noted that Gagné-Briggs' prescriptions are considerably more comprehensive (broader) than Merrill's and Gropper's, as witnessed by prescriptions for such outcomes as attitudes and motor skills and such methods as gaining attention and stating objectives.

§This prescription comes from Ausubel's work and recent schema theory and is unique among the theories in this book, including the three cognitively based theories: Landa's and Scandura's, which both emphasize information-processing routines rather than memory structures, and Collins's, which emphasizes techniques for depth of processing. Clearly, all of these prescriptions are compatible with each other.

‖This is somewhat similar to Gropper's prescriptions for "display of information," especially "tabled formats" (p. 57).

¶Again, prescriptions for this category of outcomes are unique among the theories in this book.

6. Eliciting the Performance

Here the learner is required to demonstrate the newly learned behavior to show whether or not the learned capability has been stored in long-term memory.*

Verbal information. Ask for part or all of the information; require paraphase or learners' own words.

Intellectual skill. Ask the learner to apply the concept or rule to instances not previously encountered during the learning.

Cognitive strategy. Give the learner the challenge of an unfamiliar problem to solve using the strategy.

Attitude. Place the learner in a previously unencountered situation where choices must be made; ask the learner to indicate choice of action in such real or simulated situations or in a questionnaire.

Motor skill. Provide the opportunity for the student to perform the total learned procedure.

7. Providing Informative Feedback

Here the student is informed of the degree of correctness of his or her performance. Feedback can be "built in," as in computer-assisted instruction, programmed instruction, individualized instruction, and some practical activities. It can be student initiated and immediate, or provided by the instructor or similar agent, possibly after some delay. Appropriate remedial instruction should be provided if the performance is not correct (see Events 4 and 5).†

Verbal information. Confirm correctness of statement of information.

Intellectual skill. Confirm correctness of concept or rule application.

Cognitive strategy. Confirm originality of problem solution.

Attitude. Provide direct and vicarious reinforcement of the action choice.

Motor skill. Provide feedback on the degree of accuracy and timing of the performance.

8. Assessing Performance

To ensure that the learner has learned the new capability, it is necessary to require additional instances of the performance. Assessing performance serves two functions: It establishes whether or not the new learning has reasonable stability, and it provides additional practice.‡

---

*This is the same as Merrill's "practice" (p. 204) and Gropper's "practice" (p. 54).
†Feedback is also prescribed by Merrill (p. 207), Gropper (p. 47), and Collins (p. 185).
‡This is a testing prescription rather than an instructional prescription.

Verbal information. Require that the student paraphrase, or elaborate on, the learned information.

Intellectual skill. Require that the student apply the concept or rule to a number of new instances.

Cognitive strategy. Provide a variety of novel problems to be solved.

Attitude. Ask the learner to make a choice of personal action in a real or simulated situation.

Motor skill. Require the learner to perform the total skill.

9. Enhancing Retention and Transfer

Providing additional practice with a wide variety of instances is likely to increase *retention* of all learned capabilities. For *verbal information,* requiring that the student paraphrase, or elaborate on, the learned information is recommended to enhance retention. For *intellectual skills,* arranging practice in the form of spaced reviews is particularly effective for retention. If the practice involves a variety of divergent instances, then the learned capability is more likely to be *transferred* to new situations. Gagné and Briggs do not offer more detailed prescriptions for enhancing transfer, although further discussion about transfer and various cognitive models is available in Gagné (1985) and Gagné and White (1978).*

Having identified the desired learning outcome and classified it in terms of Gagné's learned capabilities, the instructional designer specifies a series of instructional events designed to activate, support, and maintain the internal act of learning. These events can take many forms, depending on the specific learning task and the characteristics of the learner(s). Further descriptions of the nine events of instruction can be found in Gagné (1985) and Gagné and Briggs (1979).

Sequencing Prescriptions

Although Gagné is most famous for his learning-task analsyis and hierarchical sequence, Gagné and Briggs (1979) recommend different sequencing strategies for different "levels" of sequencing in a course or curriculum. During the process of designing an instructional sequence, you should start by identifying and sequencing more general goals and objectives, and progress by levels down to increasingly specific objectives.†

---

*The prescriptions here are for use of strategy components that have already been prescribed (additional practice). The only new element here is the timing of the practice—spread out over time. Surprisingly, most instructional theories have not included any prescriptions for systematic review. Reigeluth provides considerable guidance for the format and timing of reviews (p. 257).

†This "top-down" approach to sequencing is not an instructional strategy, that is, it does not indicate what the instruction will be like. Rather, it is a development procedure—directions as to what the instructional designer should do and in what order.

After identifying end-of-course objectives, which state the performance expected after the course is completed, you identify major course units, each of which requires several weeks of study. For each unit you identify terminal objectives (to be reached by the end of the unit), and you sequence the units in the most appropriate sequence. Sequencing at this first level of analysis is done largely on the basis of expert opinion and intuition, although Bruner's (1960) spiral curriculum "appears to hold much promise" (Gagné & Briggs, 1979, p. 141).*

Next, you break the terminal objectives into performance objectives, which are the specific outcomes of the instruction and which are at a level appropriate for task analysis. These performance objectives, one or more of which may make up a lesson and which may require different capabilities, are sequenced primarily on the basis of expert consensus and common sense.†

Finally, a hierarchical task analysis is done on the performance objectives, and a hierarchical sequence, based on the intellectual skills, is designed. The hierarchical analysis breaks each performance objective down into "enabling objectives, each of which may have several subordinate objectives" (Gagné & Briggs, 1979, p. 137). The enabling objectives are either essential prerequisite skills required before the performance objectives can be learned, or they are objectives that help facilitate such learning. A sequence is then developed in which the component skills are taught in a parts-to-whole sequence; first the most elemental parts at the bottom of the hierarchy are taught, followed by progressively more complex combinations of the parts. Fig. 2.2 shows an example of a learning hierarchy and hierarchical sequence of skills.‡

Hierarchical analysis and sequencing are appropriate only for intellectual skills. As discussed previously, the very important category of *intellectual skills* has been divided into five subcategories. This was done for a very good reason. The learning of any one intellectual skill depends on the prior learning of one or more simpler intellectual skills.

In order to learn to solve problems by using two or more rules, a learner must have already learned to use the various component rules. Because a rule relates two or more concepts, the learning of those concepts is an essential prerequisite to the learning of the rule. Similarly, defined concepts often have concrete concepts as critical attributes, and concrete concepts cannot be learned unless their common characteristics can be discriminated.

Most courses of instruction involve lessons having more than one type of

---

*This is the first sequencing prescription, but it is very vague. Reigeluth's "elaboration sequence" is similar to Bruner's "spiral curriculum" but provides much more detailed guidance to instructional designers.

†This is another sequencing prescription (albeit vague).

‡This is a very valuable sequencing strategy that many theorists have included in their theories, such as Gropper (p. 58) and Reigeluth (p. 253).

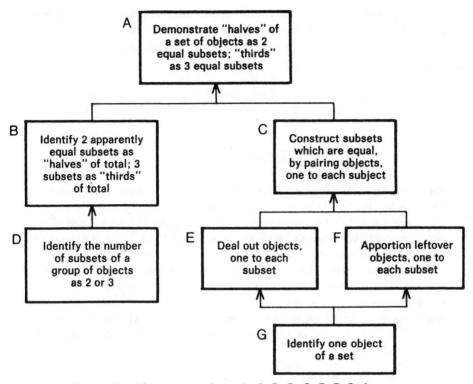

Hierarchical Sequence 1 (up a leg): D, B, G, E, F, C, A.
Hierarchical Sequence 2 (level by level): G, D, E, F, B, C, A.

FIG. 2.2. A learning hierarchy and hierarchical sequence.

learning outcome. The designer of a lesson will place emphasis on what the student can *do* as a result of instruction. Usually this implies a need to make an analysis of the *intellectual skills* involved in a lesson. Often lesson planning can best be done by making intellectual skills the major organizing factor. Verbal information, cognitive strategies, motor skills, and attitudes can then be added to the places where the most appropriate linkage occurs (Gagné & Briggs, 1979, p. 147). Regarding the sequencing of these various outcomes, the following loose "rules" apply (adapted from Gagné & Briggs. 1979, p. 144):

Verbal information. Order of presentation is not important; a meaningful context should be provided.

Intellectual skill. Subordinate skills must be mastered first. Skill sequence may be provided by verbal instruction.

Cognitive strategy. Problem situations require previously learned intellectual skills and the prior learning, or provision, of appropriate verbal information.

Attitude. Respect must be established for the human model. Verbal information relevant to choices must be previously learned or provided.

Motor skill. The executive routine must be learned, and also part skills. Intensive practice is provided on the total skill.

See Briggs (1977), Gagné and Briggs (1979), and Briggs and Wager (1981) for more detailed sequencing suggestions.

LESSON PREFACE

The remainder of this chapter illustrates how some of the Gagné-Briggs prescriptions can be applied in the design of a lesson for secondary students on basic optics and the use of the microscope. The content and objectives used in this lesson are the same as those used in other chapters of this book so as to facilitate easy comparison with the other theories and models of instruction.

This section begins with the presentation of three lessons based on different instructional strategies. In each of the lessons are circled numbers that correspond to comments presented in the following section. The comments relate specific parts of the lesson to specific prescriptions in the Gagné-Briggs theory and indicate which parts of the lesson were created solely according to the designer's discretion.

The Instructional Objectives

After completing the instruction within the three lessons, the students will be able to do the following:

1. Classify previously unencountered lenses as to whether or not they are convex lenses.
2. Define focal length.
3. Explain or predict what effect different convex lenses will have on light rays.
4. Explain the way in which the curvature of a lens influences both the magnification and the focal length of different lenses.
5. State from memory the three significant events in the history of the microscope (which are shown in the lesson).
6. Use a previously unencountered optical microscope properly.

According to Gagné and Briggs, the objectives belong to the following categories of learned capabilities: verbal information (Objectives 2 and 5); intellectual skills, specifically concepts and rules (Objectives 1, 3, and 4), and procedural learning, which involves motor skills and a sequential rule—an intellectual skill (Objective 6).

The organization of the lessons is as follows: Verbal information (Objective 5) is presented in Lesson 1; intellectual skills (Objectives 1–4) in Lesson 2; and an intellectual skill, or sequential rule (Objective 6), in Lesson 3. The reason for shifting Objective 2 to the category of intellectual skill is explained in Comment 12, and why Objective 6 is an intellectual skill rather than a motor skill is explained in the comments for Lesson 3.

Each lesson follows the guidelines for presenting the events of instruction for the particular category of learned capability. (The nine events of instruction are presented in Fig. 2.1.) The events of instruction are also referenced in the lessons themselves, at the beginning of each step in Lesson 1 between [brackets], and in the comments for Lessons 2 and 3.

The lessons provided in this chapter represent just one manner of utilizing the instructional principles of Gagné and Briggs. Because of the breadth of their work, Gagné and Briggs provide less detail regarding the selection of actual microstrategies for instruction. Therefore, many of the specific details of each lesson are left to the discretion of the individual designer.

LESSONS

LESSON 1

[1]

[2] Instructor: "What do these items have in common?" The following items are displayed:

1. Old wire-rim glasses.
2. Glass globes filled with water.
3. Two lenses combined on a pole (crude microscope).

[3] The instructor entertains answers from students, leading them to state that all are used for magnification.

[4] Instructor: "You will be learning about how lenses were invented and developed. In particular, you'll learn important names and dates in the development of magnification with glass. Pay close attention to the people and events presented in the slide presentation. You will have to know them for the final test."

[5] The instructor presents slides that trace the development of magnification with glass and does the narration and elaboration on each slide, providing directed learning. The presentation includes:

1. 1000 B.C., engraver using globe.
2. 1200 A.D., people wearing glasses similar to those already shown.
[6] 3. 1590 A.D., eyeglass lenses put together on a pole, and made into a microscope, by Zacharias Jensenn in Holland.

Instructor: "Notice that these were presented in chronological order, beginning with a very crude method of magnification, leading to a more refined one. You'll find a graphic representation of this on your worksheet."

The instructor presents students with a worksheet (see Fig. 2.3).

[8] Each student fills in the worksheet and discusses his or her answers with another student. The instructor asks for scores from the students, and provides additional feedback and discussion, answering questions and clearing up any remaining problems the learners express.

[9] Students are asked to write a short history of the development of magnification as part of the final exam. They are instructed to include names and dates in their histories.

[10] At later points in the curriculum, the instructor relates the history of the development of magnification to the history of the development of other technologies and bodies of knowledge. The names, dates, and events are all reviewed in the process.

IMPORTANT EVENTS IN THE HISTORY OF MAGNIFICATION

+	+	+	+	+
1000 B.C.	1 A.D.	1200 A.D.	1590 A.D.	1971–72 A.D.

[7] 1. Place the following events on this timeline by placing the letter of the event at the appropriate spot:
   A. First compound microscope invented
   B. Glass globes used for magnification
   C. Year of your birth
   D. Eyeglasses first used

2. Give a short history of the development of the first compound microscope. Include dates.

FIG. 2.3. Worksheet for Lesson 1.

[12] [This lesson is presented to the learner as a workbook, with each frame on a separate page.]

A LESSON ON LIGHT AND LENSES   1

In this lesson you will learn:

[13]   1. To identify any convex lens.
       2. To define and identify focal length.
       3. To graphically show the path of light as it passes through different parts of a convex lens.
       4. To predict the relationship between focal length, lens curvature, and magnification, given a set of lenses.

---

[14]   Have you ever used a magnifying glass? You may want to play with[2] one before you do this lesson. Look at lots of different objects through the magnifying glass. What happens? Do you know why? This lesson will help you learn about the magnifying glass and why it works as it does.

Follow the directions in these self-instructional materials *exactly.*   3
After you answer a question, turn the page. If your answer is correct,
[15]   continue with the directions on that page. If you give a wrong answer, turn back a page and review the information. Then see if you can answer correctly. Work at your own pace and turn in the booklet when you've finished.

All convex lenses have at least one surface that bends out, so that   4
the lens is thicker in the middle than at the edges.
These are cross-sectional side views of each lens:

[16]
[17]

These are convex lenses.   These are not convex lenses.

The middle of a convex lens is _____ than the edges.   5

Turn the page

The middle of a convex lens is *THICKER* than the edges.   6

Circle the lenses below that are *CONVEX*.
Again, these are cross-sectional side views of each lens:

[18]

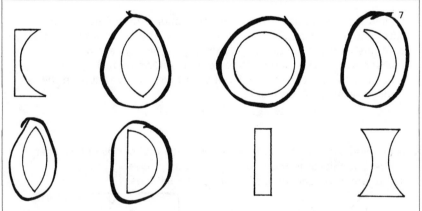

[19]

Your page should look like this because:

All convex lenses have at least one surface that bends OUT, and
convex lenses are thicker in the middle than at the edges.

Turn the page.

[20]

Do you remember what happens to light when it passes through a   8
medium like glass?

It _____.

Light *BENDS* when it passes through a medium like glass.   9

When light rays pass through a <u>CONVEX LENS</u>

[21]

Those that pass through the outer edges of the lens bend inward.
and those that pass through the middle of the lens do not bend at
all.

---

[21]

Which way do the rays coming through the outer edges of a convex[10]
lens bend?

_____

Which way do the rays coming through the center of a convex lens
bend?

_____

Rays passing through the edges bend *INWARD.*   11
Rays passing through the center *DO NOT BEND.*

----

[22]   Draw the paths of light rays through this convex lens.

[23]

[24]

Your drawing should look like this: ¹²

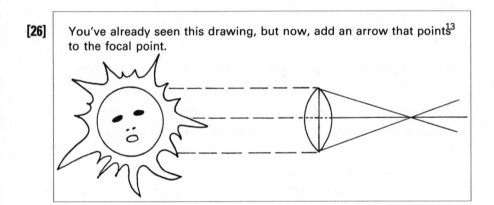

[25] Obviously, if some rays bend inward and others bend not at all, they will all intersect at some point. That point of intersection is called the <u>FOCAL POINT</u>.

[26] You've already seen this drawing, but now, add an arrow that points ¹³ to the focal point.

[27]

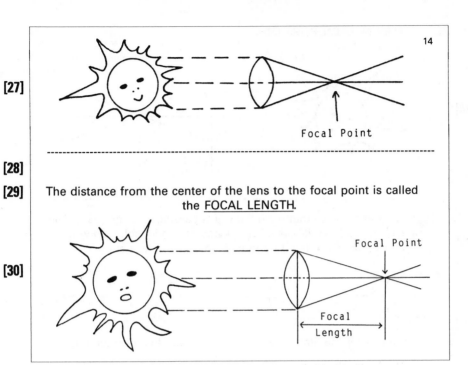

Focal Point

[28]

[29] The distance from the center of the lens to the focal point is called the <u>FOCAL LENGTH</u>.

[30]

Focal Point

Focal
Length

[31] What is focal length?   15

_____

_____

[32] The focal length is the distance from the center of the lens to the   16
focal point.

[33] On the diagram below, label the <u>FOCAL LENGTH</u>.

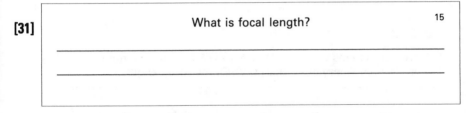

[34]

17

Focal
Length

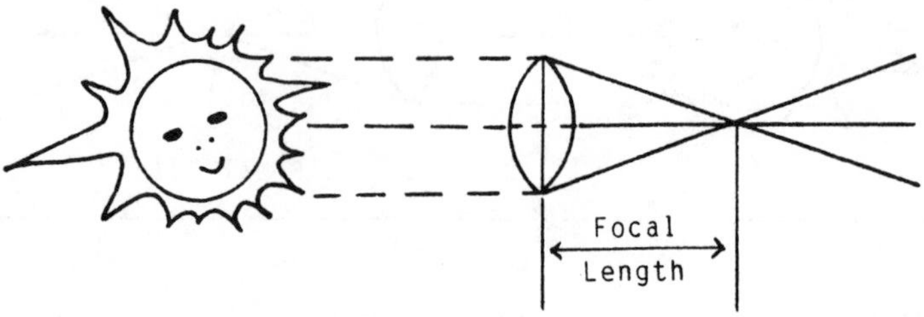

[35]

Here are some lenses that have light rays passing through them. The focal length has been labeled. What kinds of relationships do you see between the focal length and how sharply the lens curves?

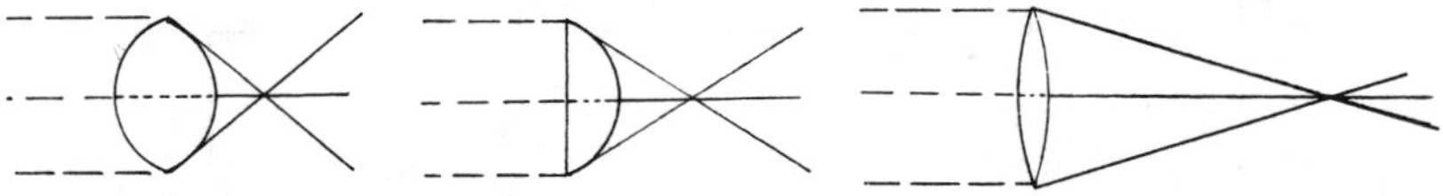

The greater the lens curvature, the _____ the focal length.

The lesser the lens curvature, the _____ the focal length.

The greater the lens curvature, the *SHORTER* the focal length.   18
The less the lens curvature, the *LONGER* the focal length.

[36]

On the lenses below, draw in the path of the light rays. remembering how lens curvature affects focal length. Label the focal point and the focal length.

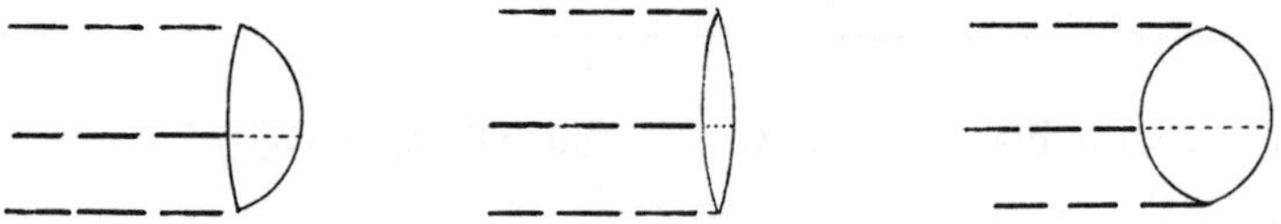

19

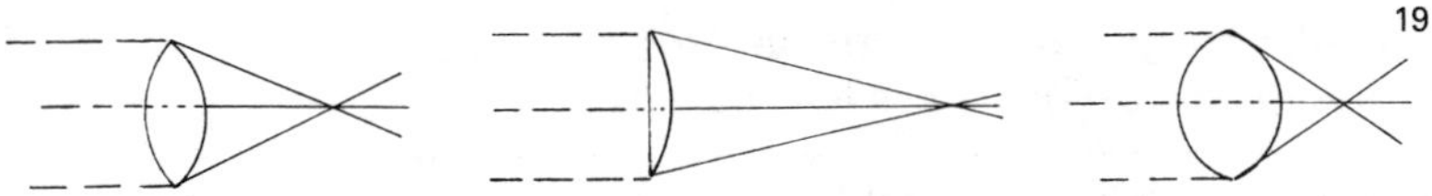

[37]

The whole point of having a convex lens is to magnify an image, to make it bigger.
If a lens has a longer focal length, it will have less magnifying power.
If a lens has a shorter focal length, it will have greater magnifying power.

20

To achieve the greatest magnifying power,
use the lens with the _____ focal length.

21

[38]

To achieve the greatest magnifying power, use the lens with the SHORTEST focal length.

Since you know that
    less magnification = longer focal length
    greater magnification = shorter focal length
and that
    less lens curvature = longer focal length
    more lens curvature = shorter focal length
What is the relationship between lens curvature and magnification?

_____ magnification = _____ lens curvature

_____ magnification = _____ lens curvature

greater magnification = greater lens curvature
less magnification = less lens curvature

22

----

[39] Which of these lenses would you use to achieve the greatest magnification?

a. _____

b. _____

c. _____

d. _____

23

d.   because it is thickest in the middle.

----

[39] On the lenses below, draw in the path of the light rays, remembering how lens curvature affects focal length. Label the focal point and the focal length, and rank in order of magnifying power.

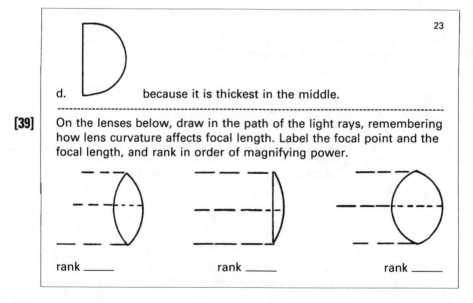

rank _____   rank _____   rank _____

[40] The teacher gives the learners a quiz upon completion of this workbook. Its items are similar to the ones that elicited student performance in this workbook. Note: Later in the course, students are given a worksheet that presents

[41] various lenses, concave and convex, and are asked to identify the convex lenses and their focal lengths, draw paths of light through them, and state their relative magnifying powers. They will also be asked to use real lenses and objects that contain lenses (e.g., microscopes) in a variety of situations.

[42]   LESSON 3

Students are seated in pairs, each pair sharing a microscope and four clean slides. The instructor presents an old pair of blue jeans, rips them, and passes them around, inviting each set of students to place a few threads on [43] one of the slides in front of them. The instructor also passes around an orange and tells students to pick off a piece of skin and place it on a slide. Students are also told to place some strands of their own hair on a slide and, finally, to place a piece of a leaf on a slide.

Instructor: "By placing these specimens on your slides, you've learned how to *dry mount* a slide. During the rest of this class you will learn another, more [44] complex skill: how to use a microscope, not only the one in front of you but any microscope in this room. Each one is slightly different from the others. Some use mirrors rather than light bulbs for the light source. In addition, the adjustment knobs can be in different places on each microscope. You will learn to correctly place a slide, direct light onto the stage, and focus the microscope in order to examine the specimens on the slide in front of you." The instructor projects a slide that shows students what they will see through their own microscopes when they correctly complete the procedure. The slide remains visible throughout the rest of the class.

Instructor: "I will now take you on a 'guided tour' of your microscope, to help [45] you recall the parts of the microscope that we have already learned. Many of the microscopes in this room are different, so you will have to examine yours and discover how each part works. Don't worry now about the order in which each part will be adjusted; just find the parts that you already know." Instructor then has students identify and manipulate each of the following:

objectives   light source
eyepiece   diaphragm
stage and clips   coarse and fine adjustment knobs

The instructor now demonstrates the correct use of a microscope. Depending [46] on the size of the group, students may gather around as the instructor demonstrates on a real microscope, or a videotape could be shown that displays the procedure.

The instructor distributes the "Memo on the Microscope" worksheet (see [47] Fig. 2.4) and says, "This list will help you to remember the correct sequence

---

MEMO ON THE MICROSCOPE

1. Direct the light source onto the stage.
2. Adjust the light coming through the diaphragm.
3. Place and secure a prepared slide on the stage.
4. Select the appropriate objective.
5. Adjust the coarse focus knob.
6. Adjust the fine focus knob.
7. Repeat steps 4–6 with other objectives as needed.

FIG. 2.4.   Worksheet for Lesson 3.

of steps necessary for using a microscope. Use the microscope in front of you and the slide with the blue jean fabric on it for your first time through the procedure."

Students are then allowed to work through the entire procedure at their own pace with their partner. While one student performs the procedure, the part-
[48] ner will provide guidance and feedback using the "Memo on the Micro-scope" sheet.

As the students work their way through the procedure, the teacher circulates, answering questions and giving whatever guidance is necessary for students
[49] to get through the exercise. The following questions ought to be raised during this time:

With which objective do you want to start looking at your specimen? Why?

When do you know that the light is correctly adjusted?

How do you know when you've adjusted the coarse focus enough?

As each pair of students finishes, the students are instructed to make sure that the view through their eyepiece corresponds with the slide shown on the
[50] wall, and to record their success on their score sheet for this unit. If they are not successful, they have another chance to correct it by going back over their handout and trying the procedure again.

Students then repeat the entire procedure with the slide of the orange peel.
[51] After that, students move to another microscope and perform the procedure again, using that microscope and the slide with the hair on it.

Finally, students will bring the leaf slide into focus on yet another micro-
[52] scope, with the instructor present so that he or she can assess the learner's performance.

[53] Later in the course the students will be required to use microscopes as a part of subsequent learning tasks.

COMMENTS

LESSON 1

Objective 5

.1. The first section of this lesson serves to present the events of instruction necessary for a student to learn Objective 5, stating important events in the history of the microscope, which is verbal information. For the purposes of this chapter, the events have been included in as close as possible to the exact order as they are presented by Gagné and Briggs. Often, these events will not occur in this order, and some may be excluded, depending on the learner's needs and characteristics.

2. *Event 1.* The *learner's attention* is gained by providing a change of stimulus in the environment. Presenting the real objects will pique the learner's interests.

3. *Event 3.* The use of objects that are familiar to the learners helps them to *recall information* they may already have learned and stimulates the recall of the context in which they will place the newly learned information (one of the conditions of learning verbal information).

4. *Event 2.* The learners are told exactly what they will have to do to show that they have met the standards for performance. Stating the *objective* serves to answer the learner's question, "How will I know when I have learned?"

5. *Event 4.* The *stimulus material* that is presented is the information that must be learned by the student. An incorrect stimulus would be to provide a list of other devices that were invented in 1920. Although that is also information, it would not help the student to master this objective.

6. *Event 5.* The instructor's narration can include answering questions from the learner and providing *learning guidance.* Gagné states that just telling the learners the answer to their questions is the correct form of learning guidance when the objective is verbal information.

7. *Event 6.* The *performance* that is elicited is a paraphrase of the information that has been given ("a short history . . ."), which is Gagné-Briggs' prescription for the acquisition of verbal information. A timeline was also added to elicit the performance, contributing to learning guidance (Event 5). Although

based primarily on designer discretion, this is also an alternative *spatial* representation of what is usually simply verbal information. It presents the stimulus in a different manner that can help students perform according to their own learning style (Dunn, 1978).

8. *Event 7*. In order to be effective, all *feedback* must inform the learner of the correctness or degree of correctness of the performance. Here the learner receives feedback that is immediate and indicates correctness, following the Gagné-Briggs prescriptions. In this instance, the designer of the lesson has decided that the feedback will come from a peer and be supervised by the instructor. Peer feedback is usually motivational to both the student and the peer. It can be an effective management strategy for the instructor. As the students report on their performances, the instructor can monitor overall performance.

9. *Event 8*. Assessment of the learners occurs here in the form of a typical essay test question. Multiple-choice, true-false, fill-in-the-blank, or matching questions could have been used instead.

10. *Event 9*. Retention and transfer of learning are aided by a spaced review that is a paraphrase of the information that was presented in this lesson. Designer discretion has placed this review at the final exam.

LESSON 2

11. *Sequencing*. Objectives 1 through 4 deal with the acquisition of intellectual skills. According to Gagné, there is a hierarchical relationship between concepts and rules. Certain simpler skills must be mastered before superordinate skills can be mastered. Identification of these prerequisite skills results in a learning hierarchy. A learning hierarchy for Objectives 1 through 4 is shown in Fig. 2.5. A proper instructional sequence is derived from the learning hierarchy by teaching the objectives from the bottom up in the hierarchy. Such a sequence for Objectives 1 through 4 is used in this lesson. It is assumed that all students have mastered entry-level behaviors and are starting instruction on the same level.

12. Self-paced instructional materials were chosen at the discretion of the designer to present these objectives (1–4). The events of instruction are handled differently in an individualized setting than they are for large-group instruction. According to Gagné, this approach allows for a greater degree of precision in the management of instructional events. Presented here on full-size pages, the booklets would best be printed on smaller pages or index cards with one frame per page.

13. *Event 2* (for all four objectives). The learners are told exactly what they will be learning and what behaviors they will have to exhibit to show that they have learned. All four objectives are presented together for this lesson (designer discretion).

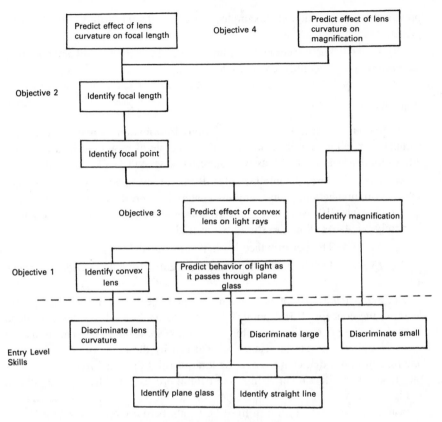

FIG. 2.5.   Learning Hierarchy.

Objective 1

14. *Event 1.* This activity helps to gain the learner's attention and also informs the learner of the lesson's objectives.

15. These are simply directions to the student, having no direct relation to the events of instruction.

16. *Event 4.* Gagné states that as the stimulus material is presented, a variety of examples should be shown. Without this variety a student might not be able to identify the many different shapes and sizes in which convex lenses can be found.

17. *Event 5.* Learning guidance is provided by the examples, nonexamples, and verbal cues.

18. *Event 6.* Here a performance is elicited for the objective to classify a convex lens by definition. Examples that have already been presented, as well as

previously unencountered examples, are used, according to Gagné's prescriptions.

19. *Event 7.* The learner receives immediate, informative feedback regarding the performance "identify convex lenses."

Objective 3

20. *Event 3.* While this may be obvious information to many students, it stimulates recall of the prerequisite to the principle of how light behaves. This allows the learners to more easily acquire the new skill.

21. *Event 5.* Here, the intellectual skill (rule) to be learned is presented via a verbal communication. This stimulus material is presented in frame 9 and quizzed in frame 10. Note that frame 10 does *not* elicit the desired performance; it merely elicits recall of the stimulus material.

22. *Event 6.* The performance is elicited in frame 11.

23. *Event 7.* Feedback about performance correctness is provided in frame 12.

24. *Sequencing.* It can be seen here that Objective 3 is prerequisite for learning the concept "focal point." One has to understand that the rays bend inward in order to understand that they intersect at some point. It occurs to us that many complex concepts in science are defined by the kinds of "relationships among concepts" that characterize the kind of rules often referred to as principles (cause-and-effect relationships and natural processes). Also note (as shown in Fig. 2.5) that focal point is taught here because it is prerequisite to the concept "focal distance," which in turn must be taught before Objective 4 (a rule).

25. *Event 4.* This frame presents the stimulus materials for a new objective.

26. *Event 6.* This elicits the performance.

27. *Event 7.* This provides feedback about performance correctness.

Objective 2

28. Objective 2 (defining focal length) entails learning the definition, which is actually the acquisition of verbal information. However, the *concept* of focal length is a prerequisite for Objective 4. Therefore, focal length must be taught as both verbal information and an intellectual skill (concept).

29. *Event 4.* This frame presents the stimulus material for both the verbal information and the intellectual skill.

30. *Event 5.* This visual representation of an example provides learning guidance both for the verbal information (as an elaboration that makes the verbal information more meaningful) and for the intellectual skill (as an example of the defined concept).

31. *Event 6*. This elicits the performance for the verbal information.

32. *Event 7*. This provides feedback.

33. *Event 6*. This elicits the performance for the intellectual skill.

34. *Event 7*. Feedback.

Objective 4

35. *Events 4 and 5*. Gagné has indicated that a discovery approach can be utilized through the same events of instruction. The stimulus material is of a slightly different nature (it does not tell the learners the relationship), but the learning guidance is quite similar (primarily examples). There is some evidence that a discovery approach enhances motivation, retention, and transfer.

36. *Event 6*. This elicits the performance.

37. *Event 4*. This is the stimulus material for the other part of Objective 4 (see Fig. 2.5).

38. Frame 21 involves stimulating the recall of prerequisite learnings (Event 3). Although these prerequisites were just learned in this lesson, they are essential to the relationship between magnification and lens curvature and should be recalled. To the extent that this frame requires a review of the intellectual skills presented in earlier frames in a different application, it can be viewed as an enhancement of retention and transfer (Event 9). On such a small scale, however (within one lesson), it may also be viewed as simply eliciting another performance of the task (Event 6). It can be seen that any given portion of the instruction may implement several events of learning.

39. *Event 6*. Frames 22 and 23 elicit the performance.

40. *Event 8*. This assesses the learners' performance for all of the objectives taught in this workbook (including objectives 1–4).

41. *Event 9*. This enhances retention and (to the extent that different lenses and representations of lenses are used) transfer.

Lesson 3

42. Lesson 3 teaches the steps for using a microscope properly. Each step includes motor skills, but the final objective is still classified as a rule. At this level, students will presumably not have to learn the necessary motor skills (e.g., turning on a switch, adjusting knobs) but instead must learn the proper *procedure* for combining these skills. Each step of the procedure could be seen as a rule by which the student must respond with a class of relationships among classes of objects and events (Gagné & Briggs, 1977, p. 67). For example, the student must bring the specimen into focus by first selecting the appropriate objective and then using the coarse and fine adjustment knobs, in that order. Gagné

classifies procedures as a type of chaining. There are four conditions that must be met in order for the learner to be successful. First, the learner must be able to perform each step in the chain in the *proper order*. Second, the steps must be performed in a *contiguous manner*, one after another. This condition concerns time lapses between successive steps of the procedure; they must be minimal. In order for the learner to be able to perform each link in the chain in the proper sequence and at the proper moment the sequence must be *repeated* by the learner. Finally, completion of the sequence must result in immediate satisfaction on the student's part (i.e., seeing the magnified object through the eyepiece). This *reinforcement* has been found to be important for the learning of chains, and delay of reinforcement makes learning more difficult. These conditions are further explained in the following comments.

43. *Event 1.* The objects presented are familiar to students but will be seen in an unfamiliar manner (i.e., magnified through a microscope), thus appealing to the students' interest. The arrangement of students in pairs represents a real school situation where equipment may be at a premium, as well as enhancing motivation for students by allowing them to work together (designer discretion).

44. *Event 2.* A complete performance objective for this lesson following Gagné's prescriptions reads: Given any microscope in the classroom and a prepared slide (situation), the student will demonstrate the correct procedure (learned capability) for using a microscope (object), by arranging the lighting apparatus and focusing the lenses (action) of any microscope in this room (tools/constraints). The essential elements of this objective are communicated to students at this time.

45. *Event 3.* It is assumed that students have already learned the actual parts of the microscope in a previous lesson. The recall of these prerequisite concepts is especially important for rule learning. Gagné's necessary internal condition for rule learning is that each concept that is a part of the rule must be previously learned. In this lesson, the instructor begins with a ''guided tour'' of the instrument itself, so that students may both familiarize themselves with the microscope and recall each of the various parts.

46. *Event 4.* The instructor presents the stimulus material by modeling the procedure that students will learn, using the same equipment. This stimulus is a demonstration of the procedure that students will be expected to perform themselves.

47. *Event 5.* The use of the handout for the microscope provides guidance for the learners by meeting the ''correct order'' condition necessary for learning a chain.

48. *Events 6 and 7.* By allowing students to perform the procedure at their own rate with prompting (if necessary) by the partner, students are able to achieve the contiguity requirement for performing a chain. The steps of the

procedure must follow each other without hesitation, and students will do this on their own without waiting for the rest of the class. The partner provides feedback as needed by each student.

49. *Event 5.* This line of questioning by the instructor provides learning guidance for the students. Instead of explicitly stating the rules that must be learned (e.g., use the lowest power objective when first examining a specimen), the instructor suggests a line of reasoning that will lead students to combine the subordinate rules and concepts for themselves. This contributes to the efficiency of learning.

50. *Event 7.* If the view through their microscope corresponds to the projected slide, the students will know that they have successfully performed the procedure. When each student is successful, immediate reinforcement occurs for the entire procedure and enhances learning for the student.

51. *Event 6.* Once the procedure for using a microscope has been learned, the student's performance must have a kind of "regularity" over a variety of specific situations (Gagné & Briggs, 1979, p. 67). In this case, the learner must be able to use different styles and types of microscopes. Therefore, once the learner has successfully completed the task on one microscope, he or she must also successfully perform the task on others. This repetition is an essential element for learning a procedure. Furthermore, all conditions for chain learning are rarely present on the first time through a procedure. Repeated practice allows students to work out problems they may encounter, as well as helping them to remember the procedure.

52. *Event 8.* This allows the learner's performance to be assessed.

53. *Event 9.* This facilitates transfer and retention.

REFERENCES

Ausubel, D. P. (1960). The use of advance organizers in the learning and retention of meaningful verbal material. *Journal of Educational Psychology, 51,* 267–272.

Briggs, L. J. (Ed.) (1977). *Instructional design. Principles and applications.* Englewood Cliffs, NJ: Educational Technology Publications.

Briggs, L. J., & Wager, W. W. (1981). *Handbook of procedures for the design of instruction.* Englewood Cliffs, NJ: Educational Technology Publications.

Bruner, J. S. (1960). *The process of education.* Cambridge, MA.: Harvard University Press.

Gagné, R. M. (1974). *Essentials of learning for instruction.* New York: Holt, Rinehart & Winston.

Gagné, R. M. (1984). Learning outcomes and their effects. *American Psychologist, 39,* 377–385.

Gagné, R. M. (1985). *The conditions of learning and theory of instruction.* New York: Holt, Rinehart & Winston.

Gagné, R. M., & Briggs, L. J. (1979). *Principles of instructional design* (2nd ed.). New York: Holt, Rinehart & Winston.

Gagné, R. M., Wager, W. W., & Rojas, A. (Sept. 1981). Planning and authoring computer-assisted instruction lessons. *Educational Technology, 21,* 17–26.

Gagné, R. M., & White, R. T. (1978). Memory structures and learning outcomes. *Review of Educational Research, 48,* 187–222.

Rothkopf, E. Z. (1970). The concept of mathemagenic activities. *Review of Educational Research, 40,* 325–336.

3

A Lesson Based on A Behavioral Approach to Instructional Design

George L. Gropper
*Digital Equipment Corporation**

FOREWORD

History

When instructional theory was born, about 1960, a behavioral orientation domi-nated learning theory and instructional practice. Skinner's programmed instruc-tion and teaching machines were highly popular. Gropper's theory of instruction is a creative synthesis of the vast majority of the knowledge about instruction that arose out of the behavioral tradition.

Unique Contributions

Part of the creative aspect of that synthesis is Gropper's conceptualization of three kinds of treatments (methods of instruction): routine treatments, which should always be used; shaping treatments, which should precede the routine treatments whenever the conditions pose learning difficulties; and specialized treatments, which supplement the other two types of treatments to meet special learning problems. This is a very useful conceptualization for instructional de-signers and teachers.

Another unique feature of Gropper's theory is the amount of detailed guidance its prescriptions provide for designers (see, e.g., his prescriptions for the size of the unit of behavior, the mode of the stimulus or the response, and exaggeration

---

*The views expressed in this chapter are those of the author and are not necessarily those of the Digital Equipment Corporation.

of stimuli). Of all the theories in this book, this one provides the most detailed guidance for designers and teachers.

Similarities

Gropper's theory prescribes a number of the same strategy components as other instructional theories, such as practice, examples, cues for learning guidance, and Gagné's hierarchical sequence. These and other similarities are identified with Editor's Notes. Also noteworthy, like the Gagné-Briggs theory, Gropper's is comprised of just one model of instruction, and variations on that model are prescribed for different situations. However, Gropper's situations are very different from the Gagné-Briggs categories of learned capabilities.

Issues to Think About

Perhaps the most important issue here is, what has been ignored? In his quest for depth (detailed guidance), what breadth has been sacrificed? And in his self-imposed restriction to behaviorally based prescriptions, has anything of value been sacrificed? If so, what? On both counts, it may be helpful to compare this theory to Gagné-Briggs', and on the latter count it may be helpful to compare it to the three cognitively based theories that follow.

Another interesting issue is, what should follow practice? Is Gropper's reinforcement the same as Gagné's feedback? How do they differ? Are they both important? Finally, how does Gropper's basis for prescribing variations in his basic model differ from the Gagné-Briggs basis? How do they compare?

STUDY QUESTIONS

1. What are the three main types of "treatments?"
2. When should each type of "treatment" be used?
3. What role do conditions play in prescribing treatments, and what kinds of conditions are important?
4. Describe each of the three kinds of routine treatments.
5. Describe each of the five kinds of shaping treatments.
6. Describe each of the five kinds of specialized treatments.
7. What other kinds of instructional strategies does Gropper prescribe?
8. On what two considerations are Gropper's instructional sequences based?

C.M.R.

INTRODUCTION: BRIEF SUMMARY
OF CLASSICAL BEHAVIOR THEORY

The Role of Practice

A central requirement in classical behavior theory is learner practice* followed by reinforcement. What does the learner practice?

Learners must practice the very performance that they are expected to learn. If they are to operate a microscope, they must practice operating one. If they are to choose from among lenses the one that will magnify an object the most, they must practice making such choices.

Reinforcement that follows practice consists either in learners finding out that their practice responses were correct (confirmation)† or in receiving something they desire following practice (reward) or both.

Discriminative Stimuli

It is not sufficient for learners just to practice performing the right responses. The responses must be performed in an appropriate context. Therefore, they must be practiced in the context that is expected to elicit them at some future time. In behavioral terms, they must be practiced *in the presence of* the discriminative stimuli that will have to elicit them.‡

Given a microscope, learners must be able to operate it. The microscope itself is the discriminative stimulus that must elicit "operating" responses. Given varied lenses, learners must be able to choose the "convex" one. Varied lenses constitute the discriminative stimuli that must elicit "choosing" responses.

Prior to instruction, discriminative stimuli do not have the capacity to elicit required responses. That is why instruction is necessary. How then can practice proceed if, to begin with, discriminative stimuli do not possess the capacity to elicit the responses that need to be practiced? A practice session cannot simply present the discriminative stimuli to learners and expect them to start practicing the appropriate responses.

Eliciting Role of Cues

The science of instruction consists of finding stimuli, other than the discriminative stimuli, that *can* elicit the responses learners must practice. In behavior theory these other stimuli are called "cues."§

Cues are selected on the basis of their capacity to elicit the responses that need

---

*Practice is specifically prescribed by Gagné-Briggs (p. 20) and Merrill (p. 204), and it is tacitly assumed by the other theorists.

†This kind of informational feedback is prescribed by Gagné-Briggs (p. 20) and Merrill (p. 207).

‡This prescription is similar to Gagné-Briggs' "present the stimulus material" (p. 18).

§Cues are similar to Gagné-Briggs' "learning guidance" (p. 19) and Merrill's "help" (p. 207).

to be practiced. A list of steps may be selected to elicit practice of those steps.* For example, a list of steps can serve as a cue to prompt learner practice in operating a microscope. Some verbal principles and examples† may be selected to prompt learner practice in choosing the lens that will magnify a specimen the most or the least.

Cues that are selected accompany discriminative stimuli. For example, learners will practice operating an actual microscope—the discriminative stimulus, with a list of steps in hand—the cue. That makes it possible to prompt the learner to practice making required responses *in the presence of* the discriminative stimuli that eventually must be able to elicit them.

Cues may also be used for purposes other than that of eliciting a desired response. One key role they play is in eliciting and *directing learner attention.*‡ They may be used to direct attention to discriminative stimuli or to isolated features of those discriminative stimuli. For example, they might be used to direct attention to features of a microscope (e.g., its component parts) or of a lens (e.g., its width at the center).

Cues may also be used to direct attention to the requirements of a practice problem. Or they may be used to call attention to required responses or they may be used to direct attention to what makes for a correct answer to a practice problem. Directing attention in these varied ways is central to all forms of instruction.

All instruction consists of some combination of:

- Cues that have the capacity to elicit required responses.
- Discriminative stimuli that must acquire that capacity.

Transfer of Control from Cues to Discriminative Stimuli

When a stimulus, either a discriminative stimulus or a cue, is capable of eliciting a response, the response is said to be under the control of that stimulus. At the beginning of instruction, only cues have control over responses to be learned; discriminative stimuli do not.

Practice with cues and discriminative stimuli working in tandem makes it possible to transfer control over responses from cues to discriminative stimuli. If, at the end of instruction, learners are given a microscope (the discriminative

---

*This kind of cue is the same as Merrill's "generality" (p. 204) and Landa's "prescription" (p. 120).

†This kind of cue is the same as Merrill's "example" (p. 204), Landa's "demonstration" (p. 121, footnote 12), and Collins' "positive exemplars" (p. 183).

‡This is the same as Merrill's "attention-focusing information" (p. 207).

stimulus), they can operate it correctly. Given a lens (the discriminative stimulus), learners can label it as "convex" or "concave." The discriminative stimuli now do possess control over required responses. Even with no cues available, they *can* elicit those responses. Control has been successfully transferred from cues to discriminative stimuli. Such is the aim of all instruction.

Fading of Cues

Instruction starts with strong cues that provide maximum help, or at least as much help as is judged necessary. It then uses progressively weaker cues that offer less and less help. For example, it may start with a complete set of cues (e.g., a list of *all* the steps involved in operating a microscope). Later it may just offer partial cues (e.g., *some* of the steps involved in operating a microscope). Ultimately, instruction ends with no cues at all. This gradual weakening and eventual elimination of cues is called "fading."*

The *gradual* fading of cues is what makes it possible for discriminative stimuli ultimately to gain control over responses. Learners are not required to make longer jumps at any stage of instruction than they are judged capable of making. Cues are faded at a rate that is in keeping with learners' estimated and increasing capacities to continue making correct responses. They are removed completely only at that point at which learners are judged able to make required responses without them.

Shaping of Component Skills

Component Skills

Any performance, whether it is operating a microscope or choosing a lens, is made up of many component skills.† Some of them may already have been learned in the past. Mastery of any type of full-blown performance depends on learning those component skills that have not been previously learned. Further, when any of the individual component skills can be anticipated to pose learning difficulties, special approaches and extra attention may be necessary.

The component skills that behavior theory focuses on include: discriminations, generalizations, associations, and chains.‡ Choosing the lens that is a "convex" lens depends on being able to discriminate (tell the difference) between convex lenses and other types. It also depends on being able to generalize (see the similarities) among varied instances of convex lenses. Furthermore, it depends on associating the label "convex" with instances of it. Operating a

---

*Merrill (p. 208) incorporates this strategy.

†This is similar to Gagné's notion that intellectual skills can be broken down into simpler component parts (p. 22).

‡This breakdown is quite different from Gagné's.

microscope depends on these same types of skills and, in addition, on chaining (linking together) a sequence of multiple steps.

Any performance is made up of and can be analyzed for its unique combination of these four types of component skills. It can also be analyzed for conditions likely to make learning the component skills difficult (see section on stimulus/response characteristics).*

Shaping

Sometimes it is possible to practice component skills as part of a total performance. At other times it may be too difficult to master them in this way—even with maximum cuing. Practicing a full-blown performance at the outset may not be feasible. Instruction must then attend to the component skills in some other, usually piecemeal, way. Each component skill or a small number of component skills may first have to be practiced in isolation.

In a behavioral approach to instruction, first dealing with component skills in piecemeal fashion and then gradually linking them into a complete performance is called "shaping." Much instruction requires such a gradual, additive approach.†

Implementing a Behavioral Approach

Classical behavioral principles offer a strategy for bringing about the behavior change called "learning." It is a strategy framed at a very high level of generality. Its implementation has in the past found varied expression. It has appeared, nearly intact, in avowedly behavioral approaches as well as, borrowed and piecemeal, in some cognitive approaches. These differing approaches simply represent variations in tactics—in the practical means chosen to implement the same set of behavioral principles.

Practitioners need guidance that is more explicit than simply being told to "transfer control from cues to discriminative stimuli" or to "fade cues" or to "shape behavior." "Engineering tactics" need to be spelled out in more concrete detail.

A behavioral theory of instruction (described in the companion volume, Gropper, 1983) attempts to do precisely that. It identifies types of objectives with which most practitioners are familiar. It analyzes each type of objective for its behavioral component skills. It identifies subject matter characteristics that could

---

*Note that this section did not describe an instructional strategy component (or prescription as to what the instruction should be like).

†This is similar in many ways to Landa's "step-by-step" approach to teaching algorithms (p. 122) and Scandura's approach to teaching rules. This is usually a macrolevel concern, that is, it deals with the structure and sequence of relatively larger portions of instruction, as opposed to strategies for teaching individual concepts or behaviors.

make it difficult to learn those skills. And it labels all these parameters as conditions—conditions for which suitable instructional treatments would be needed.

This instructional theory also identifies treatments suitable for each type of objective. It identifies additional treatments suitable for objectives that are likely to be judged difficult to learn. The theory explicitly matches treatments with conditions. All this is done from a behavioral point of view.

Conditions

Types of Objectives.   Four *categories of objectives* can account for most of what is taught in school or job settings. They include:

- Recalling or applying facts.
- Giving definitions and explanations, applying them to examples, or illustrating them with examples.
- Following procedural rules.
- Solving problems.*

Instances of these categories can be found in the lesson that appears later in this chapter.

Underlying Component Skills.   Each of these categories of objectives can be analyzed for its *underlying component skills:*

- Discriminations.
- Generalizations.
- Associations.
- Chains.

Although all four categories of objectives usually involve all four types of component skills, each category typically is distinguished by the predominance of one or two of its component skills. For example, "procedures" are distinguished by a requirement to learn a long chain. Definitions are distinguished by a requirement to learn discriminations and generalizations (involved in recognizing instances of a concept).

The distinctive mix of component skills that characterizes each specific objec-

---

*These four categories are similar to Gagné-Briggs' "verbal information," "concrete and defined concepts" (except for "giving definitions and explanations", which is verbal information), "rule using," and "problem solving," respectively (pp. 14–15), and to Merrill's "remember-instance," "remember-generality (for "giving definitions and explanations"), and "use for concepts" (for "applying them"), "use for procedures," and "use for principles," respectively (p. 203).

tive is one contributor to the "conditions" that must be accommodated by instructional treatments.*

Stimulus/Response Characteristics.   Characteristics of subject matter that might make learning difficult also contribute to those "conditions." Characteristics of stimuli can make discriminations and generalizations difficult to learn. For instance, similarities among stimuli, for example, convex lenses and other types of lenses, can make it difficult for a learner to tell them apart. Or the length of a chain can make it difficult to learn. Or the number of associations between stimuli and responses can make those associations difficult to learn.

The range of stimulus and response properties that can make learning difficult is identified in the first column of Figure 3.1.

Matching Treatments to Conditions

Any instructional theory, behavioral or nonbehavioral, needs to identify conditions and treatments. It also needs to match treatments with conditions in systematic fashion. Treatments must be found that can match the distinctive requirements posed by: (a) the types of objectives that need to be learned; and (b) the applicable mix of component skills and of stimulus/response characteristics that may make learning those objectives difficult.

As shown in Fig. 3.1, there are three major categories of recommended treatments:

- Routine treatments.
- Shaping treatments.
- Specialized treatments.

Routine Treatments

A common set of routine treatments is applicable to *all four* types of objectives. It includes:

                                        COMMENTS

- Telling the learner what and how to   27, 29, 34, 39, 50, 52
  perform (a cue that elicits desired re-
  sponses)†

---

*Hence, different methods of instruction are required for each of these four kinds of objectives, just as Gagné-Briggs (p. 13) prescribe differences in the events of instruction for each of their kinds of intellectual skills (discriminations, concrete concepts, defined concepts, rules, and problem solving), and Merrill (p. 204) prescribes different methods for his performance levels (remember-instance, remember-generality, use, and find) and content types (fact, concept, procedure, and principle).

†This kind of cue is the same as Merrill's "generality" (p. 204) and Landa's "prescription" (p. 120).

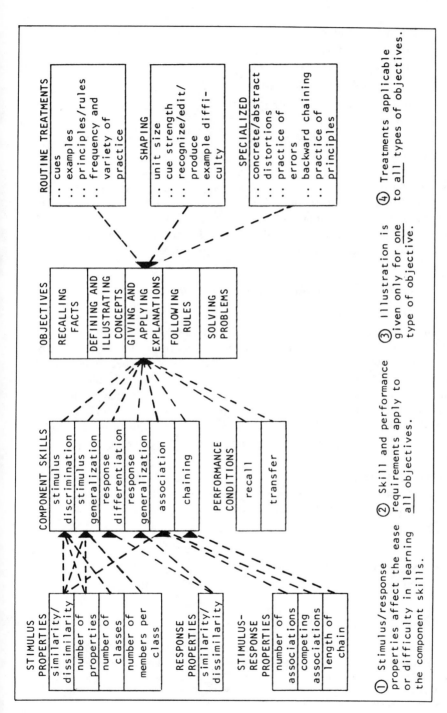

FIG. 3.1. Summary of Strategy Elements. This figure summarizes relationships among types of stimulus/response characteristics, component skills, and treatments.

53

e.g., how to follow procedures	2, 5
e.g., how to define a concept or how to classify an instance of the concept	15, 17
e.g., how to explain phenomena	42, 45
• Providing examples of the performance to be learned*	15, 17, 19, 27, 42
• Providing opportunities to practice the performance to be learned†	2, 8, 12, 15, 23, 27, 39, 44, 47, 50, 54

This overall routine strategy is appropriate for any type of objective. It calls for the practice of a complete set of skills that is to be learned. For example, learners may be asked on their first practice opportunity to practice *all* the steps involved in operating a microscope. If conditions permit, this is an ideal approach to adopt, principally for the *efficiencies* it makes possible.

Nonroutine Treatments (Shaping and Specialized)

For those conditions expected to pose learning difficulties, the same basic, routine treatments are also proposed. But the practice of an intact, full-blown performance is deferred until the closing moments of instruction. It is necessary to precede it with easier practice. This may consist of practice of individual component skills. Or it may consist of practice of an intact, total set of skills— but with large amounts of help continuing to be available. For example, learners may continue to have a list of steps in front of them on multiple practice problems—before being asked to operate a microscope without the list. Such easier forms of practice are necessary when learning difficulties are anticipated.

Shaping.   There are several ways to make early practice easier than the kind of complete performance called for in "routine" treatments. Among them are treatment types that rely on variations in:

COMMENTS

• The size of the unit of behavior practiced	15, 18, 20, 27, 32, 34, 36, 39, 42, 43, 45

---

*This kind of cue is the same as Merrill's "example" (p. 204), Landa's "demonstration" (p. 121, footnote 12), and Collins' "positive exemplars" (p. 183).

†Practice is specifically prescribed by Gagné-Briggs (p. 20) and Merrill (p. 204), and it is tacitly assumed by the other theorists.

- The amount of cuing (help) made available during practice*   2, 6, 7, 8, 10, 17, 18, 19, 21, 24, 35, 40, 43, 46, 52, 53
- The mode of stimulus or of response e.g., recognizing a response rather than producing it   22, 33
- The frequency and variety of practice†   11, 40
- The content of practice e.g., example difficulty‡   treatment not used in this lesson

These diverse techniques may be used singly or in concert to create a *graduated* learning experience. A shaping approach takes the learner from some variant of a minimal performance to a progressively more difficult one. Ultimately, the learner practices a complete, full-blown performance.§

Specialized Treatments.   Other, more specialized treatments are available to meet special learning problems:

COMMENTS

- The use of concrete examples before abstract examples   4, 9, 31, 32
- Distortion of a stimulus or response, (making either easier or more accessible because of the exaggeration)   treatment not used in this lesson
- The practice of errors to make the discrimination between the right and wrong way to do something easier¶   treatment not used in this lesson
- The practice of a series of procedural steps in a backward order   treatment not used in this lesson
- The practice of principles about procedures before practice of the procedures themselves   treatment not used in this lesson

---

*This is the same as Merrill's "attention-focusing information" (p. 207).

†Variety of practice is the same as Merrill's "divergence" (p. 208), Collins' "vary cases systematically" (p. 184) and "entrap students" (p. 185), and Scandura's "equivalence classes" (p. 164).

‡This is similar to Merrill's "range of difficulty" (p. 208).

§As represented in this section, Gropper's theory is unique in the level of detailed guidance that it provides to instructional designers for increasing the amount of "learning guidance" (Gagné-Briggs) or "help" (Merrill) when needed.

¶This is somewhat similar to Merrill's notion of "matched nonexamples" (p. 208).

When nonroutine treatments precede the routine ones (in order to make it possible for the routine ones to work), they obviously add to the length of instructional presentations. The efficiency of those presentations, a not inconsiderable issue, suffers. Accordingly, nonroutine treatments are recommended only on an as-needed basis. The "conditions" that apply to particular objectives determine whether there is such a need.*

Other Instructional Strategies

Several more general instructional strategies also have an important influence on learning: advance organizers, information displays, and sequencing. The following sections, therefore, provide a *behavioral* rationale for their use in instruction.

Advance Organizers.   Instruction may provide a learner with varied types of advance organizers, including an introduction, a statement of purposes (objectives), and self-instructional "learning hints" (see Comments 3, 16, 28, 41, and 51). How is such usage rationalized—behaviorally?

In behaviorally oriented experimentation, cues meant to elicit relevant responses or to direct attention are presented *simultaneously* with discriminative stimuli. In contrast, advance organizers are cues presented in advance of a presentation and, therefore, *in advance of* the presentation of discriminative stimuli. Whether advance organizers are presented simultaneously or prospectively, their purpose is the same. Advance organizers are meant primarily to direct learner attention. Their aim is for more generalized effects than are typically achieved with the simultaneous pairing of a specific cue and a specific discriminative stimulus. Advance organizers are meant to serve as cues calling attention *throughout* a whole lesson to multiple discriminative stimuli, to multiple presentation cues relating to them, or to multiple responses.

It is an empirical issue whether the prospective nature of advance organizers influences their effectiveness. However, if advance organizers do work, their effects are likely to be highly generative. They will achieve those effects by their capacity to direct learner attention to the ingredients of a required performance: discriminative stimuli and responses. This is but one role they can play.†

Self-Instruction.   Advance organizers may also be capable of prompting learners not just to attend to but also to *search actively* for specific kinds of information. Learning hints are meant to prompt a self-directed search for information

---

*These specialized treatments are also quite unique and provide considerably more guidance for instructional designers than any of the other instructional theories.

†Although the term "advance organizer" is not being used quite the same way as Ausubel uses it, the use of a "preinstructional strategy" is an important prescription that few other instructional theories include.

(cues or discriminative stimuli) that can facilitate learning the objectives in a given section of a lesson. Thus, they are advance organizers in the same way that objectives are. Their eliciting role is similarly a prospective rather than a simultaneous one. They relate to an immediately upcoming lesson segment.*

The inclusion of learning hints in all segments of a lesson has a more far-reaching aim as well. The expectation is that, having practiced searching over and over for the kinds of information that can facilitate learning discriminations, generalizations, associations, and chains. learners will come to do similar self-directed searches in any future instructional setting—with or without being told to do so. Whether or not such learning hints will result in acquisition of useful learning skills is an empirical question that, on the face of it, merits investigation.

Display of Information

Instructional-design theories have primarily concentrated on relevant types of information (e.g., rules and examples) needed to teach specific types of objectives. For the most part, they have neglected consideration of how that information might best be *displayed*. This represents a missed opportunity to use the ''display of information'' as a tool—as a cue to elicit attention to the content of a lesson or to elicit learner recognition of the types of information being made available or of the way to use the information.

The way information is displayed can enhance or detract from the effectiveness or the efficiency of instruction. If a display is designed to serve the same goals that informational content is meant to serve, both content and display can be made to work together toward that end. For example, presenting procedural steps in a list rather than in paragraph form might better facilitate learning of the sequence of steps. Or juxtaposing discriminative stimuli that have to be distinguished from one another might help to make the distinguishing features more obvious than a serial display would be able to do. Display techniques are additional instructional design tools—to be considered and used systematically.† (See Comments 6, 18, 30, and 52.)

Directing Attention.   One very useful way to display information is in tabular formats. Their primary purpose is to function as cues that control learner attention. Information is juxtaposed in rows or columns as a means of facilitating the learning of component skills. Such juxtaposition can cue a comparison of (direct attention to) stimuli that need to be discriminated. Or it can direct attention to the

---

*This is another preinstructional strategy that could be very useful but is overlooked by most other instructional theories.

†Although much work has been done on such ''message design'' prescriptions, instructional theories as a rule do not yet incorporate these valuable prescriptions.

similarities among stimuli that require generalization. Or it can direct attention to stimuli and responses that need to be associated.

Characterizing Lesson Content.   Display parameters can do more than just direct attention. They represent a nonverbal means of *characterizing* the types of information being offered. For example, a tabled list of procedural steps identifies or models in nonverbal fashion the sequential nature of the information being provided. Display parameters, suitably selected and designed, are capable of cuing learner recognition of the types of information being provided, as well as recognition of how that information needs to be used. Repeated use of a display convention for the same cuing purpose can create a stable tool. It can be depended upon, on multiple occasions, to elicit the same kind of responses it was originally designed to elicit.

Sequencing

"Sequence" as Facilitator.   The concept of the "transfer of stimulus control" may be used to rationalize the sequence in which the various sections of a lesson are arranged. For example, in one section of a lesson, stimulus *A* acquires control over response *A*. In the next section, stimulus *A* can now be used as a cue to elicit response *A* or a new response, *B*.

In the current lesson, learners are first taught to "use a microscope." In the course of learning to operate the microscope, they experience and, as a result, begin to understand the concept of magnification. In subsequent sections of the lesson, the word *magnification* can now be used as a discriminative stimulus with which other responses can be associated (e.g., the prediction of which lens will magnify an object the most). Thus, the order in which objectives or topics are taught can facilitate the overall progress of instruction. It is not, however, a required order. (See Comments 4 and 49.)

Sequencing of Prerequisites.   Most instruction does have a required order. Most instructional-design theories take this into account when they prescribe the sequencing of prerequisite skills before the skills that are contingent on them.* "Transfer of stimulus control" may also be used to account for this sequencing strategy. (See Comments 14, 26, and 38.)

The sequence of sections and the material within sections of the lesson in this chapter reflect both facilitating and required orders.

---

*This is a direct reference to Gagné's "hierarchical sequence of learning prerequisites" (p. 22). Reigeluth also uses this strategy on a much narrower scale (p. 253).

LESSON PREFACE

Purpose of the Lesson in This Chapter

The lesson that appears in this chapter is offered as an example of the application to course development of behavioral instructional-design principles. The design principles they illustrate were set forth in the earlier volume (Gropper, 1983).

The Instructional Objectives. The objectives for the lesson in this chapter are identical to those addressed in other chapters. They include the following performance requirements:

1. Classify previously unencountered lenses as to whether or not they are convex lenses.
2. Define focal length.
3. Predict what effect different convex lenses will have on light rays.
4. Explain the way in which the curvature of a lens influences both the magnification and the focal length of different lenses.
5. State from memory the three significant events in the history of the microscope.
6. Use a previously unencountered optical microscope.

Target Audience. The intended audience for the lesson is a sixth-grade student.

Lesson Description. The lesson is a self-paced, printed lesson.

Testing. Although tests do not accompany this lesson, the practice exercises that are scheduled *last* in each section of the lesson are suitable for testing purposes. They test for the full-blown type of performance called for in lesson objectives.

Annotation Provided in This Chapter

Although the lesson in this chapter exemplifies the application of instructional-design principles presented in the earlier volume, a lesson itself is unfortunately mute. Any example of a lesson by itself cannot testify as to how or in what ways it exemplifies a specific design theory. It takes annotation external to the lesson to identify what it is about the lesson that makes it an example of an instructional-design theory.

To supply that kind of annotation, three types of information are provided: reader introductions, numbered comments and "learning hints."

Reader Introductions. A "reader introduction" appears at the beginning of each section of the lesson. It is meant only for you, the reader of this chapter. It is not something the student would receive. It is designed to direct *your* attention to specific features of the lesson. It provides: (a) a list of the "conditions" being addressed in that section of the lesson; and (b) a list of "treatments" chosen to address them.

Itemized Comments. Callout numbers appear throughout the lesson. They are geared to numbered comments listed at the end of the entire lesson. Each comment identifies either a "condition" that is relevant to a particular place in the lesson and/or an "instructional treatment" employed (at that place) to meet the condition.

Learning Hints. In the lesson proper, learners are given "learning hints" that are intended to serve as advance organizers. The learning hints, although written for the learner, identify for *you,* the reader of this chapter, the types of skills a given lesson segment addresses. Skills to be learned constitute one element of the "conditions" a lesson must treat.

How To Read This Chapter

It is recommended that you read this chapter in a linear way—stopping only to refer to each numbered comment (at the end of the chapter) that corresponds to the callout numbers that appear throughout the lesson.*

---

*We suggest that each time you encounter a number in the margin of the lesson, first try to figure out what prescription is being implemented, and then read the corresponding comment to confirm your analysis. By keeping a finger in the Comments section and a finger in the Lesson, it will be easy to flip back and forth as you progress through the lesson.

[1]
SECTION I: How to Use a Microscope

Reader Introduction

The first section of the lesson, which begins on the next page, teaches students how to use a mciroscope. The lists below identify for you, the reader, the "conditions" judged to underlie such a goal and the "treatments" selected for addressing them.

[2]

Conditions (The learner has to learn to:)	Treatments
produce all the individual, procedural steps required to use a microscope. (FOLLOWING PROCEDURES)	A model performance is offered (a list of steps), followed by learner practice of the steps. (ROUTINE)
produce the steps in sequence.	The model performance followed by practice also addresses this problem.
recognize correct outcomes of Individual steps and of the entire procedure.	Characteristics of correct outcomes are included with the lists of steps.
perform all the steps without any aids.	Learners are weaned of the "model of performance," and they then practice using a microscope without any cues at all. (SHAPING)
transfer the learned performance to other previously unused microscopes.	Learners practice using different types of microscopes. (ROUTINE)

How to Use a Microscope

Introduction

You can use a microscope to make something that is really very small look big. This can be particularly helpful if you want to look at things that ordinarily you wouldn't be able to see with the naked eye. For example, a special lens in a microscope makes it possible for you to see objects as small as bacteria. Without a microscope you wouldn't be able to see them at all.

[3] *Purpose*

This lesson will first tell you how to use a microscope. Then, you will practice using one yourself.

[4] • You will use the microscope to look at objects.
     • You will observe what happens to the objects when you view them through different kinds of lenses.

[3] *Learning Hints*

As you read this section, *look for* the following kinds of information:

   • What steps you should use when operating a microscope.
   • In what order you should use those steps.
   • How you can tell when you have used the steps in the right way.

Assignment

   • Read the list of steps on the next page.
   • Then, do the EXERCISES that follow.

Instructions

1. Just read each step below. Do *not* work on the microscope yet. You will do that in a practice exercise.
2. As you read each step, find the part of the microscope that is mentioned in the step. The circled letters in the step and in the picture (Fig. 3.2 on the facing page) will tell you where on the microscope the part is.
3. Read across the page.

TABLE 3.1

Step #	What You Want to Accomplish	▶ What You Should Do ▶	How You Know If You Did It Correctly
1	TO GET LIGHT TO SHINE THROUGH A SLIDE YOU WANT TO LOOK AT:	Turn on the light in the microscope (if it has one). -OR-	You can see light shining through the hole.
		Adjust the *mirror* ⓐ on the microscope to allow room light to shine through the hole ⓘ in the *stage* ⓒ.	You can see light shining through the hole.
2	TO GET THE RIGHT AMOUNT OF LIGHT TO SHINE THROUGH THE HOLE:	Turn the *diaphragm* ⓑ in the direction (clockwise or counterclockwise) that makes the light brighter.	The light shining through the hole in the stage seems bright.
3	TO PLACE THE SPECIMEN ON THE SLIDE DIRECTLY UNDER THE LENS AND IN THE LIGHT:	Place the *slide* directly over the hole in the *stage* ⓒ.	You can see the specimen over the hole in the stage.
4	TO MAKE SURE THE SLIDE WILL NOT SLIP OFF THE STAGE:	Turn the *clips* ⓓ so they are over the slide.	The slide will not move.
5	TO GET THE AMOUNT OF ENLARGEMENT THAT YOU WANT:	Select the *objective* (lens) ⓔ that will give you that amount of enlargement and rotate it so that it is over the slide.	The objective (lens) almost touches the slide.
6	TO BRING THE SPECIMEN INTO PRELIMINARY FOCUS:	Look into the *eyepiece* ⓕ and turn the *coarse adjustment* ⓖ clockwise.	You can see the specimen on the slide in a reasonable amount of detail.
7	TO BRING THE SPECIMEN INTO SHARP FOCUS:	Look into the eyepiece and turn the *fine adjustment* ⓗ clockwise.	You can see the specimen in very clear detail.

64

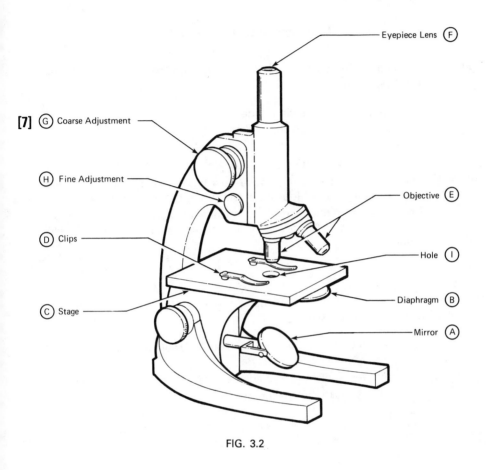

[7]

Eyepiece Lens Ⓕ

Ⓖ Coarse Adjustment

Ⓗ Fine Adjustment

Objective Ⓔ

Ⓓ Clips

Hole Ⓘ

Ⓒ Stage

Diaphragm Ⓑ

Mirror Ⓐ

FIG. 3.2

Exercise: Using a Microscope to Enlarge Objects

1

[8] Get a microscope and then use the list of steps (on the facing page) to help you do this problem.

    1. Read step #1 on the facing page.
    2. Carry out step #1 yourself.
    3. Read and then do step #2.
    4. Do the same for all the other steps.

[9]   5. After completing step #7, notice how big the specimen on the slide appears as a result of looking at it through the microscope.
    6. Take the slide off the microscope, observe the specimen with the naked eye alone, and note how small the specimen is without the microscope.

2

[10] If you still need help in using a microscope, read the list of steps on the facing page as you do this problem.

    1. Use the same microscope that you used in Problem #1. Lower a *different objective* (lens) over the slide.
    2. First bring the specimen into coarse focus; then into sharp focus.
    3. How did this make the specimen look?

      __ bigger than in   __ not as big as   __ as big as in
          Problem #1   in Problem #1   Problem #1

3

If you still need help, use the list of steps on the facing page.

[11]   1. Get a *different* microscope.
    2. View a specimen through the microscope.
    3. View the specimen through a *different* objective (lens).
    4. Did the second objective make the specimen appear as large as the first one did?

4

Do *not* read the list of the steps as you do this problem.

    1. Get *another* microscope.
    2. Get a specimen and view it through the microscope.
    3. Repeat the steps—using a *different* objective.

TABLE 3.2

Step #	What You Want to Accomplish ▶	What You Should Do ▶	How You Know If You Did It Correctly
1	TO GET LIGHT TO SHINE THROUGH A SLIDE YOU WANT TO LOOK AT:	Turn on the light in the microscope (if it has one). or Adjust the *mirror* ⓐ on the microscope to allow room light to shine through the hole ① in the *stage* ©.	You can see light shining through the hole. You can see light shining through the hole.
2	TO GET THE RIGHT AMOUNT OF LIGHT TO SHINE THROUGH THE HOLE:	Turn the *diaphragm* ⓑ in the direction that makes the light brighter.	The light shining through the hole in the stage seems bright.
3	TO PLACE THE SPECIMEN ON THE SLIDE DIRECTLY UNDER THE LENS AND IN THE LIGHT:	Place the *slide* directly over the hole in the *stage* ©.	You can see the specimen over the hole in the stage.
4	TO MAKE SURE THE SLIDE WILL NOT SLIP OFF THE STAGE:	Turn the *clips* so that they are over the slide.	The slide will not move.
5	TO GET THE AMOUNT OF ENLARGEMENT THAT YOU WANT:	Select the *objective* (lens) ⓔ that will give you that amount of enlargement and rotate it so that it is over the slide.	The objective (lens) almost touches the slide.
6	TO BRING THE SPECIMEN INTO PRELIMINARY FOCUS:	Look into the *eyepiece* ⓕ and turn the *coarse adjustment* ⓗ (clockwise).	You can see the specimen on the slide in a reasonable amount of detail.
7	TO BRING THE SPECIMEN INTO SHARP FOCUS:	Look into the eyepiece and turn the *fine adjustment* (clockwise).	You can see the specimen in very clear detail.

[13]   SECTION II: How To Recognize a Convex Lens

Reader Introduction

[14]   This section of the lesson teaches students to recognize instances of
a convex lens. The lists below identify for you, the reader,
"conditions" judged to underlie such a goal and the "treatments"
selected for addressing them.

[15]   Conditions   Treatments
The learner has to: A verbal definition of a
discriminate between instances   convex lens is provided.
of lenses that are and are not   (ROUTINE)
convex lenses.   Multiple visual examples of
generalize across varied   convex and nonconvex lenses
instances of convex lenses (see   are provided: annotation
their similarities).   identifies the features that
associate the label "convex"   make a particular instance
with instances of it.   convex or nonconvex.
                                     (ROUTINE)
                                     The label "convex" is
                                     attached to instances of
                                     convex lenses. (ROUTINE)
                                     Learners engage in graduated
                                     practice recognizing
                                     (distinguishing between)
                                     convex and nonconvex
                                     lenses. (SHAPING)
                                     Learners engage in practice
                                     identifying single instances of
                                     lenses as being either convex
                                     or nonconvex. (ROUTINE)

How to Recognize Different Types of Lenses

Introduction

You've noticed that some lenses can make a specimen look bigger than other lenses can. Why? What are the differences between one lens and another that make this happen?

One type of lens used in a microscope is called a *convex* lens.

Not all convex lenses are alike. Some are wider in the middle than other lenses. Thus, they come in different sizes. Soon you will discover that the width of a lens can affect how big the lens can make a specimen look.

[16]   *Purpose*

This section will show you how to:

- recognize a convex lens.

Learning Hints

[16] Look for the following kinds of information:

- How to tell the difference between convex lenses and other types of lenses.
- How to recognize the similarities among various examples of convex lenses.

Assignment

- Read the next two pages on lenses.
- Do the exercises that follow.

TABLE 3.3
What is a Convex Lense

		A Four Part Definition	Examples	Comment on the Examples
[17]	1.	All types of lenses have two *outside* surfaces.		a = outside surface b = outside surface c = inside the lens
[18]	2.	There are *three* types of outside surfaces: • Flat (straight). • Bent *out* from the center. • Bent *in* toward the center.		a = a *flat* surface a = this surface is bent *out* from the center a = this surface is bent *in* toward the center
	3.	CONVEX lenses have outside surfaces that bend *out* from the center. This makes the middle of the lens fatter than the ends.		a = a surface that bends *out* from the center b = a surface that also bends *out* from the center
	4.	*Definition:* A CONVEX lens must have *at least* one surface that is bent *out* from the center. And, the middle of the lens has to be fatter than the ends.		a = bends out b = bends out a = flat b = bends out from the center

TABLE 3.4
Six Types of Lenses (Three Are Convex)

Types of Lenses	Bent-Out Surfaces	Types of Surfaces	Is It a Convex Lens?
A)] B	0	a = bent in b = flat	No it *doesn't* have even one bent out surface
A)(B	0	a = bent in b = bent in	No it *doesn't* have even one bent out surface
Convex A (] B	1	a = bent *out* b = flat	Yes one surface (*a*) is bent out *And,* the middle is fatter than the ends
Convex A ((B	1	a = bent *out* b = bent in	Yes (another type of convex lens). one surface (a) is bent out *And,* the middle is fatter than the ends
A)] B	1	a = bent in b = bent *out* (a little bit)	No one surface (b) *is* bent out *But,* the middle is *not* fatter than the ends
Convex A () B	2	a = bent out b = bent out	Yes (another type of convex lens). two surfaces are bent out *And,* the middle is fatter than the ends

Answers on next page. (Don't look at them until you have finished.)

1. How many bent-out sides does each of the following lenses have?

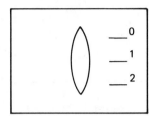
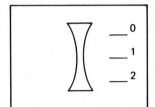
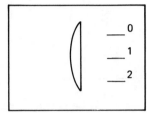

[21]   2. To be called a "convex" lens a lens must have *at least* one bent-out
[22]   surface. It must also be wider in the *middle* than at the ends. Check the
           lens in each pair that is the *convex* lens.

A.

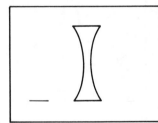
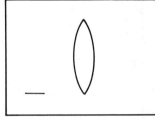

B.

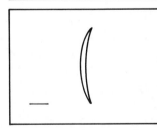
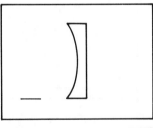

C.

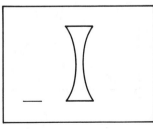

73

1. How many bent-*out* sides does each of the following lenses have?

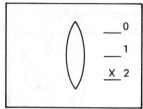

	___ 0
	___ 1
	X_ 2

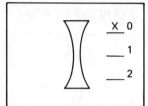

	X_ 0
	___ 1
	___ 2

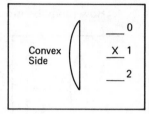

Convex Side

	___ 0
	X_ 1
	___ 2

2. To be called a "convex" lens a lens must have *at least* one bent-*out* surface. It must also be wider in the *middle* than at the ends. Check the lens in each pair that is the *convex* lens.

A.

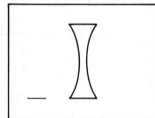

___

X

B.

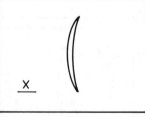

X

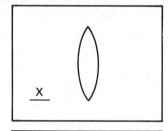

___

C.

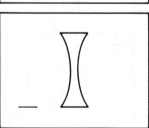

___

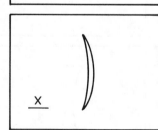

X

[23]   3. Put a check next to each lens indicating whether it is or is *not* convex.

	CONVEX	*NOT CONVEX*
	——	——
	——	——
	——	——
	——	——
	——	——
	——	——

ANSWERS TO EXCERCISE

3. Put a check next to each lens indicating whether it is or is *not* convex.

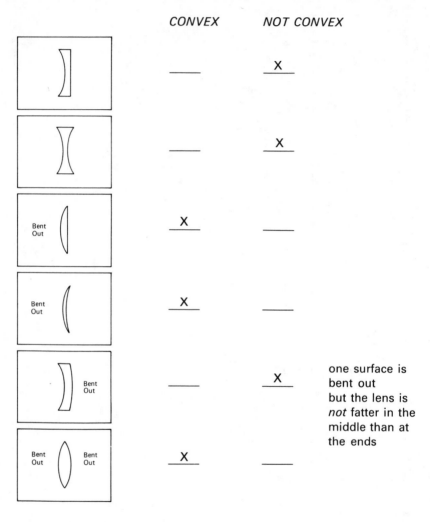

CONVEX   NOT CONVEX

___   X___

___   X___

[24]   X___   ___

X___   ___

___   X___   one surface is
bent out
but the lens is
not fatter in the
middle than at
the ends

X___   ___

[25]

SECTION III: Predicting What Will
Happen to Light Rays When They Go
Through A Lens

Reader Introduction

[26] This section of the lesson teaches: how to describe what happens to
light rays when they pass through a lens; how to predict how the
width of the lens affects what happens; and how to define "focal
length." The lists below identify the "conditions" judged to underlie
this goal and the "treatments" selected for addressing them.

[27]

Conditions	Treatments
(The learner has to learn to:)	These facts are stated and
associate and recall what happens to light rays at varied parts of a lens. (RECALLING FACTS)	learners practice stating them (or representing them in drawings). (ROUTINE)
associate the degree of bending of light rays with lenses varying in width. (RECALLING/APPLYING FACTS)	These facts are stated and learners then practice stating them or practice predicting what will happen to light rays when they pass through lenses of varying widths. (ROUTINE)

SECTION 3

Predicting What Will Happen to Light Rays
When They Go Through a Lens

Introduction

When you used a microscope, this is what happened:

1. Light rays from the mirror hit the specimen.
2. The light rays bounced off the specimen and passed through one side of the lens.
3. The lens changed the direction in which the light rays went.
4. The change in direction played a part in making the specimen look bigger.
5. When you looked into the other side of the lens you saw the enlarged or magnified specimen.

[28] *Purpose*

This section will show you how to:

- Predict what will happen to light rays when they pass through a lens.
- Predict how the width of a lens will affect how much a lens will change the direction of light rays.
- Define a new term: "focal length."

[28] *Learning Hints*

Look for the following kinds of information:

- How can you tell the difference between what happens to light rays that go through the middle of a lens and those that go through the end of a lens?
- How can you decide which size lens will change the direction of light rays the most and which will change it the least?
- How do you define "focal length"?

Assignment

Read the following pages and do the exercises after them.

*What Happens to Light Rays
That Enter Different Parts of a Lens*

Read the comments below. They describe what happens to the light rays.

[29]   1. Light rays from the sun hit a very small pencil ⓐ. Then, the light rays are reflected from the pencil in many directions ⓑ.

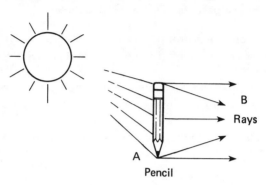

Pencil

[30]   2. The light rays enter a lens. They enter the lens at many points: ⓒ the middle; ⓓ the top; and ⓔ the bottom.

[31]

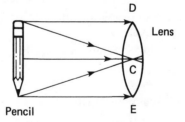

Pencil

3. The lens changes the direction of the light rays: The light going through the top of the lens is bent down ⓕ. The light going through the bottom is bent up ⓖ. The light slanting down continues to slant down ⓗ. The light slanting up continues to slant up ⓘ. Notice that the rays going through the center ⓙ of the lens do *not* bend.

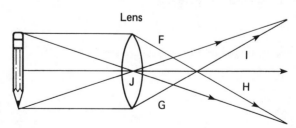

80

4. When you look at the pencil through a lens, what you see at the other end of the lens ⓚ is *bigger* than the original pencil.

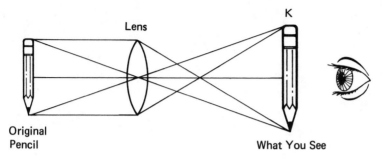

Lens

K

Original
Pencil

What You See

1. What will happen to the light rays that enter at the *top* ⓐ of the lens shown below and at the *bottom* ⓑ at the same lens?

[32]

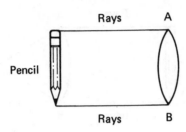

The light rays at the *top* will bend _____.
　　　　　　　　　　　　　　　　　　　 direction

The light rays at the *bottom* will bend _____.
　　　　　　　　　　　　　　　　　　　　　 direction

2. *Draw in* on the picture below what will happen to the light rays that enter the lens at the top ⓐ and what will happen to the light rays that enter the lens at the bottom ⓑ.

[33]

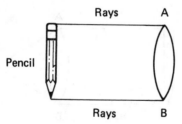

1. What will happen to the light rays that enter at the *top* ⓐ of the lens shown below and at the bottom ⓑ of the same lens?

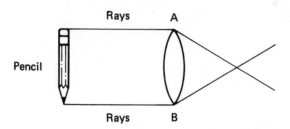

Rays   A

Pencil

Rays   B

The light rays at the top will bend <u>DOWN</u> .
                                         direction

The light rays at the bottom will bend <u> UP.</u>
                                         direction

2. *Draw in* on the picture below what will happen to the light rays that enter the lens at the *top* ⓐ and what will happen to the light rays that enter the lens at the *bottom* ⓑ.

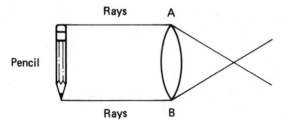

Rays   A

Pencil

Rays   B

[34]

1. Look at the three lenses below. Lens(a)on the left is the widest. Lens(c)on the right is the narrowest. Lens(b)in the middle is in between (in width).

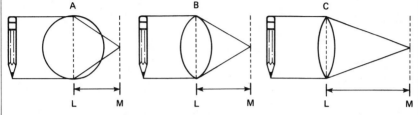

2. Read the following points about what happens to light rays when they pass through *any* lens—no matter how wide or narrow it is:

   - Light rays passing through the top and bottom of *any* lens bend.
   - The light rays at the top bend down; and the light rays at the bottom bend up.
   - Notice that the "down" rays and the "up" rays cross (intersect) on the other side of the lens—at (m).

3. How does the width of a lens affect *how much* the light rays bend?

   - The widest lens(a)made the light rays bend the most; notice that the light rays *cross over* much *closer* to the lens than in the other two examples.
   - The narrowest lens(c)made the light rays bend the least; notice that the light rays cross over the farthest away from the lens.

4. Remember the following general points about how the width of a lens affects the bending of light rays:

   - The wider a lens is, the *more* it will bend light rays; and the *more* bending there is, the *closer* to the lens will the light rays cross over (intersect).
   - The *narrower* a lens is, the *less* it will bend light rays; and the *less* bending there is, the *farther* away from the lens will the light rays cross over.

5. You're ready now to find out what the *distance* from the center of a lens(l)to the crossover point (m) is called: FOCAL LENGTH.

EXERCISE (ANSWERS ON NEXT PAGE)

[35] 1. Look at the drawings on the previous page and then answer this question:
The distance between (l) and (m) is called the "focal length" of a lens. Which lens on the previous page has the *longest* focal length?
_____a _____b _____c

[36] 2. *That* lens has the longest focal length because it bent the light rays the _____most _____least.

3. The lens that bent the light rays the *most* is lens:
_____a _____b _____c

4. Since that lens bent the light rays the most, its focal length is the _____longest _____shortest.

5. Explain how the width of a lens affects the focal length of a lens. Use the following three ideas in your explanation: (a) the width of a lens; (b) the amount of bending of light rays; and (c) "focal length."

6. Define what is meant by "focal length."

ANSWERS TO EXERCISE

1. Look at the drawings on the previous page and then answer this question:
   The distance between (l) and (m) is called the "focal length" of a lens. Which lens on the previous page has the *longest* focal length?
   _____a _____b __X__c

2. *That* lens has the longest focal length because it bent the light rays the _____ most __X__least.

3. The lens that bent the light rays the *most* is lens:
   __X__a _____b _____c

4. Since that lens bent the light rays the most its focal length is the _____longest __X__shortest.

5. Explain how the width of a lens affects the focal length of a lens. Use the following three ideas in your explanation: (a) the width of a lens; (b) the amount of bending of light rays; and (c) "focal length."

   THE WIDER THE LENS, THE MORE IT BENDS LIGHT RAYS; THE MORE IT BENDS THE RAYS, THE SHORTER THE FOCAL LENGTH WILL BE.

6. Define what is meant by "focal length."

   FOCAL LENGTH MEANS: THE DISTANCE BETWEEN THE CENTER OF THE LENS AND THE PLACE WHERE THE LIGHT RAYS CROSS OVER (INTERSECT).

[37]

SECTION IV: Predicting How Big An Object
Looks Based On The Width Of
The Lens Used

Reader Introduction

[38]   This section of the lesson teaches the relationship between the
degree of curvature (width in the middle) of a lens and the degree of
magnification. The lists below identify the "conditions" judged to
underlie this goal and the "treatments" selected for addressing
them.

[39]   Conditions

(The learner has to learn to:)

associate the degree of curvature
of a lens and the degree of
magnification it produces
(RECALLING/APPLYING FACTS)

associate the degree of curvature
and the (relative) distance a lens
must be held (away from an
object) in order for light rays to
focus on the object
(RECALLING/APPLYING FACTS)

Treatments

The relationships (in both
conditions) are described.
(ROUTINE)

(ROUTINE) Learner practice
identifying for lenses of
varing width:

the relative degree of
magnification

the relative distance from
an object in order for light
rays to focus on the object

Predicting How Big an Object Looks Based on the Width of
the Lens Used

[40]   *Introduction*

Let's review some main points:

1. Light hits an object and is reflected off it.
2. The reflected rays travel in straight lines.
3. If these rays pass through a lens, they no longer travel in straight lines; they become bent.
4. The wider the lens is, the more bending will occur.
5. Because the light rays bend, they cross each other and focus at a point.
6. The *distance* between the center of the lens and the point at which the rays come together (intersect) is called the "focal length."

[41]   *Purpose*

This section of the lesson will show you how to:

- Predict which size lens will enlarge an object the most.
- Predict how far from an object you need to hold a lens in order for the light rays to focus on that object (and still let you see it clearly).

[41]   *Learning Hints*

When you read this section, look for the following kinds of information:

- Which size lens (big or small) goes with which size enlargement (big or small)?
- How far from a lens do you have to hold an object?

Assignment

Read the following pages and then do the exercises.

[42] 1. Look at the three lenses below. Lens ⓐ on the left is the widest. Lens ⓒ on the right is the narrowest. Lens ⓑ in the middle is in between (in width).

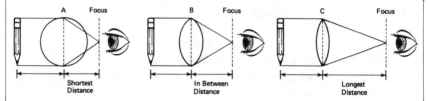

2. Figuring out how close to an object you have to hold a lens—in order to make the object look bigger.

- The wider a lens is in the middle, the more it bends light rays. The more the rays bend, the shorter the distance it takes to focus light rays.

  e.g., Lens ⓐ is the *widest*. It bends light rays the *most*. Therefore, the distance from the center of the lens to the focus is the *smallest*.

  e.g., Lens ⓒ is the *narrowest*. It bends light rays the *least*. Therefore, the distance from the center of the lens to the focus is the *longest*.

- The *smaller* the distance between the *center of a lens* and the *focal point* the *closer* you can hold an object to the lens.

  The *longer* the distance between the center of a lens and the *focal point,* means the *farther* away you hold an object from the lens.

  e.g., The distance between the center of the lens and the focal point in lens ⓐ is the *smallest*. Therefore, the object is held *closest* to lens ⓐ.

  e.g., The distance between the center of the lens and the focal point in lens ⓒ is the *longest*. Therefore, the object is held *farthest* away from lens ⓒ.

• *WIDTH OF LENS*	*DISTANCE TO FOCAL POINT*	*DISTANCE BETWEEN OBJECT AND LENS*
widest	smallest	closest to lens
in between	in between	in between
narrowest	longest	farthest away from lens

[43]

1. Look at the three lenses below. Each one is going to be held over an object that is sitting on a table. You want to look at the object through these lenses.

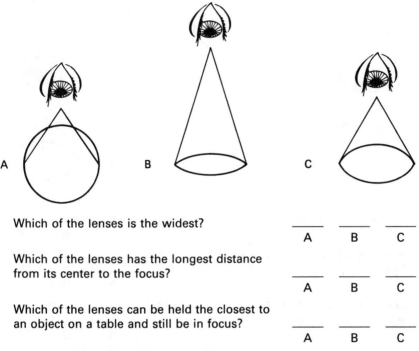

Which of the lenses is the widest?

_____ _____ _____
  A   B   C

Which of the lenses has the longest distance from its center to the focus?

_____ _____ _____
  A   B   C

Which of the lenses can be held the closest to an object on a table and still be in focus?

_____ _____ _____
  A   B   C

[44]

2. There are two different lenses. They have different widths.

Lens (1) is <u>3</u> centimeters wide

Lens (2) is <u>1.5</u> centimeters wide

Which lens can you hold <u>closer</u> to an object in order to make the object look bigger?

_____ _____
 (1)   (2)

Why? _____

_____

_____

1. Look at the three lenses below. Each one is going to be held over an object that is sitting on a table. You want to look at the object through these lenses.

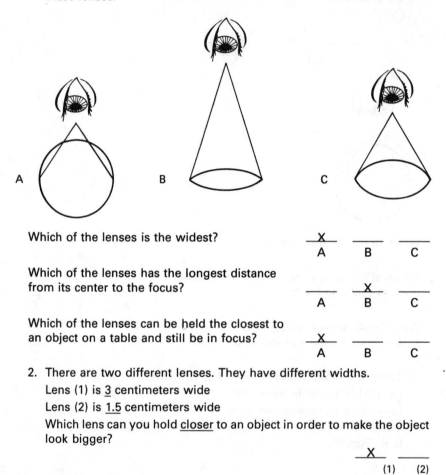

Which of the lenses is the widest?

<u>X</u> ___ ___
A   B   C

Which of the lenses has the longest distance from its center to the focus?

___ <u>X</u> ___
A   B   C

Which of the lenses can be held the closest to an object on a table and still be in focus?

<u>X</u> ___ ___
A   B   C

2. There are two different lenses. They have different widths.

Lens (1) is <u>3</u> centimeters wide

Lens (2) is <u>1.5</u> centimeters wide

Which lens can you hold <u>closer</u> to an object in order to make the object look bigger?

<u>X</u> ___
(1)   (2)

Why? THE WIDER THE LENS, THE MORE IT BENDS LIGHT RAYS, AND, THEREFORE THE SHORTER THE DISTANCE BE-TWEEN THE CENTER OF THE LENS AND THE FOCAL POINT: THEREFORE, YOU CAN HOLD THE *WIDER* LENS CLOSER TO THE OBJECT.

How the Width of a Lens Affects How Big an Object Will Look to You

Read the following points about how different sized lenses affect what you see.

1. When you look at an object through a lens:
   - you are on one side of the lens
   - the object is on the other side of the lens

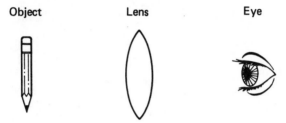

| Object | Lens | Eye |

   - what you see is bigger than the actual object; the lens has made it *look* bigger.

2. Lenses come in different sizes; some are wider in the middle than others.

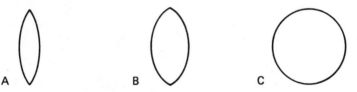

A   B   C

   - the wider a lens is, the bigger it will make an object look.

   e.g., lens "C" will make the *same* object look bigger than either lens "A" or lens "B" would.

   e.g., lens "A," the narrowest lens, will make an object look bigger; but lenses "B" and "C" will both make it look *even bigger*.

3. How big the *same* object looks when you look at it through a lens depends on how wide the lens is.

   The wider the lens, the bigger it will make an object look.

EXERCISE

1. Look at the pictures below. There are *three* different types of *convex* lens.
   - they have at least one *bent-out* surface.
   - they are wider/thicker in the middle than at the ends.
[46]
   - if you look at an object through any one of them, the object will *look* bigger.
   - but, some of the lenses will make the same object look bigger than the other lenses will.

2. After looking at the lenses, answer the questions below.

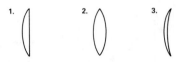

[47]
3. Which of the three convex lenses will make the object look biggest (magnify it the *most*)?

   ____   ____   ____
    1   2   3

4. Which of the three convex lenses will magnify the object the *least*?

   ____   ____   ____
    1   2   3

ANSWERS TO EXERCISE

1. Look at the pictures below. There are *three* different types of convex lenses.
   • they have at least one *bent-out* surface
   • they are wider/thicker in the middle than at the ends
   • if you look at an object through any one of them, the object will *look* bigger.
   • but, some of the lenses will make the same object look bigger than other lenses will.

2. After looking at the lenses, answer the questions below.

3. Which of the three convex lenses will make an object look the biggest (magnify it the *most*)?

   _____ _X_ _____ BECAUSE IT IS THE WIDEST LENS
     1   2   3

4. Which of the three convex lenses will magnify the object the *least*?

   _____ _____ _X_ BECAUSE IT IS THE THINNEST LENS
     1   2   3

[48]

SECTION V: Historical Facts About
Lenses to Remember

Reader Introduction

[49] This section of the lesson teaches some historical facts about lenses that learners are expected to remember. The lists below identify the "conditions" judged to underlie this goal and the "treatments" selected for addressing them.

[50]

Conditions	Treatments
(In order to RECALL FACTS the learner has to learn to:)	The facts are presented to the learner. (ROUTINE)
associate pairs of informational items:	The learner practices stating the facts. (ROUTINE)
e.g., names of inventors and the lenses they invented	
e.g., the lenses invented and the dates on which they were invented	

SECTION 5

Some Historical Facts About Lenses for You to Remember

Introduction

By now you have learned quite a bit about lenses and how they enlarge or magnify objects. This section gives you some historical background information about lenses.

[51] *Purpose*

This lesson will help you to *remember* some facts about:

- when lenses were first invented;
- who invented them;
- what they were used for; and
- what they were made of.

[51] *Learning Hints*

Look for information bearing on the following questions:

- what are the dates and what types of lenses were invented on each of those dates?
- what are the names of the inventors and the types of lenses they invented?
- which types of lenses are used for which purposes?

Assignment

In this section of the lesson, you should do the following:

- Read the facts that are presented in a table; and
- Do the exercises that follow the table.

TABLE 3.5
Some Facts About Lenses

Date	Type of Lens Introduced	Name of Inventor	How the Lenses Were Used
1000 B.C.	A glass globe filled with water was used as a magnifying lens.		Engravers used these globes to enlarge their work.
1200 A.D.	Glass lenses similar to those used today were introduced.		
1590 A.D.	Two lenses were used to create a compound microscope.	Zacharias Janssen, a Dutchman	The lenses were used in eyeglasses

EXERCISE: (ANSWERS ON NEXT PAGE)

[53]
1. If you need to, refer to the table on the opposite page as you do this practice problem:
   a. What was the earliest date when a lens was used to enlarge or magnify objects? _____
   b. What was the lens made of? _____
   c. When was a compound microscope first used? _____
   d. What was the name of the man who invented the compound microscope? _____

[54]
2. Do NOT refer to the table on the opposite page as you do this practice problem:
   a. When were *glass* lenses first introduced? _____
   b. What was the name of the inventor who used lenses as eyeglasses? _____
   c. What did the users of the first type of magnifying lenses use them for? _____
   d. What was the date? _____

103

ANSWERS TO EXERCISE

1. If you need to, refer to the table on page 102 as you do this practice problem:

   a. What was the earliest date when a lens was used to enlarge or magnify objects? <u>1000 B.C.</u>

   b. What was it made of? <u>GLASS GLOBE FILLED WITH WATER</u>

   c. When was a compound microscope first used? <u>1590 A.D.</u>

   d. What was the name of the man who invented the compound microscope? <u>ZACHARIAS JANSSEN</u>

2. Do NOT refer to the table on page 102 as you do this practice problem:

   a. When were *glass* lenses first introduced? <u>1200 A.D.</u>

   b. What was the name of the inventor who used lenses as eyeglasses? <u>ZACHARIAS JANSSEN</u>

   c. What did the users of the first type of magnifying lenses use them for? <u>TO ENLARGE ENGRAVING WORK</u>

   d. What was the date? <u>1000 B.C.</u>

SECTION I: COMMENTS

1. *Function of This Page.* This "Reader Introduction" is meant for you, the reader, and not for the student.
2. *General Instructional Strategy*
   Conditions
   - Performing *all* the steps (chaining) involved in operating a microscope is judged to be a *long* chain for this target audience.
   - Learning this chain on the basis of just *one* reading of a list of steps is judged to be too difficult for the audience.
   Treatment
   - "Routine" treatment elements are used: practice of a complete task preceded by a "how to" presentation, the list of steps.
   - Added to the "routine" are some "nonroutine" shaping elements: The learner continues to use the list of steps on multiple occasions; the list is removed altogether on the last practice attempt—a moderately large fading jump.
3. *Rationale for "Advance Organizers."* "Purpose" and "Learning Hints" are advance organizers. See the introductory section of this chapter for a rationale for their use.
4. *Sequencing Rationale.* Why are these objectives (calling for the operation of a microscope) sequenced *before* the objectives taught in the remaining sections?
   Conditions
   - Other objectives for this lesson involve either the recall of or application of explanations (relatively long chains) that relate multiple, new concepts to one another.
   Treatment
   - The scheduling of "operating" objectives first provides the learner with a *concrete* introduction to concepts involved in later objectives (a nonroutine, specialized treatment). These concepts include "magnification" and "the effects of different lenses on magnification."
   - This is viewed as an optional, facilitating sequence rather than as one based on prerequisite relationships.
5. *Routine Treatment Used.* This "routine" treatment is a list of steps identifying "how to" operate a micrscope.
6. *Display of Information.* The *display* of the list of steps (i.e., in lined rows) is designed to cue learner recognition of the serial nature of the information being provided. (See the introductory section on the uses to which the display of information can be put.)

7. *Visual Part of "How To."* A picture of the microscope is part of the routine "how to" treatment. It identifies (*cues* recognition of) parts of the microscope that will be manipulated.

8. *Routine Practice Requirement*
   - The learner practices the entire, required task or performance.
   - It is modified by a nonroutine, *shaping* treatment that allows the learner to keep the list of steps in front of him or her.

9. *Nonroutine Specialized Treatment.* Observing the magnification of the specimen serves two functions:
   - it provides *external reinforcement* to the learner, confirming that he or she has operated the microscope correctly (a routine treatment);
   - it provides a *concrete experience* with "magnification" (a nonroutine treatment).

10. *Nonroutine Shaping Treatment.* The learner is given the opportunity (a choice) to operate the microscope with less help available (*fading* of cues).

11. *Transfer.* Practice with different microscopes is intended to facilitate transfer of "operating skills" to any microscope that might have to be used.

12. *Practice with No Cues (ROUTINE).* The final stage of practice calls for operating a microscope without a list of steps (with no cues available— as called for by the objectives).

SECTION II: COMMENTS

13. The learner would not see this page.

14. *Sequencing Rationale.* Later sections teach explanations that involve the concept ("convex lens"). Accordingly, this concept is treated as a prerequisite and is sequenced (here) before the later sections that are dependent on it.

15. *General Instructional Strategy*
    Conditions
    - Being able to recognize a convex lens depends, just as it does for any class concept, on learning discriminations, generalizations, and associations.
    - There are four stimulus characteristics applicable to a lens that affect the learning of these skills: inside and outside surfaces; whether a lens surface is bent out or not; the width of the lens at the center; and the number of surfaces that bend out.

- The number of characteristics is judged likely to make it difficult for this target audience to learn the concept just on the basis of one *overall* definition.

Treatments

- Elements of a "routine" treatment are provided: a definition of the concept; examples of the concept; and practice recognizing instances.
- The lesson adds "shaping" elements to make learning easier:
  —the presentation and practice treat stimulus characteristics individually rather than going directly to practice recognizing lens types (a smaller "unit size")
  —practice in recognizing a "convex lens" is deferred to the last stage of practice.

16. *Rationale for "Advance Organizers."* See Comment 3 in SECTION I.

17. *Routine Treatment Elements*

- A definition of a "convex lens" is provided.
- Examples are provided (with annotation used to cue attention to relevant features).

18. *Nonroutine Elments Added*

- Four elements of the definition are presented individually (unit of behavior made smaller).
- The use of four rows (display) cues learner recognition of the fact that there are four considerations in defining a "convex lens."

19. *Facilitating Discriminations and Generalizations*

- *Examples* of different types of lenses are provided; annotational *cues* identify the differences among them in order to facilitate **discriminations** among them.
- *Varied* examples of convex lenses are provided: annotational *cues* identify the similarities among them in order to facilitate **generalizations** across the class of all convex lenses.

20. *Practice Requirements (Shaping)*

- Practice, like the presentation, addresses individual stimulus characteristics (a smaller unit of behavior).

21. Cues accompany practice.

22. Multiple-choice recognition practice is used (an altered practice mode) rather than full-blown practice requiring the identification of individual lenses as being or not being convex.

23. Full-blown practice (a routine element) is scheduled last (after easier shaping practice).

24. *Reinforcement*

- Reinforcement also includes annotation that *cues* recognition of characteristics that define "convexness." The annotation is used to facilitate discriminations and generalizations re: examples and non-examples (which may be difficult to tell apart because of minute differences.)

SECTION III: COMMENTS

25. The learner would not see this.

26. *Sequencing Rationale*

- Section IV, the next section, contains an explanation that relates the concepts "degree of curvature" of a lens and "degree of magnification" produced by the lens. These are new concepts to this target audience. Accordingly, this section, Section III, presents as *prerequisites* for the next section a treatment of the constituent concepts of the explanation: "how a lens affects light rays," "how the width of the lens affects the degree of bending of light rays," and "focal length."

27. *General Instructional Strategy*
   Conditions

- There are multiple objectives for this section. They involve the following skills:
  —facts (what happens to rays passing through various parts of a lens)
  —concepts (definition of "focal length")
- The ultimate skills (describing the relationship between the width of a lens and focal length) is judged to be too large a chunk of behavior to learn at once (the number of elements is too big).
   Treatments
- Routine elements are provided for each type of skill involved: how to, examples, and practice.
- Each set of skills is taught separately (a smaller unit of behavior) as part of an overall "shaping" approach.

28. *Rationale for "Advance Organizers."* See Comment 3 in Section I

29. *Routine and Nonroutine Treatments Used*
   Conditions

- The number of facts/concepts involved in describing what happens to light rays is relatively large (reflection of objects, entering lenses, deflection at both ends, change of directions, and the directions at each end). This number represents a potential learning difficulty.
   Treatments
- The "how to" approach provides a statement of *all* the facts.

30. Nonroutine elements are also used:
    the individual facts are *itemized* on the page to make learning them easier.
31. *Visual* examples are used to make the information concrete (learners are able to respond correctly to individual features of the examples).
32. *Nonroutine Practice*
    - Learners practice only a portion of the total performance (describing only the direction in which rays bend). This represents practice of a *smaller unit* of behavior.
33. Learners practice drawing rays bending in the correct direction (practice in an alternative, *concrete* mode, designed to make learning easier).
34. *Presentation Characteristics*
    - As on previous pages, a routine ''how to'' (in this case, what the facts are) is provided.
    - However, it is broken up into smaller units (nonroutine). Separate facts are presented as individual points. This is intended to make it easier to learn the multiple facts involved.

    Practice Characteristics
    Practice is made easier by:
35. presentation *cues* (drawings) being available for all these practice problems, whereby the visual examples almost completely cue (give away) the answers; and
36. facts (recall or interpretation) being practiced individually.

SECTION IV: COMMENTS

37. The learner would not see.
38. *Sequencing Rationale*
    - This is the third and final section devoted to an explanation of the relationship between the width of a lens and the degree of magnification it produces. It is sequenced after the facts and concepts that are prerequisites for the explanation treated here.
39. *General Instructional Strategy*
    Conditions
    The skills to be learned require learners to associate pairs of individual concepts (e.g., ''width of a lens'' and ''how close a lens needs to be held to an object'').
    - The individual concepts themselves are newly learned and practiced only minimally in previous sections.

Treatment

- Prerequisite concepts and facts from previous sections are reviewed (in the presentation).

- New facts/explanations are presented as a routine treatment: ("how to" = stating what the facts/explanations are).

- The facts/explanations (a relatively large chunk of behavior) are broken up into their constituent parts. This is a nonroutine treatment (using a smaller unit of behavior).

- Practice of the "ultimate" performance (stating a complete explanation or predicting which lens will magnify an object the most) is deferred until the end (the customary end point in a shaping approach).

40. *Review*

- A review is provided for prerequisite facts/concepts learned in earlier sections.

- The concepts were minimally practiced earlier and are, therefore, judged to have been weakly to moderately well learned; therefore, the review affords additional cuing (a nonroutine approach) for upcoming material.

41. *Rationale for Advance Organizers*
    See Comment 3 in Section I

42. *Routine Presentation*

- This page provides a description of relevant relationships (the "how to" element of a routine treatment for stating and/or applying explanations).

- *Examples* to which the explanations are applicable are also provided.

- The *serial treatment* of individual portions of the performance being taught is a nonroutine feature of this presentation. (This is meant to accommodate the judged difficulty in learning the complete set of skills.)

43. *Nonroutine Practice*

- This practice problem precedes and serves as preparation for the second practice problem. It requires the learner to practice parts (smaller unit of behavior) of the full-blown performance.

- The pictorial representation also provides cuing as to the correct answer.

44. *Routine Practice*

- The learner practices applying and stating a full-blown explanation (one of the objectives of the lesson).

45. *Routine Treatment*

- The presentation provides a "how to" element: stating the relationship between the width of a lens and the degree of magnification.

- Constituent parts of the statement are presented individually (nonroutinely) to make the presentation easier.

46. *Nonroutine Practice*
- The cuing (a brief review) available during practice constitutes a non-routine element—preceding routine practice in question 3.

47. *Routine Practice*
- This is the kind of practice required by the objectives and is a routine element scheduled *last* (although shaping elements preceded it).

SECTION V: COMMENTS

48. The learner would not see.

49. *Sequencing Rationale*
- This last section is sequenced *after* learners have had an opportunity to operate a microscope and to study how lenses achieve their effects.
  —One opportunity provided learners with a *concrete* introduction (non-routine) to the concept of magnification (i.e., seeing it happen); its relevance to the historical facts can now be recognized.
  —The second opportunity provided further experience (albeit abstract) with the concept of magnification.

50. *General Instructional Strategy*
Conditions
- Learners are required to recall a small number of facts (associations).
- No learning difficulty is anticipated.
Treatment
- A routine treatment is provided:
  —facts are stated ("how to")
  —learners practice recalling them

51. *Rationale for Advance Organizers.* See Comment 1 in Section I

52. *Routine Presentation*
- Facts are presented (the "how to" for "recall of facts")
- The display of the facts is intended by its very look to cue recognition of:
  —how many separate facts there are
  —what types of information are being presented (e.g., types of lenses, names of inventors)

53. *Nonroutine Practice*
Conditions
- Although the number of facts is small, recalling them just on the basis of one read-through is judged too difficult for this audience.
Treatment
- Learners are allowed to use the tabled facts (as cues) in a first practice exercise.

54. *Routine Practice:*

- Learners finally practice recalling the facts without any cues available (a full-blown performance).

REFERENCES

Gropper, G. L. (1983). A behavioral approach to instructional prescription. In C. M. Reigeluth (Ed.), *Instructional-design theories and models: An overview of their current status.* Hillsdale, NJ: Lawrence Erlbaum Associates.

4

A Fragment of a Lesson Based on the Algo-Heuristic Theory of Instruction

Lev N. Landa
The Institute for Advanced Algo-Heuristic Studies
Landamatics International

FOREWORD

History

Landa's theory evolved out of his attempt to solve some specific instructional problems when he was in the Soviet Union. In particular, he was interested in how to teach complex, unobservable, often unconscious cognitive processes. Although the cognitively oriented instructional models of Ausubel and Bruner predate it, Landa's theory is the oldest of the cognitively based theories in this book.

Unique Contributions

Perhaps Landa's most important contribution is his prescritpions for the selection of content—for deciding what to teach as well as how. For complex tasks you should teach the actual thought processes used by an expert during performance of the task. The problem is that those thought processes are difficult to identify because experts are usually not consciously aware of them. Landa has developed extensive techniques for identifying those thought processes and methods for representing them most effectively in an algorithm or heuristic prescription.

Another important contribution is Landa's instructional techniques for internalizing and automatizing those thought processes (cognitive operations). Furthermore, he was among the first to explicitly prescribe a technique for synthesis. His "snowball" approach to teaching algorithmic or heuristic processes in a step-by-step manner prescribes that, after each step has been mastered, it should be practiced together with all the preceding steps in the algorithm.

Similarities

Landa's theory also has a number of prescriptions in common with other instructional theories, such as developing algorithms at the level of elementary operations (similar to Gagné's entry level of behavior in a learning hierarchy) and the use of prescriptions (generalities) and demonstrations (examples) to teach algorithms. These and other similarities are identified in the chapter with Editor's Notes.

Issues to Think About

Among the most important issues for consideration is the extent to which Landa's algo-heuristic approach is appropriate for all kinds of school content. Are there some kinds of content or objectives for which his approach would not be appropriate? If so, which kinds? And what approaches would be appropriate for them? Another issue is whether any kinds of instructional strategy components have been overlooked for teaching algorithms. Does he include all of Gagné-Briggs's nine events of instruction? Should he?

STUDY QUESTIONS

1. What is the process through which a designer goes in order to identify the algorithms that should be taught to the learners?
2. Will the level of elementary operations always be the same for all learners?
3. What three stages of practice are prescribed to internalize and "automatize" operations?
4. What is the "snowball" method for sequencing instruction in the step-by-step approach?
5. How does an algorithmic prescription differ from an algorithmic process?
6. When should algorithmic prescriptions be included in the instruction?
7. How can the breadth or comprehensiveness of an algorithm be improved?
8. How can the generality of an algorithm be improved?

C.M.R.

INTRODUCTION: SUMMARY OF THE THEORY

There is a recurring complaint on the part of teachers and employers that students (or former students) who have a certain body of knowledge are often not able to apply it—they do not know how to think, reason, solve problems, make decisions. The Algorithmic-Heuristic Theory (AHT) proceeds from the generally accepted proposition that students should be taught not only knowledge but the ability to apply it, that is, to solve problems and make decisions. The question is how to teach the process of application of knowledge.

The AHT proposes that, in order to be able to effectively teach students how to apply knowledge and solve appropriate problems, one should know the composition and structure of cognitive operations involved in the process of knowledge application. In other words, one should know the composition and structure of the internal mechanisms of thought. It is also necessary to know how to develop such mechanisms in students in the process of instruction.

There are classes of problems that require for their solution execution of certain operations performed in a certain sequence. Such problems and the processes of their solution are *algorithmic*. An *algorithm* is precise, unambiguous, and a sufficiently general prescription as to what one should manually and/or cognitively do in order to be able to solve any problem belonging to a certain class.

There are, however, problems for which it is not known what one should specifically do in order to solve them. These problems and the corresponding processes of their solution are *creative, or heuristic*. Prescriptions that can be devised to help find a solution to such problems indicate *what* a problem solver should do in order to find a solution more easily but do not indicate *how* exactly to do this. Directions, of which such a prescription consists, contain some degree of uncertainty and do not determine the process of solution completely. Such prescriptions are *heuristic*.

The AHT has also identified problems, processes, and prescriptions that are termed *semialgorithmic* and *semiheuristic*.

With both algorithmic problems and heuristic problems, expert problem solvers and teachers are often unaware—or incompletely aware—of the processes they actually perform and therefore, while teaching, cannot impart these processes to students. As a result, students have to discover them independently. Because the process of discovery is often complex and students are not normally taught how to discover algorithms and heuristics, only a portion of them are able to make the discovery spontaneously. Those who fail to make such a discovery have difficulties in learning and problem solving and become underachievers.

In order to achieve the goals of the AHT—to be able to effectively form expert-level processes in students and novices—it is necessary to know the composition and structure of these processes. Because they are unobservable and expert problem solvers are often unaware of them, it is necessary to develop *objective methods* of penetrating experts' minds in order to identify these processes and their component mental operations.

As a learning theory, the AHT, often referred to now as *Landamatics*, analyzes and builds explanatory models of the cognitive processes that underlie expert performance, learning, and decision making. As an instructional theory, it prescribes specific methods of instruction for purposeful and accelerated development of such processes in students and novices. And as an instructional-development procedure, Landamatics is a system of techniques for:

1. Penetrating the unobservable, unconscious, and intuitive mental processes underlying expert performance, learning, and decision making for any given type of problem, task, or decision.
2. Breaking down those processes—as well as the conscious ones—into relatively elementary component operations.*
3. Describing those operations—both manual and cognitive—explicitly (i.e., building descriptive models of such processes).
4. Composing algorithmic and/or heuristic prescriptions based on such descriptions of what a student (or nonexpert) should do in his or her mind in order to learn and perform at an expert level (i.e., building prescriptive models of such processes).
5. Creating specific algo-heuristically based instructional programs and courses, on the basis of prescriptions, to effectively develop (recreate) the expert-level processes within students (nonexperts).

The development of expert-level processes in students involves effective formation of both knowledge and mental operations. The AHT has identified not only the specific nature of their interdependence and interaction but, also, how one should teach knowledge in order to effectively develop mental operations and, conversely, how to teach mental operations in order to develop high-quality knowledge and the ability to apply it accurately and unfailingly.

To determine a method of teaching, it is necessary for an instructional designer or teacher to define the type of knowledge to be taught in a given situation: whether it is an image, concept, or proposition.† In the next section we confine ourselves to instructions about teaching concepts only.

Directions for Deciding
What to Teach About a Concept‡

1. To effectively teach the concept of an object,[1] the instructional designer or teacher should identify all the object's attributes that are deemed essential for

---

*This is very similar to Scandura's process of breaking a "rule" down into "atomic components" (p. 163).

†Hence, different methods of instruction are required for images, concepts, and propositions, just as Gagné-Briggs (p. 13) prescribe differences in the events of instruction for each of their kinds of intellectual skills (discriminations, concrete concepts, defined concepts, rules, and problem solving). Gropper (p. 52) prescribes different methods for his kinds of objectives (recalling facts, defining or applying concepts, using procedural rules, and solving problems), and Merrill (p. 204) prescribes different methods for his performance levels (remember-instance, remember-generality, use, and find) and content types (fact, concept, procedure, and principle).

‡This is a selection strategy (selecting what content to teach), a macrolevel concern.

[1]"Object" is understood here in the widest sense of the word as anything for which a concept has been created: It may be a unique object (like the sun) or a class of objects (like trees).

students to know in order to be able to use the concept for theoretical and practical purposes in doing tasks and solving problems.[2]

2. All the attributes should be divided into two groups: (a) those used by the student to identify the object (i.e., to solve the identification problem) and (b) those used by the student to solve other kinds of problems (e.g., drawing inferences, building hypotheses, deciding whether the object can be used for certain practical purposes.)[3]

3. An object can usually be identified on the basis of different attributes that serve, for the purpose of identification, as the object's indicative features or clues. From all known attributes to be used as indicative features, those should be selected for instruction that have the following *psychological* properties (see also Landa, 1974, pp. 195–203). They should be:

  (a) comprehensible
  (b) sufficiently elementary
  (c) unambiguous
  (d) workable
  (e) economical (efficient)
  (f) convenient to use.[4]

4. Because each indicative feature selected should be acted upon differently depending, also, on its logical characteristics and logical functions in the process of identification, each feature should be analyzed by the instructional designer or teacher from the point of view of its *logical* properties as well (see also Landa, 1974, pp. 203–213); namely, whether the feature is (a) necessary and sufficient; (b) necessary but not sufficient; or (c) not necessary but sufficient.[5]

5. Inasmuch as it may be important and desirable to provide the students with more than one way of identifying an object (if several ways exist), it is necessary to determine all those sufficient indicative features that may serve as a basis for different methods of identification.[6]

6. Once all instructionally valuable indicative features of an object have been identified and selected and their logical properties defined, it is necessary to

---

[2]Identification of the essential attributes is done by the instructional designer or teacher in the course of designing a lesson and preparing to teach it. Comments 2–6, 18–20, 23, and 25 identify the essential attributes that were selected and taught to students within the topic "Types of lenses."

[3]In this exposition we will limit ourselves to the directions pertinent to concept formation for the purpose of identification (object classification). See Comments 2–6, 18–20, 23, 25.

[4]The indicative features of lenses with such properties are identified in Comments 2–6 and 18–20.

[5]This lesson did not have as its instructional objective teaching students general methods of operating with indicative features depending on their logical properties. For the description of such general methods and the techniques of imparting them to students, see Landa, 1974, pp. 352–386.

[6]In this lesson, there was no need to teach students different methods of identifying a type of lens.

determine the *logical structure* of indicative features, that is, the ways they are connected with each other. Specifically, it is necessary to determine whether they are connected conjunctively (by the logical connective *and*), or disjunctively (by the logical connective *or*), or have a "mixed"—conjunctive-disjunctive or disjunctive-conjunctive—logical structure. (For more detail on the types of logical structures of indicative features, see Landa, 1974, pp. 203–213).[7]

7. Having identified the logical structure of indicative features of an object, it is advisable to describe the structure in the form of an implicational (if . . . , then) proposition. In the left part of the proposition, the indicative features are given; in the right part the inference(s) to be drawn from the presence or absence of the indicative features is (are) indicated.[8]

This implicational proposition determines *what* students are to be taught with regard to the *conceptual component* of instruction. It represents a model of the *content* of psycho-logical processes that should be formed in the students' minds in order to ensure effective development of the concepts within students. This proposition, however, does not represent a model of the *operational component* of the identification process. A model of the operational process can be described only by an algorithm or a system of algorithms.

8. Once the logical structure of the concept's indicative features has been identified and explicitly stated, it is necessary for an instructional designer or teacher to develop an *algorithm* for identifying the object on the basis of these indicative features. Such an algorithm would direct what the student should do mentally in order to determine whether the object under consideration belongs or doesn't belong to the class reflected in the concept. The algorithm determines the process of effective application of the concept for the purpose of identification. But it does more. By performing operations with indicative features indicated in the algorithm, a student learns these indicative features and thus the concept itself more quickly and better. Algorithms are not only a means of teaching how to apply concepts effectively but are also a means for developing concepts more efficiently.[9]

9. Normally, on the basis of a logical structure of indicative features, it is

---

[7]The author of the lesson had determined for himself the logical properties of indicative features of lenses and the features' logical structure but—in this lesson—did not teach students explicitly how to do this by themselves, as it was not among the objectives of the lesson. However, students were implicitly taught how to operate with conjunctively connected indicative features of lenses (see Comments 10, 11, 15, 24).

[8]The author of the lesson had composed such a description for himself in the process of designing the lesson but did not teach students the general method of such a description, as it wasn't the objective of this particular lesson. However, elements of such an "if . . . , then" representation were used in the lesson (see, for example, Comment 20).

[9]See the description of the algorithm in the preface to the lesson.

possible to develop a *set* of identification algorithms rather than a single one. Being equivalent logically, they are not necessarily equivalent psychologically. This means that whereas all of them would lead to a correct solution of the identification problem, not all of them may lead to such a solution equally efficiently: some may require more operations than others, some would be more psychologically convenient and "comfortable" than others, etc. So the instructional designer's or teacher's task is to develop the most efficient algorithm.[10]*

Directions for Developing Efficient Algorithms

Because it is impossible, in a brief summary, to state all the directions pertinent to the task of developing an efficient algorithm, we will state here only some of them (for a more detailed description see Landa, 1974, chapters VIII–XI). The instructional designer or teacher should:

1. identify, through psychological analysis and diagnosis of the target population, which mental operations are elementary for them and which are not, and develop the algorithm using operations that are elementary (the notion of elementariness is relative);

2. make all the instructions in the algorithm comprehensible and unambiguous for the given student population;

3. make the set of instructions complete, so that the algorithm will be comprehensive and will provide guidance under different logically possible conditions;

4. make all the instructions as general as possible (within the range of their elementariness and comprehensibility), so that the algorithm will be as general as possible;

5. make the sequence of instructions logically reasonable and "natural" (e.g., when one wants to identify, from a large population, a female having a set of characteristics necessary to perform a special assignment, it is logically reasonable to check first whether, among all the candidates, the person is male or female and, if female, then check for the presence of other characteristics. Though a reverse sequence of checking may lead to a correct solution (i.e., be logically correct), such an algorithm would not be logically reasonable and "natural");

6. make the sequence of instructions "economically" efficient so that among a set of logically reasonable and natural algorithms, the one would be

---

[10]The algorithm for identification of the lens type seems to be such an algorithm, according to the criteria described in point 3 of this summary.

*This selection strategy provides designers with far more guidance for deciding what to teach than do most of the other instructional theories. The only other one that comes close is Scandura's.

chosen that provides for the solution of the identification problem in a minimum number of mental operations.[11]*

The algorithm so designed represents a *program* of processes that should be formed in students' minds in the course of subsequent instruction.

Directions for Designing the Teaching of an Algorithm

Once such a program has been developed, the question arises as to how should it be implemented, what are the rules to be followed by a teacher in order to actually develop algorithmic processes in students in an effective and efficient way. It should be mentioned that most of such rules are conditional rather than absolute: A method leading to positive results under one set of conditions may not lead to such results under another set of conditions.

In the following paragraphs will be given conditional rules (directions) concerning the design of instruction in mental operations within the framework of the AHT. Since not all conditions that determine the choice of instructional methods may be known and, in addition, not all conditions that are known can be listed in a short summary, the following directions will take into account only *some* of the most critical conditions.

1. The major purpose of algorithm-based instruction is to teach algorithmic processes rather than algorithmic prescriptions, the latter being just one of the means of teaching algorithmic processes.† However, prescriptions (algorithms themselves) perform an important educational function: They make students more aware of the algorithmic operations and lead to their easier and faster generalization and transfer.

Hence: If the instructional designer's or teacher's objective is to develop in students an awareness of algorithmic processes and their faster generalization, he or she should use algorithmic *prescriptions* to teach the algorithmic processes.‡

If one's objectives are more pragmatic and one wants to develop just a

---

[11]The author of the lesson (instructional designer) went through all these steps in developing the algorithm for lens identification.

*Again, these guidelines for formulating the content (what to teach) offer far more guidance than do most instructional theories.

†Algorithmic prescriptions are the equivalent of Merrill's "generalities" (p. 204); they are a strategy component. On the other hand, algorithmic processes are the content—what is to be taught as opposed to how it is to be taught.

‡This is the same as Merrill's "generality" (p. 204); Gropper's "telling the learner what and how to perform" (p. 52), and Collins's "hypothesis" (p. 184).

particular cognitive skill (manual and/or cognitive), it may make more sense to opt for not using algorithmic prescriptions to teach algorithmic processes.12

2. Knowledge of algorithmic prescriptions is not necessary for the ability to solve problems and make decisions—only the mastery of *algorithmic processes* is important here. However, such a knowledge becomes critical for the ability to *communicate* to others methods of solving problems and making decisions (this is one of the major tasks of teachers, supervisors, managers, etc.).

Hence: If the target audience for instruction is students who don't need to communicate their skills to others, then the instructional designer or teacher may teach only algorithmic processes or may decide to teach algorithmic prescriptions as well. (Direction 1 provides guidelines for making such a decision.)[13]

If, however, the target audience is students who will have to be able to communicate the learned skills to others, then students should be taught prescriptions.

3. Both the algorithmic processes and prescriptions can be given to students in ready-made form, or students may be led to *discover* them. Independent discovery is educationally much more valuable, but it requires much more time.

Hence: If an instructional designer or teacher has sufficient time available to lead students through the process of independent, albeit guided, discovery of algorithmic prescriptions and/or processes, it is advisable to do so.

If one doesn't have such time, then one has to teach algorithmic prescriptions and/or processes by presenting them to students in ready-made form. (Of course, any combination of these two approaches is possible, whereby a teacher may present some operations in ready-made form and lead students to independently discover some other operations.)[14]*

4. Both algorithmic prescriptions and processes can be introduced to students *sequentially,* in a step-by-step manner, or they can be presented to students *integrally* (as a whole). Both methods have advantages and disadvantages. The sequential method makes it easier to learn the algorithmic prescriptions and processes and facilitates their faster internalization and automatization, but it requires more time of direct teacher involvement. The integral method, having the advantage of requiring less time of direct teacher involvement, lacks those features that make the other method better.

---

[12]In the lesson, use of the algorithmic prescription for lens identification has been chosen as one of the instructional components (see Comments 7–9, 15, 21, 22, 26). Demonstrations are another type of component that can be used.

[13]As has been mentioned, we have chosen to explicitly teach students the algorithm of lens identification.

[14]In the lesson, students were led to discover the algorithm by themselves (See Comments 7, 9, 15, 21, 26).

*This is the only instructional theory in this book that provides prescriptions about when to use discovery versus when to use an expository approach.

Hence, if the teacher has sufficient time for direct interaction with students, then the sequential method is preferred.

If the teacher does not have sufficient time for direct interaction and has to use self-learning as a part of the instructional process, then he or she should use the integral method.[15]*

If the teacher opted to employ the sequential approach, then he or she should use the "snowball principle" (Landa, 1978, p. 564: 1983, pp. 198–203) as the most effective method. This method is designed to "join in" new operations to those already formed that constitute a block ("snowball") of operations. It can also be used for "joining in" new subalgorithms or algorithms to those already acquired, which provides for forming more "branched" and comprehensive algorithms.[16]†

5. Regardless of whether the integral or sequential method has been used, the teacher should consider as a specific educational objective and instructional task to provide for *internalization* and *automatization* of algorithmic operations and processes learned.‡ The techniques of internalization and automatization depend on which of the two methods (sequential or integral) has been used.[17]

6. All the above directions refer to creating and teaching identification algorithms for just *one* concept within a discipline. But the same applies to teaching other concepts as well. Each subsequent algorithm and its corresponding algorithmic process should be joined to and intergrated with the previous one(s) so that a comprehensive system of algorithms and algorithmic processes, covering the *whole subject matter area,* will gradually be built.§ Each subsequent system will be a system of a higher order, more comprehensive and general.[18]

7. As a system of concepts and cognitive operations for one subject matter is being created on each level of instruction, it is important to form *interdisciplinary* connections *between* systems of knowledge and operations developed within each of the related disciplines (say, mathematics and physics, mathematics and

---

[15]In the lesson, the sequential method was used (see Comments 9, 15, 21, 26).

*The issue of integral versus step-by-step is similar to Gropper's concern for "shaping" with a "gradualistic, additive approach" (p. 50) and Scandura's approach.

[16]In the lesson, the snowball method was used to join in the newly introduced subalgorithms to those already mastered in order to build up the comprehensive algorithm of lens identification from component subalgorithms (see, for example, Comments 22, 23, 25, 26).

†This is a sequencing strategy (macrolevel) and is similar to the forward-chaining sequence prescribed by Reigeluth for within-lesson sequencing of procedural content (p. 253). However, it also provides a measure of synthesis, such as that prescribed by Reigeluth (p. 257).

‡Scandura also prescribes the "automation" of rules (p. 165).

[17]For an example of one of the techniques of internalization and automatization, see Comments 10–15, 24, 26.

§This is similar to Reigeluth's "set synthesizers" (p. 257).

[18]The creation of a wider, more comprehensive system of algorithms wasn't the objective of this lesson.

chemistry, physics and chemistry, and so forth). This will lead to the creation of a system(s) of still higher order:[19]* The creation of this type and level of "systematism" and generality in the course of instruction enables teachers to "produce" general intellectual abilities in students in a purposeful, well-organized, reliable, and systematic way. Effective development of *specific* cognitive abilities and problem-solving skills in students, through teaching algorithms and algorithmic processes, is only one of the tasks of the AHT. Another task—and not less important—is to develop *most general, content-independent*, cognitive abilities.† The AHT provides tools and techniques to accomplish this.

LESSON PREFACE

The first learning objective stated by the editor of this book is as follows: "Students will be able to classify previously unencountered lenses as to whether or not they are convex lenses."

The thrust of the Algo-Heuristic Theory (AHT) is to develop in students concepts, skills, and abilities that are as general as possible. The stated learning objective, to develop the ability to classify lenses as to whether or not they are *convex* lenses is too narrow for the purposes of the AHT and does not allow one to reveal its "zest" and potential. In order to show how the AHT works and what are its advantages in developing more complex skills and abilities, we had to change the learning objectives and make them more general and comprehensive: "Develop in students concepts, skills and abilities which will enable them to learn and identify *any type* of lens, including varieties of convex and concave lenses." Hence, "Types of Lenses" was chosen as the topic of the lesson. Instructional objectives involved in this topic also don't give enough leeway to show different potentials of the AHT, but at least they allow one to show some.

In this chapter we demonstrate how the AHT can be applied to the design of an algorithm-based lesson on this topic. Because the other proposed instructional objectives and their corresponding topics would not demonstrate the AHT in action any better than this one, we limited ourselves to this topic. Unfortunately, this topic does not provide the opportunity to show how the *heuristic* aspect of the AHT works (there are no heuristic problems to solve in the process of identification of the type of lens). Therefore, only the algorithmic aspect is presented.

---

[19]The development of interdisciplinary connections between systems of knowledge and operations, as well as interdisciplinary algorithms wasn't the objective of the lesson.

*This level of interdisciplinary synthesis is unique among the theories in this book, with the exception of Scandura's "higher-order rules" (p. 165), which are somewhat similar.

†This corresponds to Scandura's "higher-order rules" and Gagné's "cognitive strategies" (p. 15), and is somewhat similar to Merrill's "find level of performance" (p. 203).

In the fragment of a lesson that follows, we concentrate on showing how the terminal ability to identify types of lenses can be developed on the basis of the AHT. More specifically, we show (a) what knowledge and cognitive operations should be formed in students; (b) what sequence should be used to "produce" in them effective workable concepts of the types of lenses; and (c) how to develop the ability to determine to which of the six types any given lens belongs. All other related questions (for example: the functions of each type of lens, how lenses form images) are not considered here because they are not part of the objective.

Before designing a lesson based on the AHT, it was necessary to determine indicative features of lenses that would be logically correct, workable, and economical. In order to make an indicative feature workable, it was necessary to find methods (operations) that would allow students to identify each of the indicative features. Specifically, we have in mind methods for identifying whether some curved surface is convex or concave. As soon as students have acquired and mastered the methods for identifying each of the indicative features, these features can be used in an algorithm, and students will experience no difficulties in their recognition and utilization. Both the indicative features and the algorithm will become workable.

In order to design this lesson, it was necessary to discover algorithmic identification operations that should be developed in a student's mind to enable him or her to carry out the process of identification. Textbooks usually provide students only with knowledge of the properties of each type of lens without teaching them what to do cognitively—how to think and reason—in applying this knowledge.

The analysis of the ways of explaining and characterizing some types of lenses used in a textbook that the editor has furnished to the author (namely concavo-convex and convexo-concave lenses) showed that the properties (indicative features) used in the textbook create difficulties in understanding these types of lenses, as well as difficulties in applying those indicative features to determining the type of lens.

Fig. 4.1 shows the algorithm that was designed to overcome students' difficulties in understanding and applying the knowledge of different types of lenses. The purpose of this algorithm is to provide a general and easy-to-follow method that allows a student to classify any given lens accurately and quickly.

This algorithm represents a terminal cognitive process that is to be developed in students in the course of instruction. Specific features of this algorithm and how to use it will be discussed later in the comments to the lesson itself.

The content of a lesson depends not only on the clearly defined instructional objectives, the content and structure of the terminal algorithm, and the principles and requirements of the instructional theory but also on the initial psychological state (entry level) of the students. This chapter presents a lesson under *accepted* assumptions about the entry level, and reveals the logic of the lesson and the reasoning behind it.

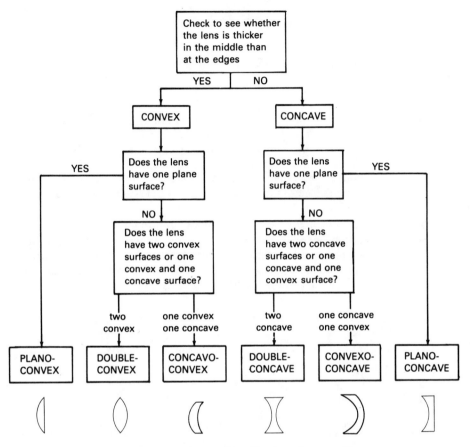

FIG. 4.1. Algorithm for the identification of types of lenses.

The lesson described in the following section is a *hypothetical* interaction between the teacher and the students. Should a teacher wish to implement the described lesson in a real-life instructional setting, he or she would adapt the lesson to each specific instructional condition, provided that he or she accepted the theory, understood the logic of instructional design, and agreed with the reasoning behind it.

LESSON

INTRODUCTION: LENSES, THEIR USES AND SHAPES

[1] STEP 1

TEACHER: What is a lens? A lens is a transparent object that has at least
one curved surface. Lenses are used to form magnified or reduced images, or to concentrate or spread light rays. Most
lenses are made of glass, but any transparent material may be
used. Sometimes plastic, less breakable than glass, is used.
Some lenses are made of transparent crystals, such as quartz.

Uses of Lenses. Lenses have many important uses. The glasses
used by people to aid their eyesight consist of lenses. Some
persons use contact lenses that fit on the eye. Optical instruments such as microscopes and telescopes have lenses. So do
binoculars, cameras, and motion-picture projectors.

How does the image formed by a lens depend on its *shape*?

For example, a lens that has the following shape will form such
an image:

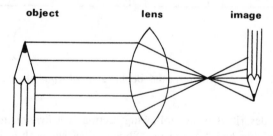

A lens that has this shape will form such an image:

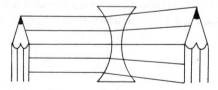

There may be dozens of other images that will be formed by
lenses having other shapes.

In order to be able to know what image a lens of a certain shape
will produce and, conversely, what shape a lens should have in

order to produce a desired image, we have to know the major shapes of lenses, how to distinguish them from each other, and what to call them. We have to be able to recognize a type to which any given lens belongs: that is, to relate it to a certain class. As soon as we know to which class (type) a particular lens belongs, we will automatically know what image this lens will form. So before we proceed to examining in detail how a lens forms an image and why different types of lenses form different images, let's study the shapes of lenses and their corresponding types.

[2] STEP 2

TEACHER: Consider these two lenses:

They have different shapes. Compare them and tell what in a lens determines its shape. What in a lens "makes" the shape?
STUDENT: The shape of its surfaces.
TEACHER: Correct. What are the shapes of the surfaces of the first lens?
STUDENT: One surface is curved and another is flat.
TEACHER: What are the shapes of the surfaces of the second lens?
STUDENT: Both of them are curved.
TEACHER: Correct. But the shape of a surface is only one of the factors that determines the shape of a lens. There is another factor. Consider these two lenses:

Are their shapes the same?
STUDENT: No, they aren't.
TEACHER: Are the shapes of their surfaces the same? Compare the lenses surface by surface.
STUDENT: Surfaces a and a_1 are the same: plane.
Surfaces b and b_1 are the same: plane.
Surfaces c and c_1 are the same: curved.
Surfaces d and d_1 are the same: plane.
TEACHER: The shapes of surfaces are the same but the shapes of the lenses are different. What makes the difference?

STUDENT: The position of the curved surfaces c and c_1 in relation to the plane surfaces a and a_1.

TEACHER: What is the difference in the position of the surfaces c and c_1?

STUDENT: Surface c is curved away from the plane surface a while the surface c_1 is curved in towards surface a_1.

TEACHER: Right. The difference in the shapes of these two lenses is determined not by the shapes of their surfaces—they are identical—but by the *relationships* between their surfaces. Curved surfaces c and c, are differently related to the similar plane surface: The first one is curved out from the plane surface, the second one is curved in toward it.

TEACHER: Can you now summarize the factors that determine the shape of a lens?

STUDENT: The shape of a lens is determined by (a) the shape of its surfaces; and (b) the relationships between the surfaces, their position with regard to each other.

TEACHER: In order to be able to recognize the type of lens when we encounter one, we have to learn first how to easily recognize the types of surfaces making the shape of a lens.

Types of surfaces will be out next topic.

PART I. TYPES OF SURFACES

Section One: *Notion of convex and concave surfaces*

1. Two Types of Surfaces—Plane and Curved.

[3] STEP 1

TEACHER: You already know how to distinguish a flat (plane) surface from a curved one. Let's refresh the notions of these surface types and have some additional practice in recognizing them. I will show you lenses with different types of surfaces. Circle the correct answer.

Surface a is: (1) plane (2) curved
Surface b is: (1) plane (2) curved
Surface c is: (1) plane (2) curved
Surface d is: (1) plane (2) curved

[4] STEP 2

TEACHER: Let's suppose that we have a rectangular transparent object. (Teacher draws such on the board.)[20]

Let's designate all the plane surfaces by letters a, b, c, and d.

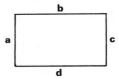

Imagine that we want to change the plane surface c in such a way that it would become curved. We want to convert the plane surface c into a curved one. To do this, imagine that you find yourself on surface a.

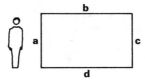

Conversion of a plane surface into a curved surface can be done in two ways. One way is to curve the surface in toward you. In this case our lens would look like this:

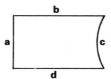

The other way to curve a surface is away from you. In this case our lens would look like this:

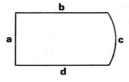

---

[20]Drawing on a blackboard is just one of the methods in presenting an image of a lens. Any other appropriate means of presentation (for example, overhead projectors) can be used.

TEACHER: We can curve not only plane but curved surfaces as well.

Imagine that you find yourself on surface a of the last lens, and you want to curve the curved surface c in toward you. What will the lens look like now?

STUDENT: (Student draws a lens looking like this:)

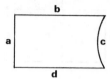

TEACHER: Here's another example. Suppose that we have a lens like this:

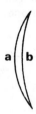

Imagine that you find yourself on surface a and want to curve surface b away from you. What will the lens look like now?

STUDENT: (Student draws a lens looking like this:)

[5] STEP 3

TEACHER: A surface that is curved away from the surface you are mentally on is called a *convex* surface.

A surface that is curved in toward the surface you are mentally on is called a *concave* surface.

Section Two: *Convex Surfaces*

1. Enhancing the Concept of a Convex Surface

[6] TEACHER: Let's suppose that we have such a transparent object:

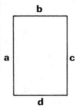

Imagine that you are on surface d and are pushing surface b away from you. What will the lens now look like?

STUDENT: It will look like this. (Student draws a lens such as this:)

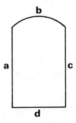

TEACHER: Let's take this last lens.

Imagine that you are on surface b and want to convert the plane surface d into a convex surface. How would you do this?

STUDENT: I would curve out surface d as if pushing it away from me.

TEACHER: What will the shape of the lens now be?

STUDENT: (Student draws:)

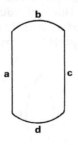

Proceeding in this way, the teacher asks students to first convert surface a and then surface c into convex surfaces. As a result, students arrive at this shape:

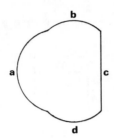

and then at this:

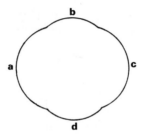

TEACHER: Let's take a lens of a different shape.

Place yourself on surface *b* and convert the plane surface *a* into a convex surface. How will you do this?

STUDENT: I will curve out surface *a* as if I were pushing it away from me.

TEACHER: What will the shape of the lens be now?

STUDENT: (Student draws:)

TEACHER: Let's take another shape.

Place yourself on surface a and convert surface b into a convex one. How will you do this?

STUDENT: I will curve out surface b as if I were pushing it away from me.

TEACHER: What will the shape of the lens be now?

STUDENT: (Student draws:)

Similar tasks are given to students using a variety of differently shaped lenses until the task is mastered.

2. Designing an Algorithm for Forming Convex Surfaces

[7] STEP 1

TEACHER: You know what to do in order to convert a plane or curved surface into a convex one. Suppose you have to explain this to someone who doesn't know how to do this. How would you explain it? Write this in the form of a prescription—a series of instructions, directions, or commands—in a step-by-step manner. For example:
First do this . . .
Second do this . . .

STUDENT: (formulates such a prescription)

1. Isolate the surface that is to be converted into a convex surface.

2. Find the opposite surface.

3. Imagine in your mind that you are on this opposite surface.

4. Curve the surface opposite you out from yourself as if you were pushing it away.

5. A surface obtained as a result of these actions is called a convex surface.

STEP 2

[8] TEACHER: A prescription such as this, which precisely indicates what one should do, and in what sequence, in order to achieve a certain result, solve a problem, or make a decision, is called an *al-*

gorithm. We have designed an algorithm for converting plane and curved surfaces into convex surfaces. As we proceed, we will develop algorithms for other problems as well.

3. Designing an Algorithm
for Identifying Convex Lenses

[9] STEP 2

TEACHER: We have devised an algorithm of what one should do in order to convert a plane or curved surface into a convex surface. Now let us suppose that we are given a curved surface and need to determine whether the surface is convex or not. What should we do in order to find the answer and solve this problem? Suppose we have such a lens:

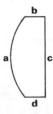

Is surface a convex? We know that a convex surface is a curved, pushed-out surface in relation to the opposite surface. What would you do in order to determine whether surface a is convex? Can you formulate an algorithm of actions?

After a discussion with students on what one should do in order to answer this question, students come up with the algorithm.

STUDENT: Here is an algorithm for determining whether or not a curved surface is convex:

1. Isolate the surface about which you need to make a judgment.
2. Find the opposite surface.
3. In your imagination, place yourself on this opposite surface.
4. Check whether the surface in question is curved out or not.
5. If the surface in question is curved out, draw the conclusion that it is a convex surface.

4. Practicing Algorithmic Identification Operations

[10] STEP 1

TEACHER: Let's consider this lens:

The question is whether the curved surface d is convex. What would you do first? Consult the algorithm.

STUDENT: I would isolate surface *d*.
TEACHER: What would you do next?
STUDENT: I would find the opposite surface.
TEACHER: What is the opposite surface?
STUDENT: It is surface *b*.
TEACHER: What would you do next?
STUDENT: I would imagine myself on surface *b*.
TEACHER: What would you do next?
STUDENT: I would check to see if surface d is curved out or not.
TEACHER: What is the answer in this case?
STUDENT: Surface *d is* curved out.
TEACHER: What conclusion would you draw?
STUDENT: Since surface *d* is curved out, it is convex.
TEACHER: That is correct.

This process is then repeated by presenting students with different lenses and having them use the algorithm to determine whether a surface indicated by (ˇ) is convex or not. To vary the lenses appropriately, we recommend using these examples:

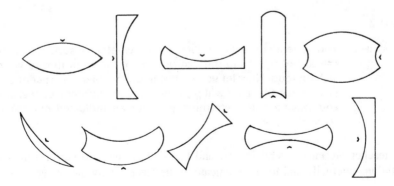

5. Internalizing and Automatizing Algorithmic Identification Operations

[11] STEP 1

TEACHER: You know now how to recognize a convex surface by following the instructions of an algorithm presented in a written form. Now remove the algorithm and let's practice identifying whether a surface is convex or not by recalling the operations of the algorithm and giving ourselves instructions out loud of what should be done to get the answer. Let us consider this lens:

In order to determine whether surface c is convex or not, what would you do first?

STUDENT: I would find the opposite surface. It is surface *a* in this case.
TEACHER: What would you do next?
STUDENT: I would place myself, in my imagination, on surface *a.*
TEACHER: What would you do next?
STUDENT: I would check if surface *c* is curved out away from me or not.
TEACHER: And in this case?
STUDENT: It is not curved out.
TEACHER: What would you do next?
STUDENT: I would conclude that it is not a convex surface.

The teacher provides the students with other lenses and has them practice solving the identification problem on the basis of algorithmic self-instructions.

[12] STEP 2

TEACHER: You have just practiced determining whether a surface is convex or not by giving the instructions of the algorithm to yourself out loud. Now let us practice in giving these instructions to yourselves silently. I will present you with different lenses, and you will have to determine whether an indicated surface is convex or not.

The teacher presents several lenses, and the students have to perform all the operations internally and to communicate to the teacher only the answer.

[13] STEP 3

TEACHER: Until now you have determined the characteristics of a surface by giving instructions to yourself out loud or silently. Now that you have learned what should be done with a lens in order to determine whether a surface is convex or not, you do not need to give yourself any instructions at all.

You can execute the necessary operations without self-instructing. Let's train in recognizing the type of surface without giving yourself self-instructions. I will show you different lenses, and you will have to give me an answer as to whether an indicated surface is convex or not.

The teacher drills the students in this mode of identification, using several other lenses as material for practice.

[14] STEP 4

TEACHER: Now you can determine whether a surface is convex or not without recalling algorithmic instructions to yourself, but you may still perform the operations of recognition in a step-by-step manner. Now I'll present you with several lenses. Try to determine whether an indicated surface is convex or not instantaneously, within one second, by just looking at the lens.

The teacher pulls out a watch and presents several types of lenses until the students are able to recognize the type of surface instantaneously.

6. Formulating an Algorithm for Finding Convex Surfaces

[15] STEP 1

TEACHER: Until now I have pointed out to you a surface on a lens and asked you whether the surface was convex or not. Now let's learn to solve another problem: I will show you a lens but won't point out any of the surfaces. It will be your task to determine whether a lens has a convex surface or surfaces and, if so, which of the surfaces are convex. Suppose we have such a lens:

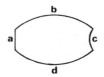

You know the algorithm as to what you should do in order to determine whether an indicated surface, for example c, is convex or not. Now suppose I don't indicate any of the surfaces to you, and I ask you whether there are any convex surfaces in the lens, and if there are, which are convex. What will you have to do in order to solve this latter problem? How would you expand the algorithm? What would you do first?

STUDENT: I would select some surface, let's say a, and see whether it is convex or not.

TEACHER: Is it convex?

STUDENT: No, it is not.

TEACHER: What would you do next?

STUDENT: I would look at another surface, let's say b, and see whether it is convex or not.

TEACHER: Is it convex?

STUDENT: Yes, it is.

TEACHER: What would you do next?

STUDENT: I would look at the next adjacent surface, c, and see whether it is convex or not.

TEACHER: Is it convex?

STUDENT: No, it is not.

TEACHER: What would you do next?

STUDENT: I would look at the last surface, d, and see whether it is convex or not.

TEACHER: Is it convex?

STUDENT: Yes, it is.

TEACHER: Your conclusion?

STUDENT: The lens has two convex surfaces, b and d.

TEACHER: Now suppose you would have to formulate an algorithm for solving this problem in order to teach someone else how to do this task. What could the algorithm be? What would the first operation be?

STUDENT: Select a surface and check whether it is convex or not.

TEACHER: Next?

STUDENT: Look at an adjacent surface and check whether it is convex or not.

TEACHER: Next?

STUDENT: Keep checking the other surfaces until you have examined all of them.

[16] STEP 2

TEACHER: Now let's practice applying the algorithm so that you will be able to instantaneously determine (just by looking at a lens) whether or not it has a convex surface or surfaces.

In developing this algorithmic skill or ability, the teacher uses the same techniques that were used with regard to the development of the skills for which the first algorithm was designed.

Section Three: Concave Surfaces

The objectives and methods used to enhance the concept of concave surfaces and develop algorithmic processes for their identification are the same as we described in regard to convex surfaces.
    The corresponding stages are these:

1. Enhancing the concept of a concave surface.
2. Designing an algorithm for forming concave surfaces.
3. Designing an algorithm for identifying concave surfaces.
4. Practicing algorithmic identification operations.
5. Internalizing and automatizing algorithmic identification operations.
6. Formulating an algorithm for finding concave surfaces.

PART II: TYPES OF LENSES

[17] Section One: The Notion of Convex and Concave Lenses

1. Forming the Concept of Convex and Concave Lenses

STEP 1

TEACHER: Until now we have dealt with different types of surfaces of a lens, and we noticed that surfaces may relate to each other in different ways. For example, a plane surface may be combined with a concave surface. In this case we would have a lens with such a shape:

A plane surface may be combined with a convex surface. In this case we would have a lens with such a shape:

A convex surface may be combined with another convex surface. In this case we would have a lens with such a shape:

A concave surface may be combined with another concave surface. In this case we would have a lens with such a shape:

There are many other ways of combining two or more surfaces that would create lenses of many diverse shapes.

Among all possible shapes of lenses, six shapes are most frequently used in different optical devices, each of them creating a specific image of an object that we will consider later. These six shapes are as follows:

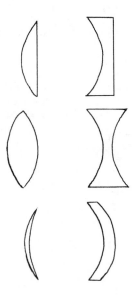

TEACHER: Compare all the lenses in the left-hand column with each other, and all the lenses in the right-hand column with each other. What is common to all the lenses in the left-hand column, and to all the lenses in the right-hand column, which distinguishes these groups of lenses from each other?

STUDENT: Both surfaces of all the lenses in the left-hand column converge to one point. The surfaces of the lenses in the right-hand column do not converge to one point.

TEACHER: That's right. How else do the lenses in the left-hand column differ from the lenses in the right-hand column?

STUDENT: The lenses in the left-hand column are thicker in the middle than at the edges. The lenses in the right-hand column are thinner in the middle than at the edges.

[19] STEP 3

TEACHER: The lenses in the left-hand column are called "convex lenses" and those in the right-hand column "concave lenses."

[20] STEP 4

TEACHER: You have established that convex lenses differ from concave ones by two indicative features: (a) convex lenses usually converge to one point while concave ones don't; and (b) convex lenses are thicker in the middle than at the edges while concave lenses are thinner. Suppose someone encounters lenses like these:

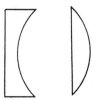

and he doesn't know how to determine which of them is convex and which is concave.

In order to help him, you have to indicate distinguishing features of each type of lens. We know two such distinguishing indicative features.

Is it necessary to use both of them in order to classify a lens, or is it sufficient to use just one of them?

STUDENT: It is sufficient to use just one of them.

TEACHER: How would you define convex and concave lenses using the first indicative feature? State the definitions according to this model: ·
If a lens . . ., *then* the lens is convex.
If a lens . . ., *then* the lens is concave.
Put in place of dots the first distinguishing indicative feature, which refers to converging of surfaces to one point.

STUDENT: *If* a lens has surfaces which converge to one point, *then* the lens is convex. *If* a lens has surfaces which do not converge to one point, *then* the lens is concave.

TEACHER: Now construct definitions using the second indicative feature.

STUDENT: *If* a lens is thicker in the middle than at the edges, *then* such a lens is convex.
If a lens is thinner in the middle than at the edges, *then* such a lens is concave.

TEACHER: Now we have two definitions for each type of lens. Are these definitions equally good? Is it all the same which of them to apply?

STUDENT 1: Yes, they are equally good.

STUDENT 2: It is all the same which of them to apply.

TEACHER: Sometimes two or more definitions are equally good, but sometimes it is not so. One—although not the only—way to determine whether two definitions are equally good is to find out if both of them can be applied to *all the possible objects* of the given type and lead to the correct conclusion(s). Let's consider our convex lenses:

In these examples application of either indicative feature leads to the same correct conclusion, that each of the lenses is convex. Can you, however, think of any convex lenses which have the second feature (they are thicker in the middle than at the edges) but do not have the first one, i.e., they do not converge to one point?

STUDENT: Yes, such lenses are possible.

TEACHER: How is that possible?

STUDENT: If we cut edges in our lenses.
            Originally we had such lenses:

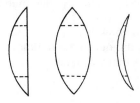

            and now we'll get such ones:

TEACHER: Which of our two definitions of convex lenses would apply to
            both cases and lead to the correct conclusion that each of the
            lenses is convex?
STUDENT: The second one.
TEACHER.   That's right. Then which definition of the two is better?
STUDENT: The second one.
TEACHER: Why?
STUDENT: Because it applies to a larger variety of lenses and leads to a
            correct conclusion in a greater number of cases.
TEACHER: That's true. We may also say that it is better because it is more
            general. Now state again the definitions of convex and concave
            lenses that you have chosen as more general and therefore
            better.
STUDENT: *If* a lens is thicker in the middle than at the edges, *then* such a
            lens is convex.
            If a lens is thinner in the middle than at the edges, *then* such a
            lens is concave.

2. Designing an Algorithm for Identifying Convex and Concave Lenses

[21] STEP 1

TEACHER: Suppose you were given a lens and had to recognize the type to
            which the lens belongs—convex or concave. What would you
            do in your head in order to recognize whether a given lens is
            convex or concave? Describe your actions in a step-by-step
            manner, and formulate it in the form of an algorithm. What
            would you do first?
STUDENT: I would first check if the lens is thicker in the middle than at the
            edges.

TEACHER: What might be the answer to this question?
STUDENT: A lens may be thicker or thinner in the middle than at the edges.
TEACHER: If a lens is thicker in the middle, then what type of lens would it be?
STUDENT: It would be a convex lens.
TEACHER: If the lens is thinner in the middle?
STUDENT: It would be a concave lens.

[22] STEP 2

TEACHER: The algorithmic prescription that you have formulated as to the sequence of actions to be performed can be represented in a diagrammatic form. This is how it can be done:

The teacher writes the algorithm on the blackboard. (See Fig. 4.2.)

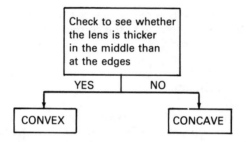

FIG. 4.2.   Algorithm for distinguishing between concave and convex lenses.

Section Two: Varieties of Convex Lenses

[23] **1.** Identifying Indicative Features of Different Types of Convex Lenses and Designing a Corresponding Algorithm

TEACHER: Among all the types of convex lenses, the following three types are the most frequently used in optical devices:

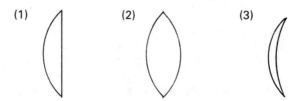

What is common to all these types of lenses?
STUDENT: All the lenses are thicker in the middle than at the edges.
TEACHER: Our task now is to find indicative features that would differenti-

ate between the different types of convex lenses. What distinguishes the first type of convex lens from the other two types?

STUDENT: It has one plane surface.

TEACHER: How do you think such a convex lens, which has one *plane* surface, could be called?

STUDENT: Perhaps a plane-convex lens?

TEACHER   Your guess was nearly correct. This type of lens is called a plano-convex lens. Let's get back to our algorithm [Fig. 4.2] and extend it.

We will be considering at the moment only the left branch of the algorithm dealing with convex lenses. If following the algorithm you have established that some given lens is convex, what question would you ask next in order to distinguish plano-convex lenses from the other two types?

STUDENT: The next question that I would ask would be: "Does the convex lens have one plane surface?"

TEACHER: That's right. And if it has a plane surface, what conclusion would you draw?

STUDENT: The lens is plano-convex.

TEACHER: And if it doesn't?

STUDENT: Then the lens belongs to one of the other two types of convex lenses.

TEACHER: Let's extend the algorithm and add to it the questions that you have just formulated. (See Fig. 4.3.)

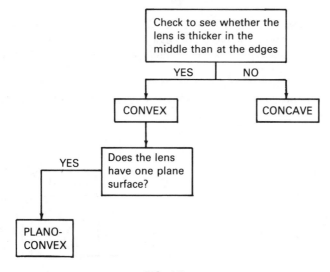

FIG. 4.3

TEACHER: Now we have to find indicative features that differentiate the two remaining types of convex lenses:

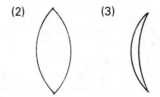

(2)   (3)

What distinguishes them from each other?

STUDENT: One of them has two convex surfaces, and the other has one concave and one convex surface.

TEACHER: What might a lens with two convex surfaces be called?

STUDENT: Convexo-convex?

TEACHER: You are right, but in physics it is more commonly called a double-convex lens—which has the same meaning as convexo-convex. And what do you think a lens that has one concave and one convex surface might be called?

STUDENT: Perhaps concavo-convex.

TEACHER: You are right. All lenses we are now dealing with are convex. In the previous cases, the indicative features that distinguished one type of convex lens from another were indicated by a word preceding the word *convex*. For example:

>   plano-*convex*
>
>   convexo-*convex* or double-*convex*
>
>   concavo-*convex*

If the distinctive feature of the third type of convex lens is that it has a concave surface, then the word *concave* should also be put before the word *convex* (i.e., concavo-convex) by analogy with plano-convex and convexo-convex or double-convex.

Let's present the classification of convex lenses in a diagrammatic form. (See Fig. 4.4).

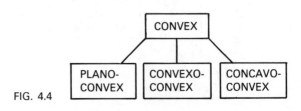

FIG. 4.4

Let's extend the algorithm by adding to it additional steps that would allow us to distinguish between double-convex and concavo-convex.

Students, with the assistance of the teacher, come up with the following extension of the algorithm (See Fig. 4.5).

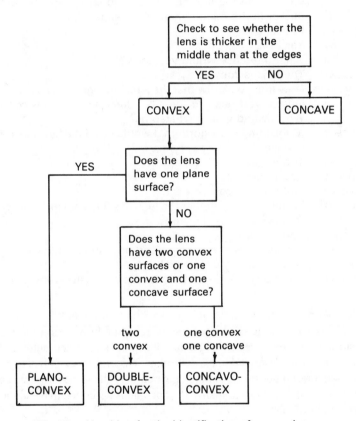

FIG. 4.5.   Algorithm for the identification of convex lenses.

2. Practicing Algorithmic Identification Operations

[24] STEP 1

TEACHER: Now we'll practice using the algorithm to identify types of convex lenses. I will present you with lenses of different types, and you will have to identify and name each of them by following the algorithm.

Let's consider this lens:

What kind of lens is it? What should you do first to determine its type?

STUDENT: (Consulting the algorithm) I should check whether the lens is thicker in the middle than at the edges.

TEACHER: In our case?

STUDENT: Yes, it is.

TEACHER: What inference would you draw?

STUDENT: The lens is convex.

TEACHER: Now that you know that the lens belongs to the class of convex lenses, you need to identify which type of convex lens it is. What would your next step be?

STUDENT: (Consulting the algorithm) I would see if the lens has one plane surface.

TEACHER: In our case?

STUDENT: No, it does not.

TEACHER: What would you do next?

STUDENT: I would check whether the lens has two convex surfaces or one concave and one convex surface.

TEACHER: And in our case?

STUDENT: The lens has one concave and one convex surface.

TEACHER: What would you do next?

STUDENT: I would conclude that the lens is a concavo-convex lens.

The teacher repeats this exercise using a variety of different types of lenses until the students have mastered the process of recognition by using the algorithm. The subsequent objectives should deal with internalizing and automatizing the operations that are described in the algorithm. The sequence of objectives and the instructional techniques used should be essentially the same as were used when we had to internalize and automatize the operations described in the algorithm for identification of surfaces.

Section Three: Varieties of Concave Lenses

The instructional techniques to be used here are essentially the same as were used with regard to convex lenses. The corresponding steps are these:

1. Identify indicative features of types of concave lenses, and design a corresponding algorithm.
2. Practice algorithmic identification operations.

This section concludes with formulation of the right-hand branch of the algorithm (Fig. 4.6), which represents a subalgorithm for concave lenses.

TEACHER: Let's formulate the algorithm for identifying concave lenses. How would such an algorithm look?

STUDENT: It might look like this:

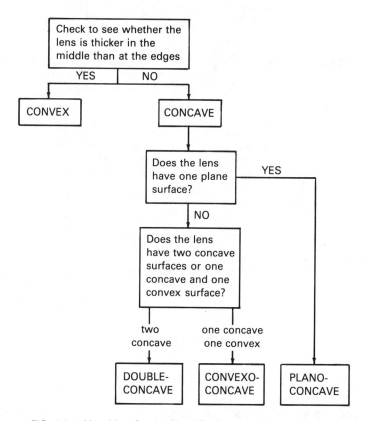

FIG. 4.6.   Algorithm for the identification of concave lenses.

Section Four: Constructing a Comprehensive Algorithm for Identification of Any Type of Lens and Practicing Its Use

[25] **STEP 1**

TEACHER: Now that we know separate algorithms for identification of both convex and concave lenses, let's put them together in one comprehensive algorithm. How would such an algorithm look?

STUDENT: It might look like this [See Fig. 4.7]:

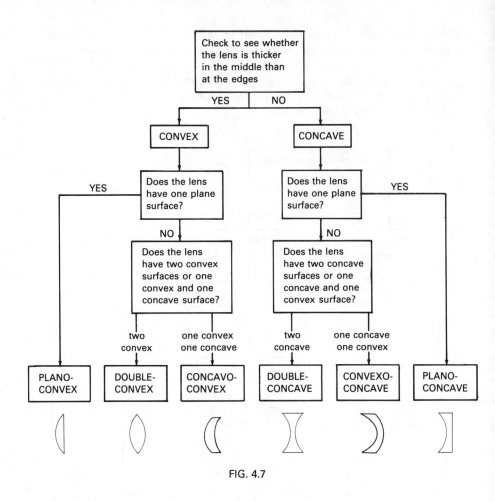

FIG. 4.7

[26] STEP 2

TEACHER: Now let's practice applying the entire algorithm to identify any lens that you might confront.

Instructional methods used here are essentially the same as those used for internalization and automatization of subalgorithms for identifying convex and concave lenses. Since the component subalgorithms have already been internalized and automatized, the synthesizing of the component subprocesses into one single process does not represent any difficulty for students.

END

150

COMMENTS

1. In order for students to be motivated to study types of surfaces and types of lenses—material that, by itself, may be relatively boring—they have to know and understand what is the practical use of lenses and why it is practically important to be able to identify types of lenses.

Hence the *instructional objective* of this step is:

Impart the information to the students that there exist different kinds of lenses which differ in their shape, with each shape forming a specific image. Different kinds of lenses, forming different images, are used for different purposes.

This step is carried out in a conventional manner, through explanation and demonstration. The AHT does not prescribe specifically how to conduct such an explanation and demonstration (there are different ways of doing so). One of the possible ways is that presented in the textbook. We'll reproduce it with some additions serving our purpose.

2. In order to be able to identify types of lenses, students have to have correct concepts of lens types. There are different ways and methods of forming concepts of objects. The AHT proceeds from the proposition that, when possible, it is educationally preferable to have students identify—or at least to present to them—basic concept-forming phenomena (objects' ingredients, components, attributes, etc.), whose various combinations or relationships *generate* various types of objects and their corresponding concepts. Students should also be taught processes of actively and independently *generating* different types of objects (and their corresponding concepts) by using specific generating *operations*. The AHT strongly advocates the active *generative* approach to forming concepts, as opposed to the passive *receptive* approach.

These considerations determine the *instructional objective* of this step:

Impart knowledge that the shape of a lens as a whole is determined by (a) the shapes of its surfaces; and (b) how surfaces relate to each other.

Concept-forming basic phenomena and their relationships may be imparted to students in a ready-made form, or students may be induced to discover them on their own. As is well known, methods of independent or guided discovery are educationally superior for transfer learning and should be used when time permits. The AHT prescribes how to teach students to independently discover algorithms and nonalgorithmic methods of thinking, but it has not developed any specific method of guiding students to discover common and distinctive features of objects. Commonly used methods (e.g., showing students two or several objects and having them compare them with the aim of identifying common and distinctive features) are quite good and effective. To reach the objective of this step, we used these known methods.

3. It is assumed here that students already know the difference between flat (plane) and curved surfaces and have the ability to recognize them. That is why this step may be viewed as a review of prerequisite knowledge and skills. Any review may be carried out, however, in different ways. As psychological research has shown, very often students are able to recognize objects that are presented in a "standard position" or "typical form." A nonstandard position or nontypical form often precludes students from recognition. One of the effective instructional means to prevent the formation in students of narrow concepts and/or to overcome them if they have already been formed is to vary the position and form of the objects being studied. We use this means. This review therefore has an additional function—to confront students with known objects in positions and forms that are perhaps new for them and thus enhance their experience and make sure that the narrow concepts of plane and curved surfaces they might have had will be overcome.

4. Curved surfaces are divided into two categories (types): convex and concave. In order to be able to identify and distinguish them, it is necessary to have a correct concept of them. The concepts of convex and concave surfaces are *relational concepts.*

The AHT proceeds from the proposition that the best way of forming relational concepts and developing the ability to identify *relations* (which in turn underlie the ability to classify objects on the basis of their *relational characteristics*) is to explicitly teach students the cognitive *operations of relating.* People who are able to identify relations are always performing operations of relating, although, very often, they are not aware of them. Students' difficulties in identifying relations and classifying relational objects are frequently caused by the fact that they were not explicitly taught operations of relating.

Processes of relating are diverse, depending on the nature of relations to be cognized and identified. But all of them include three kinds of operations: (a) isolation of an object that represents a reference point in establishing a relation; (b) isolation of an object to be related with the first one; and (c) the operations of relating the first object with the second one. For example, in a relation "John is taller than Peter," John is a reference-point object, Peter is a to-be-related object, and there are operations involved in establishing the relation "taller." If a person performs incorrectly at least one of the operations (for example, isolates Peter as a reference-point object and John as a to-be-related object), he or she will immediately establish a wrong relationship and arrive at a wrong conclusion: "Peter is taller than John."

As has been mentioned, the AHT proceeds from a proposition that the best way to cognize something in-depth, so as to be able to easily and reliably identify it, is to *generate* it, when and if it is possible and time-efficient to do so. This is true in regard to the cognizing of (a) relationships between objects; and (b) the process of application of the formed concepts and cognitive operations.

As is indicated in the AHT, one of the types of operations by which relationships between objects are established, cognized, and identified is *transformation* (or *transformational*) *operations*. With respect to our topic, we want students to better understand the relational nature of the concepts of convex and concave surfaces and later be able to unambiguously identify corresponding types of lenses. Therefore, we chose the operational-generative approach to forming these concepts. We uncovered operations underlying the ability to determine the reference-point surface, the to-be-related surface, and transformational operations of curving a to-be-related surface outward and inward from the reference-point surface, which in fact *generate* convex and concave surfaces.

Teaching students these operations has the purpose of creating in them the *active operational concepts* of the convex and concave surfaces and a *general cognitive method* of identifying them. This approach leads to forming much more general concepts of the convex and concave surfaces and a much more general method of their identification than is normally the case with conventional instruction. The method that students learn here will enable them to generate and identify all the types and varieties of simple lenses as different particular cases of the application of the same general cognitive procedure.

Hence the *instructional objective* of this step is:

> Give students an idea of curving plane and curved surfaces—curving inward and curving outward—by using operations of transforming a surface.

5. After the students have mastered the operations of determining the reference-point surface, determining the opposite surface, and curving the opposite surface outward and inward, they have practically acquired the concepts of convex and concave surfaces without knowing their names and their formal definitions. Now the students are prepared to understand these definitions and the meaning of the terms *convex* and *concave* surfaces. Therefore, it is time to introduce them. The instructional approach chosen introduces the concepts of both types of surfaces simultaneously and in contrast to each other. Because the definitions to be given are based on operations of transforming surfaces, these definitions are operational and easy to apply to the task of identification.

The *instructional objective* of this step is:

> Introduce the notions of convex and concave surfaces and their corresponding definitions.

6. As is known from instructional practice and psychological research, any concept, however skillfully it is introduced, should be associated with a variety

of objects whose irrelevant attributes are varied. Otherwise the concept and its corresponding term tend to be associated in the minds of students with some irrelevant features that will inadvertently narrow the generality of the concept. To prevent this from happening and to enhance the concept(s) learned, it is necessary to provide students with a large and varying empirical basis. This should also lead to faster concept generalization.

Instructional Objective:

Generalize and enhance the notion of convex surfaces by having students apply transformation operations to varying examples.

7. *Instructional Objective:*

Have students describe the operations of converting plane and curved surfaces into a convex surface in the form of a prescription (generative algorithm) indicating what one should do in order to make the conversion and in what sequence.

This instructional objective follows from one of the principles of the AHT, namely, that students have to be taught not only algorithmic and heuristic operations involved in solving problems of certain types but also ways of becoming aware of these operations and formulating explicit algorithms and heuristic prescriptions on their basis.

8. *Instructional Objective:*

Introduce the term *algorithm.*

9. Operations involved in generating an object and forming its concept are not necessarily the same as those that are involved in identifying an object and relating it to a certain class. Therefore, along with *algorithms for generating objects,* students should be taught *algorithms for their identification.* These algorithms can be given to students in a ready-made form, or students can be encouraged to discover them on their own. Students also can be guided to design them independently by becoming aware of their own identification operations and spelling them out explicitly should they happen to have learned or discovered those operations earlier.

The AHT advocates the two last approaches as educationally more valuable. Because, however, independent discovery of an algorithm is often a time-consuming process, the AHT does not exclude providing students with the ready-made algorithms when the time necessary for independent or guided discovery is not available. An analogy: It is better to equip a person with a ready-made technique for swimming and have him learn it than to throw him into water with a hope that he may be lucky enough to discover the technique independently and not drown.

Instructional Objective:

Have students develop an identification algorithm for determining whether or not a given surface is convex.

10. *Instructional Objective:*

Develop in students the ability (skill) to identify convex surfaces by practicing the identification operations indicated in the algorithm.

11. Knowledge of cognitive operations to be performed in order to solve problems and make decisions is a necessary but not sufficient condition for mastering efficient cognitive skills and abilities. Another necessary condition is *internalization* of these operations. The latter involves as one of its characteristic features *automatization* of operations.

Expert performers and learners don't execute all their cognitive operations in a *sequential* manner. Very often operations (or at least a portion of them) are carried out *simultaneously* or *almost simultaneously*. Expert performers and learners do not constantly give themselves instructions as to what they should do in order to solve problems and make decisions. Cognitive operations are actuated in their minds not so much by instructions or self-instructions as by external objects themselves (conditions of the problem) and other operations. In other words, there is a distinctive difference between the format and psychological regulation mechanism of cognitive operations performed by expert problem solvers and novices.

Often the final format of cognitive operations characteristic of expert performers is viewed as something given or developed "by itself." Actually, in conventional instructional process these characteristics are developed (when and if developed!) spontaneously through a lengthy experience.

The AHT proceeds from the proposition that the final, expert-level format of cognitive operations can be—and should be—created in a purposeful and controllable way in the process of specifically organized instruction. And this can be reliably done by a gradual transforming of *sequential* and *conscious* algorithmic operations into *simultaneous* and *nonconscious* (to be more precise, *post*conscious) operations which we have called *algorithmoid* (see L. Landa, 1976, 1978).

The AHT has developed a method for such a transformation, which clearly defines the techniques for "producing" cognitive processes with the desired properties and the steps of which such a "producing" consists.

Instructional Objective:

Have the students internalize the instructions of the algorithm and use them as out-loud self-instructions.

12. *Instructional Objective:*

Further internalize the process of self-instructing by having students give self-instructions to themselves silently.

13. *Instructional Objective:*

Internalize the operations still further and automatize them by eliminating in students the process of self-instructing at all.

14. *Instructional Objective:*

To transform sequential, algorithmic operations into automatic, simultaneous ones which would lead to the formation of a pattern-recognition cognitive mechanism and would allow students to solve the problem of identification on a pattern-recognition basis.

15. By now students have learned and mastered an algorithmic process for identifying whether a *given* (indicated, pointed out) surface is convex or not. The next instructional objective is to develop in students operations for *searching* for convex surfaces in a lens and finding them if they are present.

These *searching operations* are quite specific and not formed automatically as a result of developed operations of identification of a given surface. The specificity of searching operations consists in sequential mental isolation of surfaces in a lens with the aim of applying to each of the isolated surfaces the algorithm for identification of the surface type.

The specificity of the searching operations is obvious from everyday experience. There are people who can easily find a misplaced thing in a room and those who can't. The latter may have a sought-for thing "under their nose" and not see it. If someone would point out this thing to them, they would immediately recognize it, which means that the identification process is functioning well. What they cannot do is sequentially and systematically *isolate* different objects in a room and put them in the focus of their attention for further checking (identifying) as to whether the isolated object is the sought-for object or not.

Developing in students the searching operations is a prerequisite for subsequently developing in them the operations of identifying a type of lens. Without the ability to isolate, check, and identify all the surfaces in a lens, a student may overlook some surfaces and therefore not be able to recognize the type of lens.

The AHT requires uncovering of all "small and unnoticeable" operations involved in the terminal mechanism of knowledge and skills and their application. It also requires specific training in these operations. As in other cases, sequential operations will have to be turned into simultaneous operations so that a student will be able to isolate (see) different types of surfaces instantaneously or almost instantaneously.

Instructional Objective:

(a) To develop in students an ability to find out if a lens has a convex surface or surfaces and, if it has, which surface(s) is convex; (b) to lead students to design an algorithm for *finding* convex surfaces in a lens (and not only *identifying* a type of surface when it is already isolated and presented to them).

16. *Instructional Objective:*

Provide students with practice in the application of this last algorithm, so they can develop an ability to instantaneously determine whether a lens has a convex surface or surfaces and, if it has, which of them are convex.

17. *Instructional Objective:*

Show students that the shape of a lens is determined by the relationships of the shapes of its surfaces.

18. After students have received a general idea about how the shape of a lens is determined by the relationships of the shapes of its surfaces, it is necessary to lead them to the isolation of the relevant relationship that determines the distinction between convex and concave lenses, namely that convex lenses are thicker in the middle than at the edges, whereas concave lenses are the opposite. These indicative features will be used later in the algorithm for identification of lens type.

As in all situations when students have to come to know something new, this new knowledge may be imparted to them in a ready-made form or students can be induced to discover it on their own. As has been mentioned, the AHT advocates the discovery method as more educationally valuable and uses it when it is possible and advisable.

Instructional Objective:

Get students to ascertain distinguishing features of convex and concave lenses.

19. *Instructional Objective:*

Introduce the names of the types of the lenses under study.

20. The AHT proceeds from the proposition that students should be taught not only general methods of acquiring and applying knowledge but *general methods of constructing theories* as well, which includes *general methods of constructing definitions*. The latter ability, in turn, implies knowledge of how to make the decision as to which of several possible definitions is best, if any, and why.

Students should be taught cognitive operations involved in choosing the best definition out of several possible.

Instructional Objective:

> Get students to construct possible definitions of convex and concave lenses and to come up with some principles or methods of how to choose the best one among them.

21. As was discussed in the introductory comments, to know something and to be able to apply the knowledge to solving problems are two different psychological phenomena with two different underlying mechanisms. This applies to definitions as well. One may know a definition of a type of object but not know what to *do* with each particular encountered object and the indicative features pointed out in the definition in order to identify whether the object belongs to the given class or not. It is rare for a definition to be simple like ours, which comprises only *one* indicative feature. But it is not unusual for a definition (or any other theoretical proposition) to be complex, comprising *many* indicative features structured in a complicated logical way.

In *all* the cases, whether simple or complex, in order to be able to apply a definition (and any other theoretical proposition) and identify objects on its basis, it is necessary to convert a definition into an algorithm. In simple cases most students do this spontaneously and apply algorithms (or perform algorithmic processes) nonconsciously. In more complex cases, however, they are often not able to come up with an algorithm (or discover an algorithmic process) spontaneously and therefore don't know how to apply the definition correctly. As a result, students make errors in identifying objects to which a definition applies, although they know the definition and can accurately reproduce it.

If the objective of this lesson had been just to teach students how to distinguish convex and concave lenses, it might not have been necessary to devote much effort to teaching them the identification algorithm for these types of lenses. On the basis of these simple definitions, students would easily know how to classify a lens. Because, however, we have extended the lesson's objectives and want students to be able to identify the varieties of each type of lens as well, teaching them how to pass from a definition to an algorithm starts making sense. The identification algorithm for the general categories of lenses—convex or concave—would later become the first step (a subalgorithm) for the identification of the variety of lenses belonging to each category.

Instructional Objective:

> Have students design an algorithm for the identification of convex and concave lenses on the basis of the definition they came up with.

22. *Instructional Objective:*

Give students an idea of how to represent an algorithm in flowchart (diagram) form.

23. *Instructional Objective:*

Have students identify the indicative features of different varieties (types) of convex lenses and design a corresponding algorithm.

24. *Instructional Objective:*

Have students practice identifying the types of convex lenses by using the algorithm.

25. *Instructional Objective:*

Have students construct a comprehensive algorithm for identification of any type or variety of lens by putting together subalgorithms for identification of convex and concave lenses.

26. Now that the algorithmic processes ensuring instantaneous and automatic recognition of types of convex and concave lenses have been developed separately in students as subskills, these algorithmic processes should be synthesized. This synthesized process corresponds to the comprehensive algorithm.
Instructional Objective:

Practice the comprehensive algorithm in order to internalize and automatize the entire identification process.

REFERENCES

Landa, L. (1974). *Algorithmization in learning and instruction.* Englewood Cliffs, NJ: Educational Technology Publications.
Landa, L. (1976). *Instructional regulation and control: Cybernetics, Algorithmization, and heuristics in education.* Englewood Cliffs, NJ: Educational Technology Publications.
Landa, L. (1978). Some problems in Algo-Heurstic theory of thinking, learning and instruction. In J. M. Scandura and C. J. Brainerd (Eds.), *Structural/process models of complex human behavior.* The Netherlands: Sijthoff & Noordhoff.
Landa, L. (1983). The Algo-Heuristic theory of instruction. In C. M. Reigeluth (Ed.), *Instructional-design theories and models: An overview of their current status* (pp. 163–207). Hillsdale, NJ: Lawrence Erlbaum Associates.

A Lesson Design Based on Instructional Prescriptions From the Structural Learning Theory

George H. Stevens
American College of Healthcare Executives

Joseph M. Scandura
University of Pennsylvania

FOREWORD

History

Scandura developed a cognitive theory of learning and from that derived a theory of instruction. Like Landa's instructional theory, but unlike the theories of Gagné-Briggs and Gropper, it was not an attempt to integrate the work of others. (It was, however, intended to "accomodate" other theories.) Its focus reflects Scandura's conviction that the most important focus for instructional theory is deciding what to teach.

Unique Contributions

Perhaps Scandura's most important prescription is for the selection of content. He prescribes that all content should be taught in the form of rules, and that higher-order rules (which are very different from what Gagné calls higher-order rules) should be used in place of lower-order rules whenever possible.

Another unique contribution is Scandura's prescription to require mastery of each equivalence class (homogeneous type of problem) for each rule. In individualized instruction each student would be tested for mastery of each equivalence class and would only be taught paths (portions of rules) for those equivalence classes that were not yet mastered. Although related to the notion of "divergence of examples and practice" prescribed by many instructional theorists, equivalence classes represent a unique way of operationalizing and identifying the categories of divergence.

A third unique contribution is Scandura's sequencing prescription. He prescribes teaching the simplest unmastered path through a rule first and then proceeding to teach progressively more complex unmastered paths until the entire rule has been mastered. Reigeluth's procedural elaboration sequence is an extension of this strategy.

Similarities

Scandura's theory has several prescriptions in common with other instructional theories, such as teaching at the level of atomic rules (similar to Landa's level of elementary operations and Gagné's entry level of skills) and prescriptions to automate rules. These and other similarities are identified with Editor's Notes.

Issues to Think About

Perhaps the most important issue here is the extent to which other kinds of instructional strategy components have been overlooked. Does Scandura include all of Gagné-Briggs's nine events of instruction? Should he? Furthermore, to what extent should Scandura's prescriptions be viewed as an elaboration that should be integrated into the Gagné-Briggs framework? Can it be integrated? If so, how?

STUDY QUESTIONS

1. Define and give an example of each of the three components that comprise a rule.
2. What is the process through which a designer goes in order to identify the solution rules that should be taught to the learners?
3. What is a higher-order rule, and how does it differ from Gagné's higher-order rules?
4. Will the level of atomicity always be the same for all learners?
5. What happens when a rule or path of a rule becomes "automated"?
6. How do you decide what paths of a solution rule should be taught to each learner?
7. How do you decide how to sequence the paths that should be taught to a learner?
8. How can the breadth or comprehensiveness of an algorithm be improved?

C.M.R.

INTRODUCTION TO THE THEORY

In Structural Learning Theory (SLT) all knowledge is represented in terms of *rules*. Structural learning rules (not to be confused with production rules commonly used in other cognitive theories, e.g., Newell & Simon, 1972) include both declarative and procedural forms of representation. Specifically, rules have three components: domain, range, and operation. The *domain* consists of internal cognitive structures corresponding to the sum total of relevant environmental elements of a learning situation. It is the content upon which a learner operates to produce results specified in objectives. The *range* consists of those structures that the learner expects the rule to produce and that correspond to the variety of behaviors or decisions a learner can make with regard to a domain (evaluation or manipulation of a domain) and still complete an objective. An *operation* or procedure is the sum of all decisions and subsequent actions by a learner to produce a specific range element.

Applied to lesson design, the SLT provides a process for the selection of lesson content from a body of knowledge. It also provides a method for determining the optimal presentation sequence for teaching those rules that are selected for instruction.

The primary requisite in designing a lesson based on the SLT is a structural analysis of the content (e.g., see Scandura, 1982, 1984a,b). This analysis defines the cognitive processes (rules) that must be learned in order to master a set of lesson objectives (i.e., a given problem design). The rules, then, become the content to be taught.* Depending on the objective, one or more rules may be needed to solve tasks associated with that objective.† A rule that is used to solve a problem is a *solution rule* for that problem.

Instructional application of these rules begins with an analysis of the objective in order to identify all of the component decisions and resultant actions required of a learner to satisfy the behavior specified. Each of these components should be a single unit of behavior, or an individual decision. When each component of the solution rule is of this magnitude, that is, when further refinement has no distinct behavioral consequences for learners, it is said to be *atomic.*‡

When atomic components of a rule are sequenced such that their performance will complete an objective, they form one *path* through the solution rule for that objective. A path, then, is that sequence of atomic rules that results in the satisfaction of an objective to a specific level of difficulty. A solution rule can have many paths, each of which defines an *equivalence class* (or type) of prob-

---

*The major prescription of the SLT is, therefore, a selection strategy (macrolevel): prescribing what content to teach.

†Rules serve a similar function to Landa's "algorithm."

‡Atomic rules are equivalent to Landa's "elementary operations" (p. 116).

lems within the objective.* Different paths represent different levels of complexity implied by the conditions of the objective, or the domain elements provided in the learning situations. When a path through a solution rule is less complex than other paths through the same rule, it is *subordinate* to those more complex paths. Generally, subordinate paths are taught first in SLT-based lessons.† It is the atomic nature of solution rule components, and the accurate identification of all subordinate paths through the rule, that provide the diagnostic power of the SLT in the selection and sequencing of lesson content and subsequent remediation requirements.

After defining atomic skills and decisions, the SLT requires the development of a test for all paths through a solution rule. This test will determine learner competence on paths of the rule and, further, on the skills within a path. An advantage to testing based on the SLT is that testing need be done on only a small number of the paths through a rule to determine precisely the level of learner competence at a given objective. This is the result of sequencing test items based on the hierarchical structure of the paths, and on the equivalent nature of multiple tests of a single path. Tests of a solution rule in the SLT would not examine each path but would selectively test paths through a rule until a learner could not correctly perform at a tested path. Instruction would then begin at the level of the most subordinate path at which the learner was unable to perform. The equivalence class includes all examples of rule solution for a specific path. All examples within a class test the same ability of a learner and, hence, are equivalent for purposes of testing and instruction.

The implication of this is that, to the extent the prior structural analysis is adequate for all students in the target population, repetition in a unit of instruction and testing of a given path is not necessary within an equivalence class. If a learner performs at one test item from an equivalence class, it is assumed that he or she will perform at all other items within the class. This assumption does not generalize beyond an equivalence class.

The SLT can be applied to instruction for learners with no skill or previous experience in a subject (naive learners), learners with competence at the solution rules for problems that are built upon the atomic rules for the solution (neophytes), or more advanced learners who successfully integrate atomic rules for solution via higher-order rules. *Automation* of rules is the redefinition of a rule to

---

*This is a unique and useful way to identify Merrill's "divergence" (p. 208), Gropper's "variety of practice" (p. 55), and Collins's "vary cases systematically" (p. 184) and "entrap students" (p. 185).

†This is a sequencing strategy (macrolevel). This was a precursor to, and is similar to, Reigeluth's "elaboration sequence for a procedural orientation." Note that it is very different from Gagné's "hierarchical sequence of prerequisite skills" (p. 22) and Landa's "snowball" sequence for the "step-by-step" approach (p. 122). In what ways does it differ from each? Can you think of situations in which a subordinate path in Scandura's system would not be a learning prerequisite for its superordinate path?

incorporate several atomic rules into a single cognitive step.* Both of these processes result from the application of *higher-order* rules (see Scandura, 1981).†

When learners have successfully automated rules, those rules then provide a basis for applying the SLT to more complex training in a given subject matter (e.g., see Scandura & Scandura, 1980).

LESSON PREFACE: PLANNING AND STRUCTURAL ANALYSIS

The greatest strength of the SLT is its ability to allow an instructor to quickly and accurately select content and sequencing requirements for training that will provide only that instruction needed by a learner. Indeed, the primary differences between an SLT-based lesson and other lessons are the precision of content selection and sequencing and their match to learner needs, and the validity of supporting test elements for the instruction. This difference is significant and requires structural analysis of content in the lesson-planning phase (see Durnin, Scandura, 1973; Scandura, 1977; Scandura, Stone, & Scandura, 1985; Microsystem 80 Series, A and C; Microtutor II Series, A). Because the "action" in applying the SLT occurs long before the lesson begins, an example of its application must also begin at that point of structural analysis. Specific decisions regarding message medium and delivery strategy selection in using the SLT depend on secondary objectives (which are unspecified in the present case), and so will not be addressed in this example. Such decisions require analysis of learner traits and logistic variables in addition to the content and behavior variables which are treated by the SLT.

Structural Analysis: Lesson on Microscopes

Analyzing the structure of the objectives for this lesson shows that each of the six is very specific, in that each requires only a single rule of knowledge. (For details on how to perform a structural analysis, see Scandura, 1984.) Each rule within the objective contains a single "triple" comprised of a domain, range, and operation (a restricted type of procedure) (see Scandura, 1970, 1971, 1984). None of the objectives requires use of higher-order rules; that is, none of the identified rules acted upon other rules (see Scandura, 1971). Finally, the rules

---

*Automation of rules is similar to what Landa calls "automatization of operations" (p. 122).

†The selection of higher-order rules (which in essence replace numerous lower-order rules in instruction) is a very important aspect of the SLT and is similar to Landa's "general, content-independent abilities" (p. 123) and Gagné's "cognitive strategies" (p. 15), and is somewhat similar to Merrill's "find" level of performance (p. 203).

associated with the various objectives are treated independently of one another (although they may share component decisions and/or operations). Consequently, in the following analysis, relationships due to common components are not taken into account—although they could be by simply creating a single rule hierarchy showing relationships among paths of all six rules.

The rules associated with Objectives 1 through 5 specify decision-operation combinations similar to that of Objective 6. Given this, and the fact that Objective 6 has a greater number of paths, this objective is the basis for the illustrative lesson plan on microscopes. This lesson "blueprint" is presented in detail after a presentation of the domain, range, operation, and equivalence classes associated with the solution rules for each objective. It is these that result from structural analysis and, hence, that are the products of lesson planning with the SLT.

The structure of the solution rules for the remaining five objectives is also presented, but in less detail. The similarity between the types of decisions and operations in Objective 6 and the remaining objectives make a detailed treatment of all rules redundant.

Objective: Structural Analysis Products

A detailed description of the domain, range, operation, and equivalence classes follows for each path in the solution rule for Objective 6.

Solution Rule Domain. In this solution rule, the domain consists of all microscopes with multiple magnification capabilities and electric or reflective light sources. The domain items selected for a test of any given path depends upon the route through the solution rule (path) selected.

Solution Rule Range. The range of acceptable outputs for this rule consists of focused scopes with either electric or reflective sources, with N objectives.

Solution Rule Operation. The solution rule operation consists of rule components 1 (operation), A (binary decision), 2 (operation), 3 (operation), 4 (operation), 5 (operation), 6 (operation), 7 (operation), B (decision), 8 (operation), and 9 (operation). These components are organized as in the following solution procedure:

1. Turn objective so lowest power is straight down.
   A. Is there a built-in light?

YES	NO
2. Turn on light.	3. Adjust mirror to maximize light visible through microscope.

4. Adjust diaphragm.

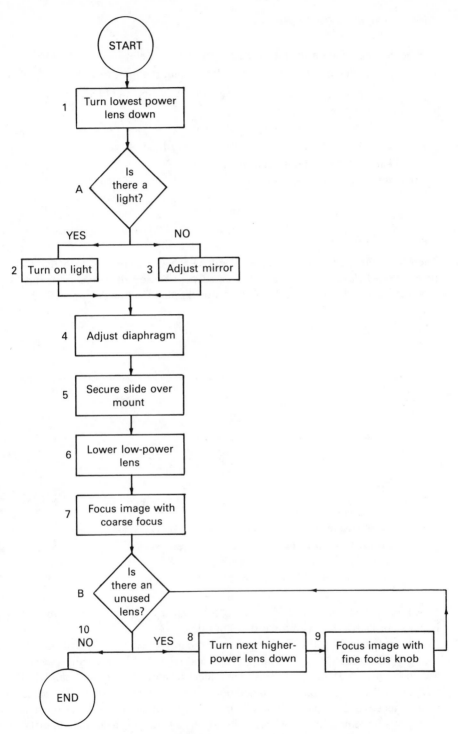

FIG. 5.1. Flowchart of solution rule for Objective 6.

5. Secure slide on mount over hole.

6. Lower the low-power objective slowly until it almost touches the slide.

7. Lock in eyepiece and turn coarse focus adjustment until specimen is in rough focus.

   B. While there is an unused objective:

8. Turn the next higher-power objective into field of sight.

9. Turn fine focus until detail is in focus.

(10. No unused objective, then END.)

Solution Rule Paths

[1] There are four paths of this focusing rule, each corresponding to a distinct (equivalence) class of to-be-focused microscopes. These paths are conveniently represented as subgraphs (subflow charts) of the full solution rule in Figs. 5.2 and 5.3:

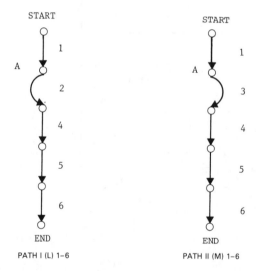

A. Microscopes with a single objective, a single focus knob using a mirror light.

FIG. 5.2. Paths identified: I.   PATH I (L) 1–6   PATH II (M) 1–6

All four paths were identified from the structural analysis of the objective; that is, all were discovered within the solution rule.

Take note that all paths involving (L) are progressively more difficult, as are all those following (M). As such, paths (I) and (III) are hierarchically related, and so are paths (II) and (IV). This hierarchical relationship requires path III to have all of the steps of path I, and additional operations or decisions. The same requirement applies to paths IV and II. It is this type of heirarchical clarification what gives Structural Learning Theory its power, by allowing a designer to make

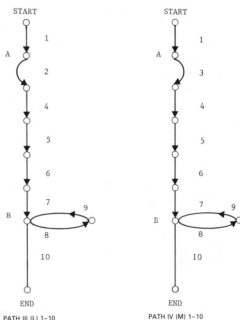

B. Microscopes with more than one objective, and both coarse and fine focus knobs.

FIG. 5.3. Paths identified: III. PATH III (L) 1–10   PATH IV (M) 1–10

assumptions about learner ability on all higher-level paths based on inability to perform on a tested path.

Equivalence Classes for Each Path

PATH	CONCEPT (CLASS) DESCRIPTION	STEPS
I.	Any focused microscope with a light, a single objective, and only one focus knob.	1, A, 2, 4, 5, 6
II.	Any focused microscope with a mirror, a single objective, and only one focus knob.	1, A, 3, 4, 5, 6
III.	Any focused microscope with a light, multiple objectives, and both a coarse and a fine focus.	1, A, 2, 4, 5, 6, 7, B, 8, 9, 10
IV.	Any focused microscope with a mirror, multiple objectives, and both a coarse and a fine focus.	1, A, 3, 4, 5, 6, 7, B, 8, 9, 10

The solution rule as shown represents the "final report" of the structural analysis that must be performed on the learning problem. It includes all of the operations and decisions needed to perform successfully on the domain to produce outcomes specified in Objective 6. As such, it is a cognitive and behavioral task analysis. One assumption made by such rules is that each of the cognitive components (decisions and/or operations) is elementary or "atomic" (i.e., either fully available to a learner or completely unavailable—partial knowledge may not be represented without further refinement of a component). Each numeric element in the rule is a single component (cognitive operation/decision) that must be completed as part of the solution. This rule is the output of the structural analysis, and the result is the specification of all critical domain attributes (i.e., equivalence classes) that will then become the learning environment for the lesson.

Although the analysis contains ten possible operations and two decisions to be made by a learner, it must be stressed that no single microscope can provide all of the variations identified in the analysis. Consequently, not all of the decisions and/or operations may be necessary to successfully focus any given microscope.

In review, if a designer were given the goal to be achieved, structural analysis would produce the design in Table 5.1.

If learners could perform all paths in the solution rule (i.e., if learners already knew the rule) and automatization (i.e., complete mastery) of the material were desired, then further practice on the solution rule may be expected to result in a more efficient version of the rule (see Scandura, 1981). For example, such a rule might have only two operations or components: (a) "Set up microscope for viewing;" and (b) "Bring specimen into focus." This simplified or "automated" solution rule would then be taught and practiced at this level of specificity until the desired behavior were mastered across the range of outputs.

TABLE 5.1
Structural Analysis of Objective

Domain (unspecified)	Operation (unspecified)	Goal Behavior

⎯⎯⎯⎯⎯⎯⎯⎯⎯⎯⎯⎯⎯⎯

STRUCTURAL ANALYSIS

specific list of all:

Domain Elements	Solution Procedure	
In this lesson, these would be:		
• Microscope	• Solution procedure as	Focused Microscope
• Objectives (multiple)	identified on page 7	
• Focus knobs	• Enumeration of possible	
• Electric light source	paths through the solution	
• Reflective light source	rule as specified on pp. 9–	
• Specimens for	10	
viewing (mounted)		

Atomic vs. Automated Rules

Here is a comparison of atomic and automated steps to a solution rule:

"ATOMIC" ELEMENTS *OF ORIGINAL SOLUTION RULE*	*"AUTOMATED" SOLUTION RULE*

"ATOMIC" ELEMENTS
OF ORIGINAL SOLUTION RULE

1. Turn objective so lowest power is straight down.
   A. Is there a built-in light?

Yes	No

2. Turn on light.   3. Adjust mirror to maximize light visible through microscope.
4. Adjust diaphragm.
5. Secure slide on mount over hole.
6. Lower the low-power objective slowly until it almost touches the slide.
7. Look in eyepiece, and turn coarse focus adjustment until specimen is in rough focus.
   B. While there is an unused objective:
8. Turn the next higher-power objective into field of sight.
9. Turn fine focus until detail is in focus.
10. No unused objective, then END.

"AUTOMATED" SOLUTION RULE

1. Set up microscope.

2. Bring specimen into focus.

What constitutes "atomicity" of a path or component of a rule is, of necessity, somewhat arbitrary. Identifying paths makes it possible to specify all those behaviors that will allow a learner to achieve the prescribed goals. Depending upon the ability level of any given population, valid assumptions might be made by a designer that would change the level of specificity of the "atomic" components of a rule. For example, if a designer knew that a given audience could *already* focus a microscope, the solution procedures could combine steps 6 through 9 into a single operation that states, "Focus the specimen in view." The risk here is that of assuming more than is justified as regards learner ability. In general, atomicity provides a "least common denominator" of all individuals in the target population.

An equivalence class may be defined as that concept containing all instances representative of a given path. In the present lesson, each equivalence class represents a set of objective/light source combinations.

Test Development

The final step in preparing for a lesson based on the SLT is the development of an adaptive test based on the paths of the solution rule. This test is derived directly from the equivalence classes for the solution rule. Test items selected from any given equivalence class should require the learner to complete all steps in the path corresponding to that equivalence class. The test developed for the solution rule of Objective 6 need contain only four test items, one for each of the four paths. Sample test items corresponding to the four paths are given below.

		PATH
[2]	_TEST ITEM_	_TESTED_

1. "Using the multiple-stage, light-powered microscope, focus the specimen with all magnifications in the proper sequence."   III

2. "Using the single-stage, light-powered microscope, focus the specimen using the proper sequence of operations."   I

3. "Using the multiple-stage, mirror-powered microscope, focus the specimen with all magnifications in the proper sequence."   IV

4. "Using the single-stage, mirror-powered microscope, focus the specimen in the proper sequence."   II

With Objective 6 presented in detail, the remaining five objectives are briefly described. The domain, range, solution procedure, and equivalence classes for each objective will be presented. In this group of objectives, there is only one equivalence class for each objective, as there is only one path associated with each skill. This is not normally the case with more complex learning situations.

The behavior required to satisfy _Objective 1_ is concept classification. The rule for concept classification, applied to this objective, has a domain of all lenses, a range of two classes of lenses—convex and nonconvex—and a solution rule, or operation, as follows:

1. Is the center of the lens thicker than the edge?

Yes	_No_
The lens is convex.	The lens is nonconvex.

The analysis presents all subject material and decisions that are necessary for objective achievement. The solution procedure statement shows only one possible path through the rule. This is similar to the decision required at step two of the solution procedures for Objective 6.

A test to determine the necessity of instruction would be the random presentation of examples and nonexamples of convex lenses for learner classification. As there is only one step to the solution rule, instances should vary over the range of lenses for each learner. The equivalence class for this rule would contain all lenses with corresponding labels of "convex" or "nonconvex."

Objective 2 requires a learner to recall a definition when presented with a request for that definition. The domain of this skill involves a request for the definition of the term *focal length*, either verbatim and/or paraphrase. The range is any response that contains the equivalent of "the distance from the lens to the focal point, on either side of the lens." The solution rule for this rule might have two paths. One path would correspond to verbatim recall of a given definition, while the other would correspond to a paraphrase of that definition. The equivalence class for the first path would contain essentially one element; the given definition. The equivalence class for the second path would include any reply that contained the critical elements of the definition.

Objectives 3 and 4 share a common domain: all convex lenses, or diagrams of such lenses, light rays, focal lengths, and image magnifications created by the interaction between light rays and given lenses. The third and fourth objectives together cover a range of three principles. The cause and effect relationship expressed by Objective 3 as follows: If a lens curvature is greater than a given standard, then light passing through the lens is bent at a greater angle than light through the standard.

Objective 4 includes the principle described in Objective 3, and also the following cause-effect relationships: (a) If light is bent to a greater degree through a given lens than through a standard, then the focal length of that lens is shorter than the standard; (b) If the focal length of a lens is shorter than a standard, then its power of magnification is greater than that of the standard. The range of the rule would also include separate cause-effect statements describing light bent to a smaller degree than a standard, and corresponding focal lengths.

The solution procedure for these two objectives can be combined into what resembles a concept classification procedure, as shown for Objective 1, and can be taught as such.

SOLUTION PROCEDURE
FOR OBJECTIVES 3 AND 4:

1. Is lens curvature greater than the standard?

Yes	*No*
Light refraction is greater than standard.	Light refraction is less than standard.

2. Is light refraction greater than standard?

Yes	No
Focal length is shorter than standard.	Focal length is longer than standard.

3. Is focal length shorter than standard?

Yes	No
Magnification is greater than standard.	Magnification is less than standard.

The path that satisfies Objective 3 (e.g., students will explain or predict what effect different convex lenses will have on light rays) is the completion of step 1 of the procedure. Steps 1, 2, and 3 are required for satisfaction of Objective 4, which requires a learner to explain or predict how the curvature of the lens influences both the magnification and focal length of different lenses. Because the solution rule for Objective 4, presenting Objective 3 first will facilitate the learning of Objective 4. Correct performance on a test of Objective 3 becomes the input for a test of steps 2 and 3 of Objective 4.

Objective 5 has a domain that includes a request for three significant events in the history of the microscope, and a range that is a learner response that includes those events. The solution procedure for Objective 5 would be an association of those events with the request. Testing and instructional sequences for this objective would be similar to those used for Objective 2, which also links the domain and range of a rule with an associative procedure.

LESSON

After lesson preparation through structural analysis, and the development of
[3] a test of each path in the solution rule of lesson objectives, the prepared test must be implemented. In our illustrative lesson, the test previously described will be offered to a student named Sally, as follows:

1. "Using the multiple-stage, light-powered microscope, focus the spec-
[4]   imen with all magnifications in the proper sequence." (Sally's re-
       sponse is incorrect.)
2. "Using the single-stage, light-powered microscope, focus the spec-
[5]   imen using the proper sequence of operations." (Sally's response is
       correct.)

3. "Using the multiple-stage, mirror-powered microscope, focus the specimen with all magnifications in the proper sequence." (Sally's response is incorrect.)

4. "Using the single-stage, mirror-powered microscope, focus the specimen in the proper sequence." (Because Sally failed the test on path 3, testing on path 4 is unnecessary. (See the following section.) Sally's response is assumed incorrect.)

[6] The single-stage, mirror-powered microscope (path II) entails the most atomic path at which the learner requires instruction and therefore is the first area for instruction. After this, the more complex skills for multiple-focus scopes (paths III and IV) will be taught.[1]

The content and sequence of the lesson prescribed by the test administered to student Sally follows:

[7]

PATH	SOLUTION COMPONENT	CONTENT
II	3 "Adjust mirror."	• Adjustment of mirror to maximize light flow through eyepiece.
III, IV	8 "Turn next higher power lens down."	• Differentiation of objectives from other microscope parts. • Differentiation of objective power by size of objective (length of tube). • Manipulation of objective wheel through clockwise rotation.
III, IV	9 "Focus image with fine focus knob."	• Differentiation between coarse focus knob (a known variable) and fine focus knob (an unknown variable), which is attached to the coarse focus.

---

[1]In the absence of secondary objectives pertaining to such things as learning strategies, recommendations provided by the Structural Learning Theory for delivery of instructional messages are limited to the task at hand rather than including methodological prescriptions. Indeed, "once (structural) analysis has been completed, designing an effective instructional strategy follows directly and precisely from the theory" (Scandura, 1983). Specifically, one knows (a) what the student is to be able to do, (b) what the student must learn in order to do that, and (c) the most effective sequence for instructional presentation. It must be understood, however, that the above can only be as complete and/or useful as the structural analysis from which it derives.

Transition to Next Path

Briefly describe similarities and *differences* between the path for which instruction has been provided. Highlight those differences by comparing one scope from each path's equivalence class.

> *REPEAT:* Repeat transition sequence until all paths have been taught.
>
> *TEST:* Test learner performance as was done in the content sequence identification.
>
> *FEEDBACK:* Provide evaluative/corrective feedback to learner.
>
> *IF:* All paths are not performed properly.
>
> *THEN:* Repeat lesson at a higher level of detail/specificity, beginning with the last path at which the learner was able to perform successfully. This can be done by redefining the level of atomicity of the paths and providing feedback on the learner performance at the level of individual *steps* in completion of any given path. This testing of instruction is intermingled so the student progresses to the next path only after the prerequisites have been mastered.
>
> *IF:* Path performances are correct, and automation of the skill is desired by the designer.
>
> *THEN:* The steps of the solution procedure can be reduced to two subsuming steps:
>
> 1. "Set up Microscope for Viewing"
> 2. "Bring Specimen into Focus"

This simplified or automated solution rule would then be taught at this level of specificity until the desired behavior was mastered. This rule could be taught as in the process used in the "neophyte" solution procedure. Differences would be greater emphasis on the practical component of the presentation form in the instruction of the two-step automated rule. This practice will maximize path completion with association of fewer steps, thus improving long-term rule retention.

The SLT does not specify how the content in the outline is to be taught and so will not be prescribed in a lesson plan.

After instruction at these content areas, a test of the paths requiring these components will be completed to evaluate learner competence. Based on learner performance, remediation can then be provided specific to the skills requiring development.

COMMENTS

1. Objective 6 has two groups of subordinate/superordinate paths, and yet each group is independent of the other. These groups are paths associated with a light-powered microscope and those associated with a mirror-operated scope. Assumptions made on one group of paths cannot be generalized to the other without testing to verify learner competence.

2. The test constructed for Objective 6 will be presented such that learners will be evaluated at a level of skill complexity greater than the most subordinate path in any group of paths. If learners cannot perform at this level, then they will be tested at a more subordinate level until the existing competence level is determined. This is reflected in the test sequence of path III first and then path I. Path III is superordinate to I. The same logic produces the testing sequence of path IV to path II; paths IV and II are independent of III and I. An alternate test sequence of IV-II, III-I would be equally effective to the presented sequence of III-I, IV-II.

3. The first contact a learner will have in a lesson based on the Structural Learning Theory is an individualized test of key paths to the rule. Prototypical example problems are selected from equivalence classes and presented to the learners on the preceding test element. The result is that although two learners may begin on the same element from the same equivalence class, they may not take the same test, if their performances are at all different.

When structural analysis has identified learning needs in each path of the rule, each path at which the learner is not competent becomes an element selected for instruction.

4. The hierarchical organization of learning material that resulted from structural analysis allows the instructor to make valid assumptions about student competence with few test items. The assumptions made are: (a) if a learner is competent on a given path, he or she is competent on all subordinate paths; (b) if a learner is not competent on a given path, he or she is not competent on any superordinate paths. In Objective 6, this assumption is exemplified by the inability of a learner to focus a specimen using a microscope with multiple objectives. Given this, it can be assumed that the learner would also fail at a higher path that requires use of multiple objectives and multiple focus knobs.

5. The next step in testing based on the Structural Learning Theory is to determine learner competence at a subordinate path. This learner is competent at the simplest path. If the learner were not competent at this path, further testing of component behaviors of this simplest path would be necessary to indicate learning needs. In this example, however, as the learner is competent at this path, instruction would begin with the next path in the hierarchy.

6. The two independent path sequences that were identified were tested

yielding the results illustrated in Fig. 5.4 for this one learner, compared to the standard on the left.

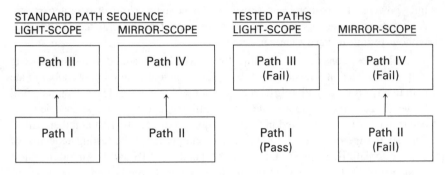

FIG. 5.4

Results of Test: For this one learner, on light-scope paths, instruction should begin at path III, while mirror-scope instruction should begin at path II.

Instruction on path I of the rule is unnecessary, as learner performance on the diagnostic test indicated competence at operation of a scope with an electric light source and a single focus adjustment.

If more specific identification of content needs is required, the prior structural analysis and corresponding diagnostic test procedures could be carried out at a more detailed level on each path to identify specific behaviors (steps) to be taught.

A diagram of the content to be taught, expressed as steps for each path, is shown in Fig. 5.5.

7. With content selection complete at the path level of specificity, sequencing proceeds in a simple-to-complex order. Subordinate paths, as identified in structural analysis, are taught before more complex superordinate paths.

Although the Structural Learning Theory does mandate a simple-to-complex instructional order, there is some flexibility in a case such as this lesson. In this case, there are two independent path sequences to the complete rule. These hierarchies are first, those paths that proceed using a light-powered base, and second, those paths that involve the use of a mirrored scope. Because these paths hierarchies are independent, paths II and IV must be taught in that order. Path II is subordinate to path IV in the same hierarchy. Path III is independent of paths II and IV (in the sense that path III includes steps not included in II or IV). Hence, no particular sequence of instructional presentation is prescribed by the Structural Learning Theory. Because of this fact, there are three acceptable instructional sequence alternatives:

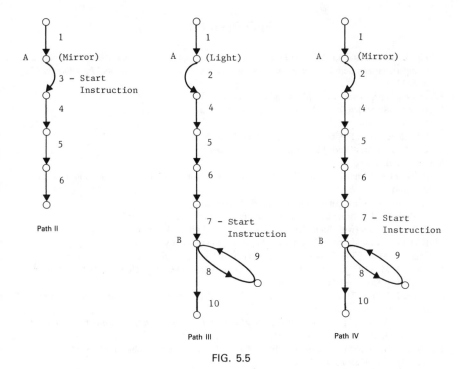

FIG. 5.5

OPTION ONE	*OPTION TWO*	*OPTION THREE*
1. Path II	1. Path III	1. Path II
2. Path IV	2. Path II	2. Path III
3. Path III	3. Path IV	3. Path IV

Regardless of which sequence option is chosen, skills from one independent path sequence could be generalized to the other path sequence to facilitate learning efficiency. For example, if sequence option one were chosen, the learner would first gain familiarity with the use of not only a mirror light source (path II) but also multiple-objective scopes (path IV). The latter could then facilitate the learning of path III, inasmuch as the learner already knows how to turn on the light (path I) and shares the other previously learned steps. Similarly, if option two were selected, the skills of operating multiple objectives and focus adjustments (path III) and mirror light source (path II) would contribute to later learning path IV.

This type of generalization is accommodated in SLT by taking components of the various paths into account in prescribing instruction and by performing all testing and instruction in a dynamic interactive manner (see Scandura & Scandura, in press).

REFERENCES

Durnin, J. H., & Scandura, J. M. (1973). An algorithmic approach to assessing behavior potential: Comparison with item forms and hierarchical analysis. *Journal of Educational Psychology, 65,* 262–272.

Microcomputer Software by J. M. Scandura, Director.

MicroSystem80 Series, Borg-Warner Educational Systems

    A Critical Reading, Fall 1980 (8-disk system)

    B College Board Preparation, Winer 1980 (12-disk system)

    C Language Arts-Word Structure, Fall 1982 (8-disk system)

MicroTutor II Series

    A Tutorial Arithmetic, Fall 1982 (12-disk system for addition, subtraction multiplication, division)

    B EZ Author & EZ Author Plans Authoring systems, Spring 1983

    C SUPRAS Authoring system with ''intelligent'' interface, Spring 1983

    D Reading Sills (with John Dawkins), Summer 1983 (10-disk system)

    E Tutorial Mosaic (over 170 titles produced in collaboration with others)

Scandura, J. M. (1970). Role of rules in behavior. *Psychological Review, 77,* 516–533.

Scandura, J. M. (1971). Deterministic theorizing in structural learning: Three levels of empiricism. *Journal of Structural Learning, 3,* 21–53.

Scandura, J. M. (1977). *Problem solving: A structural/process approach with instructional implications.* New York: Academic Press.

Scandura, J. M. (1981). Problem solving in schools and beyond: Transitions from the naive to the neophyte to the master. *Educational Psychologist, 16,* 139–150.

Scandura, J. M. (1984). Structural analysis. Part II: Toward precision, objectivity and systematization. *Journal of Structural Learning, 8,* 1–28.

Scandura, J. M. (1984b). Structural analysis. Part III: Validity and reliability. *Journal of Structural Learning, 8,* 173–193.

Scandura, J. M., & Scandura, A. B. (1980). Structural learning and concrete operations: An approach to Piagetian conservation. New York: Praeger.

Scandura, J. M., & Scandura, A. B. (in press). ''The intelligent rule tutor: A structural approach to intelligent tutoring.'' In David H. Jonassen (Ed.), *Instructional Designs for Microcomputer Courseware.*

6

A Sample Dialogue
Based on a Theory
of Inquiry Teaching

Allan Collins
Bolt Beranek and Newman, Inc.

FOREWORD

History

This is the most recently developed of the instructional theories in this book. In contrast to all the other instructional theories in this book, this one was not derived from or based on a learning theory of any kind. It was developed almost purely inductively by "observing" expert teachers, cataloging the strategies that they used, and developing prescriptions as to when to use each of those strategies.

Unique Contributions

Perhaps the most unique prescription of this theory is for the use of a discovery approach. Learners are required to formulate hypotheses (discover generalities) based on observation of varied cases (examples), presumably to force greater depth of processing of the new knowledge. Another feature is the use of an inquiry approach. Questions provide the focus and direction for the instruction, presumably to improve motivation.

This work was supported by the National Institute of Education under Contract No. HEW-NIE-400-80-0031 and the office of Naval Research under Contract No. N00014-85-C-0026. My thanks to Albert Stevens, who has collaborated with me on the research that led to this paper, and to Dedre Gentner, who made many helpful comments on an earlier version of the paper.

Another unique feature of this theory is that many of its strategies are intended more to develop higher thought processes (cognitive strategies) than to develop content-specific knowledge. Furthermore, this is the only theory that provides prescriptions for teaching independence of thought (intellectual freedom).

Similarities

This theory does have a number of strategies for teaching content-specific knowledge, and many of them are similar to prescriptions in other theories, such as the use of positive and negative exemplars (examples and nonexamples), varying cases systematically (example divergence), and tracing consequences to a contradiction (feedback). These and other similarities are identified in the chapter with Editor's Notes.

Issues to Think About

As with many of the instructional theories in preceding chapters, perhaps the most important issue is whether there are situations for which this approach would not be advisable. For what kinds of situations is it and is it not appropriate? Group-based learning? Foreign language vocabulary? But there are other important issues as well. How cost-effective is it? Have any important strategies been overlooked? Can it (should it) be integrated into the Gagné-Briggs framework? If so, how?

STUDY QUESTIONS

1. When and why does one present positive or negative exemplars?
2. When and why does one vary cases systematically?
3. When and why does one select counterexamples?
4. When and why does one generate hypothetical cases?
5. When and why does one have the learner consider alternative predictions?
6. When, why, and how does one entrap learners?
7. When and why does one trace consequences to a contradiction?
8. When, why, and how does one have the learner question authority?
9. How do you know which strategy to use when?

C.M.R.

INTRODUCTION TO THE THEORY

By analyzing the work of a variety of teachers who use an inquiry method of teaching (Collins, 1977; Collins & Stevens, 1982, 1983), we have formulated a theory of inquiry teaching in terms of the goals, strategies, and control structure

TABLE 6.1
Different Instructional Techniques

1. Selecting positive and negative exemplars (2, 7)
2. Varying cases systematically (3, 6, 7, 9, 13, 16)
3. Selecting counterexamples (6, 14)
4. Generating hypothetical cases (6)
5. Forming hypotheses (3, 4, 7, 9, 15)
6. Testing hypotheses (3, 8, 9, 10, 12)
7. Considering alternative predictions (4, 10)
8. Entrapping students (3, 6, 7)
9. Tracing consequences to a contradiction (14)
10. Questioning authority (11)

Described by Collins and Stevens (1983). Numbers in parentheses refer to the numbered comments in the text after the dialogue, where each strategy is discussed.

different teachers use. In this chapter I illustrate the theory by an extended inquiry dialogue on the nature of lenses. Thus, this chapter shows how the theory can be applied in detail to one specific context.

Inquiry teachers have two overall goals. One is to teach a deep understanding of a particular domain so that students can make novel predictions about the domain. The other is to teach students to be good scientists so that they can learn to construct general rules and theories on their own, and be able to test them out.* The dialogue tries to encompass both these goals of inquiry teaching. In general, inquiry teachers do not try to teach facts and concepts per se, except insofar as they fit into a general framework or theory of a domain.

The ten general strategies inquiry teachers use to accomplish these goals are shown in Table 6.1. We describe each of these strategies briefly:

1. *Selecting Positive and Negative Exemplars.* In selecting cases, teachers often pick paradigm cases where the values of all the relevant factors are consistent with a particular value of a dependent variable.† For example, to illustrate convexity of a lens, a teacher might choose an example where both surfaces curve outward (a positive exemplar) and one where both curve inward (a negative exemplar).‡

2. *Varying Cases Systematically.* In selecting cases, teachers often pick a comparison case that varies from the previous case in a systematic way. For example, the teacher might systematically vary the distance between a lens and a

---

*These two goals correspond to Gagné's "intellectual skills" and "cognitive strategies," repsectively.

†This is the same as Merrill's "example" (p. 204), Gropper's "example of the performance" (p. 54), and Landa's "demonstration" (p. 121, footnote 12).

‡This is what Merrill refers to as a "nonexample."

piece of paper so the student will see how light rays from the sun (a) cross over; (b) come to a focal point; or (c) fail to come together as the lens moves closer to the paper.*

3. *Selecting Counterexamples.* If a student forms a hypothesis that is not completely true, the teacher will often select a case that satisfies the student's hypothesis but violates the hypothesized prediction. For example, if a student thinks a magnifying glass always makes letters appear larger, the teacher might hold the glass halfway between the letter and the student's eye.

4. *Generating Hypothetical Cases.* Teachers often generate hypothetical cases in order to force students to reason about situations that are hard to reproduce naturally. For example, if a teacher wants the student to think about what happens to the sun's rays as they go through a lens held far above a piece of paper, the teacher might ask the student to predict where a hypothetical spot on the sun would appear in the image on the paper.†

5. *Forming Hypotheses.* Inquiry teachers continually try to make students predict how a dependent variable varies with one or more independent variables or factors. For example, the teacher might ask the student to formulate a hypothesis about what focal length depends on (i.e., curvature of a lens) and how it depends on it (i.e., the more the curvature, the less the focal length).‡

6. *Testing Hypotheses.* Once the student has formulated a hypothesis, the teacher wants the student to figure out how to test the hypothesis. For example, if the student thinks that focal length will be less the more curved the lens, then the teacher might ask how this hypothesis could be tested (e.g., by comparing how high above a piece of paper lenses of different curvature must be held so that the light through them comes to focus).§

7. *Considering Alternative Predictions.* Tutors often encourage students to consider whether a prediction different from the one they have in mind might be correct, in order to foster differential diagnosis as a strategy. For example, if a student thinks that an image turns upside down as one moves a lens toward one's eye, the tutor might ask the student to consider whether instead it might turn the image right side up.‖

8. *Entrapping Students.* Inquiry tutors often suggest incorrect hypotheses in

---

*This is similar to Merrill's "example divergence" (p. 208) and Gropper's "variety of practice" (p. 55), except it appears to apply to examples rather than to practice.

†This strategy component is unique among the theories in this book and seems likely to facilitate depth of cognitive processing in the learners.

‡This strategy component is also unique among the theories in this book, and it seems intended primarily to achieve Collins's second goal: "to teach students to be good scientists." Hypotheses themselves are similar to Merrill's "generality" (p. 204) and Gropper's "telling the learner what and how to perform" (p. 52).

§Same: This is unique and primarily targeted toward the second goal.

‖Same: This is unique and primarily targeted toward the second goal.

order to get students to reveal their underlying misconceptions. For example, a tutor might ask whether, as one moves a lens closer to a piece of paper, a light shining through it will come more and more into focus (it does not).*

9. *Tracing Consequences to a Contradiction.* Tutors often trace the implications of a student's answer to a contradiction with some other belief the student holds. This forces students to build consistent theories. For example, if the student draws rays of light through a lens bending more when they go to the eye than when they come from the sun, the tutor might ask if the student really thinks the rays will bend more in one case than the other.†

10. *Questioning Authority.* When students ask what the right answer is, or seem to rely on a textbook, inquiry teachers try to get students to conduct their own experiments and reach their own conclusions. For example, if a student asks the teacher whether a lens that is more curved has a shorter focal length, the teacher might plead ignorance and encourage the student to conduct an experiment to find out.‡

In running an inquiry dialogue with students, teachers maintain an agenda of goals and subgoals that is continuously updated throughout the dialogue. They start out with very high-level goals that spawn subgoals governing the selection of problems and initial questions. But as students answer these initial questions, they reveal misconceptions and holes in their knowledge that in turn generate subgoals for the teacher to diagnose and correct.§

LESSON PREFACE

The goal of this paper is to apply the theory outlined to teaching specific material about the nature of lenses. The content to be taught is summarized in six basic objectives given us by the editor:

1. Students will be able to classify previously unencountered lenses as to whether or not they are convex lenses.
2. Students will be able to define focal length.
3. Students will explain or predict what effect different convex lenses will have on light rays.

---

*This is basically the same as Merrill's "divergent practice" (p. 208) and Gropper's "variety of practice" (p. 55).

†This is a unique form of feedback that requires the learner to think more deeply about an error than does typical correct-answer or process feedback.

‡This unique strategy component seems intended primarily to achieve the second goal, also (teaching students to be good scientists).

§This is primarily a sequencing strategy (macro level).

4. Students will explain the way in which the curvature of a lens influences both the magnification and the focal length of different lenses.
5. Students will be able to state from memory the three significant events in the history of the microscope.
6. Students will be able to use a previously unencountered optical microscope properly.

The lesson as written addresses only the first four objectives. I have omitted any teaching of the procedure for using a microscope and the historical facts about lenses that were suggested for inclusion in the lesson. The inquiry method can be very effectively used to teach procedures or history, but in order to do so the inclusion of the procedures and history must be well motivated. For example, an inquiry dialogue about the procedure for using a microscope might try to get the student to invent the correct procedure by considering all the things that could go wrong at each step in the procedure. To teach history the inquiry teacher would have to know how various events led to other events, so that the teacher can get students to try to predict how history unfolded. However, in the materials submitted to us, the procedure consisted of a series of steps without any reasons given for the steps, and the history consisted of three unrelated facts. So without a great deal of work it would have been difficult to develop either into an inquiry dialogue.

The dialogue that follows is derived from interviews with two actual children, but it has been drastically shortened and edited to emphasize the strategies described in "Introduction to the Theory" above. Although only one student is depicted, inquiry teachers often conduct such a dialogue with groups of students. If done well, the fostering of multiple hypotheses and argumentation among groups of students can make the method more effective.

LESSON:
THE INQUIRY DIALOGUE

[1]   1. T: Do you know what the piece of glass in this magnifying glass is called?
        2. S: A lens?
        3. T: That's right, it's called a lens, like the lens in a camera or the lens in your eye. Why do you think it is curved?
        4. S: So you can see things magnified.
        5. T: How does it magnify things?
        6. S: By bending the light.

7. T: Right, the light bends as it enters and leaves the glass. Do you know which way it bends?

8. S: No.

9. T: Have you ever held a lens under the sunlight?

10. S: Yes.

11. T: What happened?

12. S: Well, there was a bright spot of light.

13. T: So how must light rays bend as they go through the lens?

14. S: They must bend together to a point.

15. T: Right. Do you know what that point is called?

16. S: No.

[2]

17. T: It's called the focal point or focus. The light is focused together at that point. Do you know what the shape of the lens in the magnifying glass is called?

18. S: No.

19. T: It's called convex. What do you think the difference is between a convex lens and a concave lens?

20. S: Concave would be inward.

21. T: That's right. Concave lenses curve inward just like caves do, and convex lenses curve outward like a ball or a globe. What would a lens shaped like this be called? (See Fig. 6.1a.)

22. S: Concave?

23. T: That's right. Suppose you had a lens shaped like this (see Fig. 6.1b), what would its shape be?

24. S: Convex.

25. T: Right. Suppose you had a lens that was flat on one side and curved on the other like this (see Fig. 1c). What kind of lens would that be?

26. S: A half-convex lens?

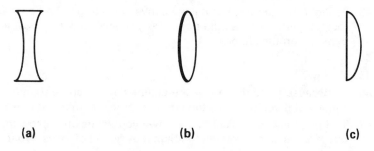

(a)   (b)   (c)

FIG. 6.1. Three lenses for the student to identify.

[3] 27. T: It would be a convex lens, and it would bend the light a little differently than a lens that was curved on both sides. So what happens if you hold a magnifying glass in the sun and bring it slowly down over a piece of paper?

28. S: It makes the paper start burning.

29. T: Yes, with the sun you can make it burn. As you come closer to the paper, what happens?

30. S: Well, the light comes together.

31. T: So as you move the lens closer to the paper, the light comes more and more into focus?

32. S: Yes, I guess so.

33. T: Well, let's try it and see what happens. We'll use this flashlight as our sun, and I'll hold it up here. And you move the glass from halfway down toward the paper. What happens?

34. S: The light comes more and more in focus, and then it seems to spread out again.

35. T: So it doesn't keep getting more and more in focus as you go lower.

36. S: No. There is a point about here (holding the lens about half a foot above the paper) where it seems to be most in focus.

[4] 37. T: That's right. When the light is in focus on the paper, the distance above the paper is the focal distance or focal length. What do you think the focal length depends on?

38. S: The way the glass curves.

39. T: How do you think it depends on the curvature of the glass?

40. S: When you use a convex lens, the point where it comes to one point would be closer than when it is concave, I think.

41. T: Well, suppose I had a concave lens. The light rays might bend together, they might bend apart, or they might go straight through. Which do you think will happen?

42. S: I don't know. Maybe the beams of light would come in and bend apart.

43. T: Right. So you have to have a convex lens to get the light rays to focus together at a single point. Do you still think the focal length depends on the shape?

44. S: Yeah.

45. T: How?

[5] 46. S: Because if it's down low the beams haven't come together to a single point yet. But if it's too far they come together and they cross.

47. T: Right, they cross. And that's why if you get down too low they go out of focus, and if you get too high they go out of focus. What is the point called where they come together?

48. S: The focus point?

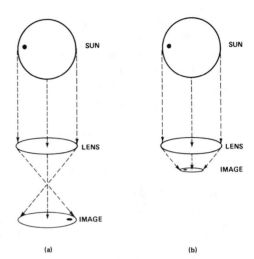

FIG. 6.2. Two sketches by the teacher of the sun's image projected through a convex lens (the dot represents a sunspot).

(a)　　　　　　　(b)

49. T: Yes, the focus or focal point. And what is the distance called from the focal point to the lens?

50. S: The focal length.

[6] 51. T: Suppose I draw a picture of the sun shining down on my lens, and there is a spot on the sun over on the left side. (See Fig. 6.2a.) Now where would that spot be in the image of the sun that falls on the paper?

52. S: I guess on the left side.

53. T: Well, let's see. Suppose I draw a picture of the rays coming down through the lens and bending together to the focal point and falling on the paper. Now where would a sunspot over on the left side of the sun appear on the image of the sun on the paper? (See Fig. 6.2a.)

54. S: On the right side.

55. T: Why do you think it would be on the right side?

56. S: Because the beams cross.

57. T: Is the whole image reversed, then?

58. S: Yes, all the beams cross over.

59. T: Suppose I lower the lens below the focal point in the picture. Would the sunspot still be on the right side of the image, when it is on the left side of the sun? (See Fig. 6.2b.)

60. S: I don't think so, because the beams haven't crossed over yet.

[7] 61. T: Yes, that's right. Now look at this other magnifying glass. What kind of lens does it have?

62. S: It has a convex lens too?

63. T: That's right. Is it as curved as the other one?

64. S: No, it's less curved.

189

65. T: Okay. Do you think its focal length will be the same as the other one?

66. S: No, it will be different, I think.

67. T: Then will it be greater than or less than the other one?

68. S: Well, if you hold it in the light, the beams will bend less, so they'll take longer to come together. So I guess its focal length will be greater.

69. T: Perfect. So how would you say focal length is related in general to curvature of the lens?

70. S: Well, it must be that the less curved the lens is, the greater the focal length.

[8]   71. T: That's right. Do you think that applies to concave lenses as well, or just to convex lenses?

72. S: I don't think concave lenses have a focal length because the light beams never come together.

73. T: If you had a concave mirror, would the light rays come together at a point?

74. S: Yes, I guess so, because they would come in and bounce off the mirror at an angle, so they would come together at a point.

75. T: Would that be a focal point?

76. S: Yes, I guess so, since they would all come together there.

77. T: That's right. And what would be the focal length?

78. S: I guess the distance from the focal point to the mirror.

79. T: Yes, to the center of the mirror. The focal length of a concave lens is measured in just the same way. So do you think your statement that the less the curvature of the lens, the more the focal length applies to concave lenses as well?

80. S: Let's see. If the glass is curved less, then the beams will come together further out, so I guess it's true for concave lenses, too.

[9]   81. T: That's absolutely correct. Suppose I hold the magnifying glass over the newspaper and slowly move it away from the page. What will happen?

82. S: The glass magnifies the image at first, and then it goes out of focus as you raise it up, I think. Somewhere the image turns over, because I've seen an upside-down image in the magnifying glass.

83. T: Okay, let's try it and see what happens. When you hold the magnifying glass right up against the paper, what happens? (Fig. 6.3 shows the results of the experiment schematically.)

84. S: It looks just like the paper.

85. T: So it doesn't magnify the print when it's right next to it. As you raise it slowly up, what happens?

86. S: The print gets larger until it starts to go out of focus.

87. T: That's right, it magnifies the image more, the further from the

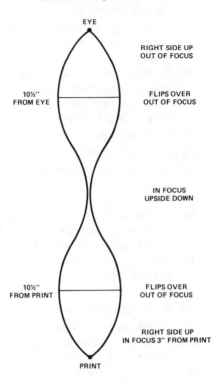

HEIGHT OF LENS BETWEEN EYE AND PRINT
(Width Indicates Magnification)

EYE

RIGHT SIDE UP
OUT OF FOCUS

10½"
FROM EYE

FLIPS OVER
OUT OF FOCUS

IN FOCUS
UPSIDE DOWN

10½"
FROM PRINT

FLIPS OVER
OUT OF FOCUS

RIGHT SIDE UP
IN FOCUS 3" FROM PRINT

PRINT

FIG. 6.3. Schematic diagram of the results of the mini-experiment carried out by the teacher and student shows height of lens between eye and print (width indicates magnification).

paper you raise it. In the other magnifying glass, we saw that the lens wasn't as curved. If you held it up the same distance from the paper, do you think it would magnify the letters more or less or the same amount as this one?

88. S: Well if it's not as curved, I don't think it would magnify the print as much as this one.

89. T: That's right. The magnification is less, the less curved the lens is. Now bring the magnifying glass very slowly up, holding it over the headline. What do you see?

90. S: Okay. I've got an image again, and it's upside down.

91. T: As you raise it up is the image getting smaller or larger or staying the same size?

92. S: It's getting smaller. Now it's staying about the same size. When it's half way to my eye it doesn't magnify the print much at all.

[10]

93. T: Okay. What do you think will happen if you raise it up further toward your eye? Will it get smaller or larger? Will it turn over again?

94. S: I think it will stay upside down and the same size, since the dis-

tance from the newspaper is so large that the light rays from it won't change any more.

95. T: That's a really good hypothesis. Let's test it to see if it is correct. Raise the lens slowly from the point of sharpest focus up toward your eye.

96. S: Okay, the image seems to stay the same size. Wow, now it is getting larger and more blurry again. Now it's gone completely out of focus. As it gets near my eye I can see the print again. It's right side up and kind of fuzzy.

97. T: Does it get smaller or larger as you bring it close to your eye?

98. S: It gets smaller, but it never seems to come into focus really.

[11]

99. T: Okay. Your hypothesis was a good one, but it didn't turn out to be correct. Can you guess how far up from the page the image flips over?

100. S: Maybe at the focal length. No, that doesn't seem right because that's where the print would be magnified best. Maybe twice the focal length? You must know the right answer. What is it?

[12]

101. T: I may think I know the right answer, but I could be wrong. Let's try to measure where it occurs. How can we measure the focal length of this lens?

102. S: We could use a ruler.

103. T: Yes, but what would we measure?

104. S: I guess we should measure the distance from the lens to the paper when the light is focused on the paper.

105. T: That should work. So why don't we do it? I'll hold the light up here, and you take the ruler and hold the lens so the focal point is right on the paper. How high is the lens when you do that?

106. S: About $10\frac{1}{2}$ inches from the paper.

107. T: Okay, so that's the focal length. Now what should we measure?

108. S: I guess the distance from the newspaper where you get the best focused image that is magnified, and the distance where the image flips over.

109. T: Okay, what do you measure them to be?

110. S: Well, you get the best magnified image about 2 or 3 inches above the paper, and the image goes blurry above that. It must flip over at about the focal length.

111. T: That's right. Where do you think the image flips over as you bring the lens up to your eye?

112. S: It must flip over at one focal length there, too.

113. T: Measure it and see.

114. S: Yes, it's just about at one focal length it flips over.

[13]

115. T: Okay. Let's try to draw a picture of what is happening to the light rays, like we did for the sun shining down through the lens. Suppose

we first draw what happens when the lens is near the print and the eye is way out here somewhere to the right. Now the focal point of the lens will be over here to the left of the printed letter A. Can you draw how the rays going out from the letter A will bend in the lens? (See Fig. 6.4a.)

[14]   116. S: Well, they'll go out toward the lens and then bend inward toward the eye.

117. T: If the letter is inside the focal length, will the rays bend enough to come together again like you've drawn them?

118. S: I think so.

119. T: In the first picture we drew, with the light rays from the sun, how did the rays come into the lens?

120. S: They came straight in.

121. T: How did they bend?

122. They bent together at the focal point.

123. T: So they bent just enough to come together at the focal point. Now in your picture you have the rays going from a point on the A inside the focal length, and then bending in toward the eye.

124. S: That's right. They bend toward the eye, where you see them.

125. T: So then you must think the rays coming from the letter A will bend more than those coming from the sun in the other picture.

126. S: No, the rays should bend the same amount.

127. T: Right. How would you have to change your picture then?

128. S: I guess the rays coming out from the letter would be going straight after they go through the lens (see Fig. 6.4b).

[15]   129. T: Right. If you continue the rays coming out of the lens (by dotting them) back to where the letter is, then you can see how the letter is magnified. Notice they don't come together like the actual rays, so

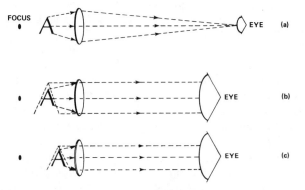

FIG. 6.4.   Three sketches by the student of how the light rays travel through a lens when the lens is held near the letter A.

that the letter appears to be the height between the dotted lines and not the actual height.

130. S: Yeah, I see.

131. T: You said earlier that the image would be less magnified for the other lens that is less curved. Can you explain why that is in terms of the picture we just drew?

132. S: Well, the rays would bend less as they go through the lens, so the difference between the dotted image and the real letter would be less.

133. T: That's right! Can you also explain why the letters don't appear to be magnified when the lens is right up against the print, in terms of the picture we drew?

134. S: Maybe the rays coming out of the lens don't diverge from the rays coming into the lens as much.

135. T: Why don't you draw a picture and see if that is true.

136. S: What do I draw?

137. T: Well, draw the same picture as before, but with the *A* closer to the lens.

138. S: If I draw the letter right next to the lens, then the rays will hit the lens. I guess they will bend less than before. (See Fig. 6.4c.)

139. T: Why would they bend any differently than before?

140. S: Will they bend the same as before?

141. T: That's right. Now dot in the continuation of the rays going to the eye.

142. S: There is less divergence between the real rays and the imaginary ones. So how much the figure is magnified depends on how close the letter is to the lens. (See Fig. 6.4c.)

[16]   143. T: That's perfect. The dotted imaginary rays form what is called a virtual image. It's called virtual because it's not real. Okay, see if you can draw the picture for the case where the lens is in the middle and there is a reversed image. Treat the rays as if they go in a straight line from the letter to the lens.

144. S: Okay. The rays go straight from the letter to the lens, and then they bend together when they go through the lens. They come together at a point and cross over. Somewhere after that they reach the eye, so the image looks reversed. (See Fig. 6.5a.)

145. T: That's fine. The image you see when the rays cross over is called the real image. Can you say how the picture is different for the case when the eye is close to the lens?

146. S: Then the eye is up here before the rays reach the point and cross over. So the print looks right side up. (See Fig. 6.5b.)

147. T: Very good. I think you understand now everything I wanted to teach you about the way lenses work.

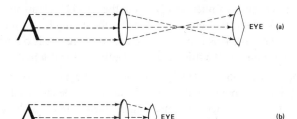

FIG. 6.5. Two sketches by the student of how the light travels through a lens when the lens is held away from the print.

COMMENTS

In the comments below I have tried to emphasize how the ten strategies shown in Table 6.1 are involved in the dialogue, and how goals and subgoals are generated in carrying on the dialogue.

1. In lines 1 to 17 the teacher sets the initial goal of establishing the basic terminology about lenses that they will need for the rest of the dialogue. The teacher tries to find out what the student knows a priori, in order to build on that knowledge. This is preliminary to **Objective 2** of the lesson, "Defining focal length."

2. In lines 17 to 27 the teacher is still establishing basic terminology, in this case the distinction between convex and concave lenses. The strategy is to present different cases of convex and concave lenses and test whether the student can identify them. This illustrates Strategy 1 in Table 6.1, **selecting positive and negative exemplars** to make the student learn the distinction. This part of the dialogue is aimed at **Objective 1,** "Classifying lenses as to whether or not they are convex."

3. Lines 27 to 37 make up the last section of the dialogue directed to the goal of establishing basic terminology. In this case the subgoal is to teach the concept of focal length (**Objective 2**). First the teacher gets the student to **form a hypothesis** (Strategy 5 in Table 6.1) about how the image of the sun will change as the lens is moved closer to the paper (lines 27–32), and then to conduct a mini-experiment (lines 33–37) to **test that hypothesis** (Strategy 6). One kind of **entrapment** (Strategy 8) that inquiry teachers use occurs in line 31—there the teacher formulates the student's suggestion into an explicit hypothesis that is incorrect, to which the student accedes in line 32. This whole section also illustrates how the teacher **varies cases systematically** (Strategy 2). In particu-

lar, there are three cases of interest: (a) where the lens is high up and the image is out of focus; (b) where the lens is held at the focal length and the image is in focus; and (c) where the lens is near the paper and the image is out of focus. This section is directly aimed at **Objective 2,** "Defining focal length."

4. In lines 37 to 45 the teacher establishes the new goal of **forming a hypothesis** (or rule) about what factors focal length depends on (Strategy 5). This goal is not fully satisfied until much later (line 80) in the dialogue. In line 40 of this section of the dialogue the student reveals a misconception about how light bends in a concave lens. The teacher pursues the subgoal of correcting this misconception by asking the student in line 41 to **consider alternative predictions** (Strategy 7) about the bending of light in a concave lens. Once the student understands this correctly, the teacher returns in line 43 to the original goal of determining what focal length depends on. This is in pursuit of **Objective 4,** "Explaining how curvature of a lens influences focal length."

5. In line 46 the student again leads the conversation away from the teacher's goal, by talking about the rays crossing. The student's answer is a non sequitur (a common occurrence in dialogues), and yet the teacher picks up on it to review the terminology introduced earlier for focal point and focal length (lines 47–50). This is reviewing for **Objective 2.**

6. In lines 51 to 61 the teacher continues the discussion introduced by the student in line 46 about the light beams crossing. **Generating a hypothetical case** (Strategy 4) of a spot on the sun, the teacher asks the student to hypothesize where that spot would appear in the image of the sun on the paper. When the student guesses the left side, the teacher **chooses as a counterexample** (Strategy 3) the case where the paper is far enough below the lens so that the beams cross over and the image is on the opposite side. In line 59, the teacher **systematically varies the case** (Strategy 2), so that the spot falls on the other side and asks the student if it will still be on the right side of the image. This suggestion is another example of how inquiry teachers use **entrapment** (Strategy 8). This section relates to **Objective 3,** "Predicting the effects of convex lenses on light rays" and **Objective 4,** "Explaining how curvature of a lens affects focal length."

7. In lines 61 to 70, the teacher returns to the prior goal of establishing the relation between the focal length and the curvature of a lens (**Objective 4**). He does this by introducing another lens with less curvature than the first, thus **systematically varying cases** (Strategy 2) again. First he reviews whether the student can identify the type of lens in line 61 (Strategy 1—**selecting a positive exemplar**). Then in line 65 he asks the student whether it will have the same focal length as the other lens, in order to get the student to **form a hypothesis** (Strategy 5) about how focal length depends on curvature. The wording of this question is a slight **entrapment** (Strategy 8). Line 67 again exemplifies the way teachers get students to **consider alternative predictions** (Strategy 7). In line 70

the student formulates a quite general rule relating lens shape to focal length. This section is particularly addressed to **Objective 3,** "Predicting the effects of different convex lenses on light rays," as well as **Objective 4.**

8. In lines 71 to 80 the teacher pursues the subgoal of determining whether the rule the student had formulated applied to concave as well as convex lenses— **testing hypotheses** (Strategy 6). To do this he first had to show the student how to measure focal length of a concave lens by analogy to a concave mirror. This allowed the student (in line 80) to make the generalization of the rule relating focal length to curvature of the lens. This section relates to **Objective 4** and completes the overall goal the teacher started pursuing in line 41.

9. In lines 81 to 92 the teacher starts on a new goal to establish how an image is magnified and where you see an upside-down image versus a right-side-up image. In line 81 he presents the problem to the student of predicting how the image of letters on a page will change as you move a lens through different positions. This again is **systematic variation of cases** (Strategy 2). After the student **makes a hypothesis** in line 82 (Strategy 5), the teacher suggests another mini-experiment to **test the hypothesis** (Strategy 6). In line 87 the teacher asks the student to compare the degree of magnification for two different cases (Strategy 2 again—**systematic variation of cases**). This section serves **Objective 4,** "Explaining how curvature of a lens affects magnification."

10. In line 93, after they have completed half the experiment, the teacher asks the student to **revise the hypothesis** about how the image will change, given what has happened so far in the experiment (Strategy 7). The student makes a conjecture, which is incorrect, but because the conjecture is well reasoned, the teacher in line 95 is very encouraging. This is a strategy used frequently by the teachers who wanted to foster hypothesis formation by their students. In lines 95–99 the teacher has the student **test his revised hypothesis** (Strategy 6), and points out again that it was a good hypothesis, even though it turned out to be incorrect. This relates to **Objective 3,** "Predicting the effects of convex lenses on light rays."

11. In line 99 the teacher starts pursuing the subgoal of determining where the image flips over with respect to focal length. In line 100 the student appeals to authority (i.e., the teacher) to provide the correct answer, but in line 101 the teacher **questions his own authority** (Strategy 10) in order to encourage the student not to accept the answers given unquestioningly. This strategy is common among inquiry teachers who emphasize theory formation in their teaching. This section relates in **Objective 2,** "Defining focal length."

12. In lines 101 to 114 the teacher gets the student to invent a procedure for measuring focal length of a lens. Then he has the student measure where the image turns over in terms of focal length. In both these efforts he is getting the student to learn how to **test hypotheses** (Strategy 6). In getting the student to

invent a procedure for measuring focal length, the teacher is gradually turning over the thinking to the student so that he will learn to form and test hypotheses on his own. This section also relates to **Objective 2.**

13. Starting in line 115 and for the rest of the dialogue the teacher tries to get the student to draw representations for the various situations (or cases) that they established in the little mini-experiment. Again the teacher is using a strategy of **systematically varying cases** (Strategy 2), so that the student can see how the representations change from case to case. These drawings relate to both **Objectives 3 and 4.**

14. In line 116 the student makes a mistake in his drawing, by having the light rays bend more than they actually do, given the letter A is inside the focal point. In line 119 the teacher **picks as a counterexample** (Strategy 3) the previous picture they drew where the rays from the sun came in straight and bent together to the focal point. Then the teacher asks a series of questions through line 125 that **trace the consequences** (Strategy 9) of the student's mistake in his drawing until he sees the contradiction (in line 126) with the way the rays bent in the previous drawing. Socrates was particularly fond of this consequence-tracing strategy, and it may be particularly useful in getting students to give up wrong hypotheses. This section is particularly aimed at **Objective 3,** though **Objective 4** is also relevant.

15. In lines 129 to 143 the teacher tries to get the student to **form a hypothesis** (Strategy 5) from his drawing as to how two factors (curvature of the lens and distance from the object) affect magnification. He does this by introducing dotted lines that represent how the image appears, as opposed to how it is. This serves to introduce the notion of a virtual image. This is particularly relevant to **Objective 4.**

16. In lines 143 to 147 the teacher gets the student to represent the other two cases: (a) where the lens is midway between the paper and the eye and the image is upside down; and (b) where the lens is near the eye and the image appears right side up. Here the teacher is using **systematic variation of cases** (Strategy 2) in order to get the student to learn the rules for representing different configurations of eye and lens. This is particularly relevant to **Objective 3.**

The hypothetical student in the dialogue, while naive, is the best kind of student. The dialogue is perhaps a bit unrealistic in that the student leads the tea on very few detours. These were avoided in order to present the basic goals, strategies, and control structure of inquiry teachers in a concise and coherent form. Even though real students are likely to be less intelligent and to lead dialogues astray much more often, I think the dialogue gives a good flavor of how the best inquiry teachers guide a discussion. They try to get students to analyze problems like scientists—to systematically consider different cases, to form and test hypotheses, to look for counterexamples. The kinds of experiments the teacher and student perform here together illustrate this well. It is a time-consuming way to teach, but if the goal is to teach students to solve problems or invent theories in a creative way, this may be the only method we have.

REFERENCES

Collins, A. (1977). Processes in acquiring knowledge. In R. C. Anderson, R. J. Spiro, & W. E. Montague (Eds.), *Schooling and the acquisition of knowledge*. Hillsdale, NJ: Lawrence Erlbaum Associates.

Collins, A., & Stevens, A. L. (1982). Goals and strategies of inquiry teachers. In R. Glaser (Ed.), *Advances in instructional psychology* (Vol. 2). Hillsdale, NJ: Lawrence Erlbaum Associates.

Collins, A., & Stevens, A. L. (1983). A cognitive theory of interactive teaching. In C. M. Reigeluth (Ed.), *Instructional design theories and models: An overview*. Hillsdale, NJ: Lawrence Erlbaum Associates.

7

A Lesson Based on the Component Display Theory

M. David Merrill
University of Southern California

FOREWORD

History

Merrill's theory began as an explicit attempt to integrate the current knowledge about instruction. It arose out of a review of literature that he did with a student for the *Review of Research in Education* in 1973. Hence, it was primarily inductively developed from empirical research findings. Like Gagné-Briggs's theory (but unlike all the other preceding theories in this book), its prescriptions are drawn from multiple perspectives: behavioral, cognitive, and humanistic. However, it is still a much narrower theory than Gagné-Briggs's because it deals only with the cognitive domain, and within the cognitive domain, it deals only with microlevel strategies (for teaching an individual concept, principle, etc.) and does not include all of Gagné-Briggs's events of instruction. In exchange for its narrowness, it provides considerably more guidance to instructional designers and teachers. This theory is indicative of the highly integrative, multiperspectived approach to prescriptive theory construction that is sorely needed at this point in the evolution of our knowledge about instruction.

Unique Contributions

Perhaps the two most outstanding contributions of Merrill's are his classifications of performance levels and content types as bases for prescribing strategy components. His identification of the four primary presentation forms and his cataloging of a wide variety of secondary presentation forms and interdisplay relationships are also of great value. Finally, his notion of learner control and training learners to use it to their best advantage show great promise.

Similarities

Due to its integrative roots, Merrill's theory has many prescriptions in common with other instructional theories. Generalities, examples, practice, and feedback are all prescribed by many other theories in some form; and some of the secondary presentation forms (attention-focusing devices, alternative representations, mnemonics, etc.) and interdisplay relationships (easy-to-difficult sequence of examples) are prescribed by other theories as well. These and other similarities are identified in the chapter with Editor's Notes.

Issues to Think About

Have any important strategies been overlooked by Merrill? Can (should) Merrill's theory be integrated into the Gagné-Briggs framework? If so, how? Does Merrill's theory in turn provide a framework within which the prescriptions of other theories can be integrated? If so, what gaps need to be filled by prescriptions from other theories?

STUDY QUESTIONS

1. Define and give an example of each of the four levels of performance.
2. Define and give an example of each of the four types of content.
3. Compare and contrast each of the four primary presentation forms.
4. Define and give an example of each of the secondary presentation forms.
5. Define and give an example of each of the interdisplay relationships.
6. What differences in the instruction are required by the levels of performance?
7. What differences in the instruction are required by the content types?
8. What features should the instruction have in order to facilitate learner control?

C.M.R.

INTRODUCTION TO COMPONENT DISPLAY THEORY

Component Display Theory (CDT) is not a method but, rather, a theory about those components that comprise every instructional presentation. In order to use Component Display Theory a designer must select an instructional method that incorporates the prescriptions of the theory appropriate for the performance and subject matter content to be taught. In the overview section of this chapter

Component Display Theory is briefly outlined. The reader is referred to chapter 9, Component Display Theory, in Reigeluth (1983) for a more complete presentation of the theory. In the second section of this chapter five lesson fragments are presented representing the application of CDT to five different instructional objectives concerning lenses and the microscope. Section three indicates the specific prescriptions from CDT that were used in preparing each lesson fragment.

SUMMARY OF CDT

Component Display Theory is comprised of three parts: a two-dimensional performance-content classification system, a taxonomy of presentation forms, and a set of prescriptions relating the classification system to the presentation forms.

The Performance/Content Matrix

CDT holds that instructional outcomes, represented either by objectives or test items, can be classified on two dimensions; student performance (Remember Instance, Remember Generality, Use, and Find) and subject matter content (Fact, Concept, Procedure, and Principle).* A *generality (rule)* is a statement of a definition, principle, or the steps in a procedure. An *instance (example)* is a specific illustration of an object, symbol, event, process, or procedure. *Use* means to apply a generality to a specific case(s). *Find* means to find a new generality. A *fact* is an association between a date and event or a name and part. A *concept* is a set of objects, events, or symbols that share common characteristics. A *procedure* is a set of steps for carrying out some activity. A *principle* is the cause-and-effect relationships in a process. As represented in this chapter, CDT is appropriate only for cognitive outcomes and does not include psychomotor or affective objectives. The classification system is summarized in Fig. 7.1.

Presentation Forms

CDT also assumes that all instructional presentations are comprised of a series of discrete displays or presentation forms. Any presentation can be described as a sequence of such presentation forms together with the interrelationships between such forms.

---

*The remember, use, and find levels of performance correspond to Gagné's "verbal information," "intellectual skills," and "cognitive strategies," respectively (pp. 14–15), and to Gropper's "recall facts," "apply or illustrate definitions and explanations and follow procedural rules," and "solve problems," respectively (p. 51). The find level is also somewhat similar to Scandura's "higher-order rules" (p. 165).

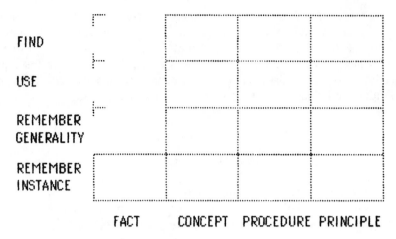

FIND

USE

REMEMBER
GENERALITY

REMEMBER
INSTANCE

FACT   CONCEPT PROCEDURE PRINCIPLE

FIG. 7.1. The Performance Content Matrix.

Four Primary Presentation Forms (PPF) can be described by the two dimensions of content mode (generality or instance) and presentation mode (expository or inquisitory). *Expository* means to present, tell, or show; *inquisitory* means to question, ask, or require practice. The symbols in the table are shorthand for expository generality *(EG)*; expository instance *(Eeg*—the little *eg.* is the abbreviation for example); inquisitory generality *(IG)*; and inquisitory instance *(Ieg)*. The Primary Presentation Forms are summarized in Fig. 7.2.*

Primary Presentation Form—
Performance Consistency Prescriptions

CDT is based on the Gagne assumption of different conditions of learning for different outcomes. Each of the different performance levels in the performance/content (P/C) matrix is associated with a different combination of primary presentation forms.† When the necessary presentation forms are present, student achievement and learning efficiency are increased; when the necessary presentation forms are not present or are inappropriate, there is a decrement in student achievement and learning efficiency. The combination of primary presentation forms associated with each performance level of the P/C matrix is

---

†Generality *(EG)* is similar to Gropper's "telling the learner what and how to perform" (p. 52), to Landa's "prescription" (p. 120), to Scandura's "rule" (p. 163), and to Collins's "hypothesis" (p. 184). Example *(Eeg)* is similar to Gropper's "example of the performance" (p. 54) to Landa's "demonstration" (p. 121, footnote 12), and to Collins's "positive exemplars" (p. 183). Practice *(Ieg)* is similar to Gagné-Briggs's "elicit the performance" (p. 20) and to Gropper's "practice" (p. 54).

† The use of some classification of objectives as the basis for prescribing methods of instruction is also an important part of the theories of Gagné-Briggs (p. 13) and Gropper (p. 52).

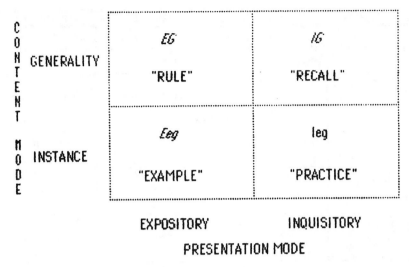

FIG. 7.2. The Primary Presentation Forms (PPF).

illustrated in Fig. 7.3 (see Comments 1, 7, 16, 21, and 30). The subscripts indicate specific interdisplay relationships required. The N (as in $Ieg.N$) means *new* or previously unencountered. This means that the examples presented should be different from those used in previous parts of the instruction. The P (as in $IG.P$) means *paraphrase*. The statement of the generality required from the student in practice should be a paraphrase, rather than a verbatim statement, of the generality.

Primary Presentation Form—
Content Consistency Prescriptions

Different kinds of content require different manifestations of the four primary presentation forms. To be consistent, the primary presentation form must contain the information necessary to present the content. Fig. 7.4 summarizes the fundamental elements that should be present in the PPFs for each type of content. The underlined words represent alternative labels by which the PPFs are sometimes called. There is not space to elaborate this table. The following information will suggest the type of elaboration implied. An adequate *definition* for a concept should include the concept name, an identification of the superordinate concept involved, the attributes that distinguish instances of one coordinate concept from another, and the relationships of these attributes to one another. An adequate classify practice (Ieg) for a concept should present a new object, symbol, or event (instance of the concept); this instance should have all the relevant attributes present; the instance should use a form of representation that presents all

205

P/C CLASSIFICATION	PRESENTATION	PRACTICE	PERFORMANCE
If the instructional objective is classified as ...	Then the PPF's required for a consistent presentation are ...	And the PPF's required for consistent practice items are ...	And the PPF's required for consistent test items are ...
FIND		legs.N IG.N	legs.N IG.N
USE	EG → Eegs	legs.N	legs.N
REMEMBER GENERALITY	EG → Eeg	IG.P	IG.P
REMEMBER INSTANCE	Eeg	Ieg	Ieg

FIG. 7.3.   Performance—PPF consistency.

EG = Expository Generality   Ieg = Inquisitory Instance
Eeg = Expository Instance   .N = New
IG = Inquisitory Generality   .P = Paraphrase

P/C CLASSIFICATION	PRESENTATION		PRACTICE	
If the instructional objective is classified as ...	Then the EG required for a consistent presentation has ..	Then the Eeg required for a consistent presentation has ..	Then the Ieg required for a consistent presentation has ..	Then the IG required for a consistent presentation has ..
FACT	NO Generality	symbol - symbol symbol - object symbol - event A B	symbol - ? object - ? event - ? A ?	NO Generality
CONCEPT	Definition • name • superordinate • attributes • relationships	Example • name • object, etc. • all attributes • representation	Classify • new object, etc. • all attributes • representation ? (name)	State Definition • name • paraphrase ? (Definition)
PROCEDURE	Process • goal -- name • steps • order • decision/branch	Demonstration • goal -- name • materials • execution • representation	Demonstrate • goal • new materials • response mode ? (execution)	State Steps • goal • paraphrase • response mode ? (steps, etc.)
PRINCIPLE	Proposition: • Name • concepts • relationship	Explanation • name • situation • representation	Predict • name • new problem • response mode ? (prediction)	State Relationship • name • paraphrase • response mode ? (proposition)

FIG. 7.4.   Content—PPF consistency.

of the relevant attributes; and, finally, the student should be asked to supply the name [? (name)] or indicate if the instance shown is a member of the concept class. The comments in Section 3 of this chapter provide additional elaboration for PPF—Content consistency (see Comments 2, 9, 17, 24, 31). These prescriptions are cross-references to the tables in the introduction. For additional elaboration see our chapter in the companion volume (Reigeluth, 1983).

Adequacy Prescriptions: Secondary Presentation Forms

Secondary Presentation Forms (SPF) represent information added to the primary presentation forms to enhance the learning that occurs. A presentation that is more adequate, that is enhanced by the addition of appropriate secondary presentations, will promote an increment in the achievement and learning efficiency of students participating in the instruction. Fig. 7.5 indicates those secondary presentation forms that have been shown to improve achievement. The *prime* ($'$ as in $EG'h$) means that this is an enhancement of the expository generality. The subscript h means that the secondary presentation is the use of attention-focusing information or *help* with the primary presentation form (see Comments 8, 11, 18, 22, 23, 33).* The subscript p (as in $EG'p$) means that the secondary presentation is *prerequisite* information, related to the primary presentation form, that the student should have learned from a previous part of the instruction but that is repeated to facilitate the student's recall of necessary prerequisite information (see Comments 8, 23, 32).† The subscript r (as in $Eeg'r$) means that the secondary presentation is an alternate *representation* of the information, such as the restatement of a generality, the presentation of an instance in a different context, the use of an alternate medium to present the information, and so forth (see Comments 8, 11, 14, 22, 23, 25, 32). The subscript mn (as in $EG'mn$) means *mnemonic*. A mnemonic is a memory facilitator that assists the student to remember (see Comments 19, 32).‡ FB (as in $FB'ca$) means *feedback*.§ The ca subscript (as in $FB'ca$) means *correct answer* feedback (see comments 3, 20); the subscript h (as in $FB'ca,h$) means *helped* feedback. Helped feedback is attention-focusing information or working the problem for the student to show how it should have been done (see Comments 14, 25, 38). The subscript u (as in $FB'u$) associated with feedback for the find level means feedback intrinsic to the *use* of the new generality. For example, the best feedback for designing a computer program, which is finding a new procedure, is to see if it works. The most important secondary presentation forms associated with each performance level are indicated in Fig. 7.5.

---

*This is similar to Gagné-Briggs's "learning guidance" (p. 19) and Gropper's "cues" (pp. 47, 55).

†This is Gagné-Briggs's "stimulate recall of learning prerequisites" (p. 18).

‡The prescription of mnemonics is unique among the chapters in this book.

§The use of feedback is also prescribed by Gagné-Briggs (p. 20), Gropper (p. 47), and Collins (p. 185).

P/C CLASSIFICATION	PRESENTATION			PRACTICE	
If the instructional objective is classified as ...	Then the SPF's required to augment the PPF's for an adequate presentation are ... (with an EG)	(with an Eeg)		And the SPF's required to augment the PPF's for adequate practice items are ... (with an IG)	(with an Ieg)
FIND				*FB's*	
USE	*EG'h EG'p EG'r*	*Eeg'h Eeg'r*			*Ieg'r FB'ca*
REMEMBER GENERALITY	*EG'mn*	*Eeg'r*	*FB'ca,h*	
REMEMBER INSTANCE					*FB'ca*

FIG. 7.5.   Performance adequacy: Secondary presentation forms.

Adequacy Prescriptions: Interdisplay Relationships

In addition to material that can be added to the primary presentation forms, the relationship between these forms also affects the learning that will occur. Fig. 7.6 summarizes the interdisplay relationships that have been found to contribute to student performance. *Divergent* means that subsequent instances are different in their variable attributes (see Comments 13, 27, 35, 37, 38).* *Range* means that there is a range of difficulty represented by the instances (see Comments 15, 28, 37).† *Matching* means that examples are matched to nonexamples in that the attributes they share with the superordinate concept are the same, but the relevant attributes are different. Matching also means that when procedures or principles are being taught, the student is shown inappropriate applications or activities matched to the correct way to execute the activity (see Comments 12, 29, 36).‡ *Fading* means that the amount of help provided via secondary presentation forms is gradually eliminated (see Comments 11, 12, 14, 22, 33).§ *Random order* means that a set of facts are presented in a different order each time (see Comment 4). *Chunking* means that a student is required to remember only five to

---

*Divergence is similar to Gropper's "variety of practice" (p. 55), Collins's "vary cases systematically" (p. 184) and "entrap students" (p. 185), and Scandura's "equivalence classes" (p. 55).

†This is also prescribed by Gropper (p. 55).

*This is similar to Gropper's "practice of errors" (p. 184) and Collins's "select counterexamples" (p. 49), except that Collins's counterpart just applies to principles.

§This is Gropper's "fading of cues" (p. 49).

208

P/C CLASSIFICATION	PRESENTATION	PRACTICE	PERFORMANCE
If the instructional objective is classified as . . .	Then the IDR's required for an adequate presentation are . . .	And the IDR's required for adequate practice items are . . .	And the IDR's required for adequate test items are . . .
FIND		*Divergent Range*	*Divergent Range*
USE	*Divergent /Range Matching Fading*	*Divergent /Range NO Matching Fading in FB*	*Divergent /Range NO Matching NO Help*
REMEMBER GENERALITY			
REMEMBER INSTANCE	*Random Order Chunking*	*Random Order No delay 100%*	*Random Order No delay 100%*
ALL LEVELS	*Isolation Learner Control*	*Isolation Learner Control*	*Isolation Learner Control*

FIG. 7.6. Performance adequacy: Interdisplay relationships.

seven new items at one time. *No delay* means that the student can recall the association of a fact immediately (see Comment 6). *100%* means that all facts must be learned (see Comment 5). *Isolation* means that the primary presentation forms are clearly identified for the student (see Comments 10, 26, 34). *Learner control* means that the student can determine how many instances to study, when to receive help, and other strategy decisions.* More detail concerning these interdisplay relationships is provided in the comments section of this chapter and in the chapter in the companion volume (Reigeluth, 1983).

LESSON PREFACE: SAMPLE SEGMENTS

This chapter does not attempt to present a comprehensive lesson dealing with the microscope. Each of the theorists represented in this volume were given a set of objectives, a set of test items, a list of generalities, and some text material related to the microscope. As a consultant faced with the same array of material, the author would have engaged in task analysis that would have yielded additional

---

*All of these last prescriptions are unique among the theories in this book, except that Reigeluth also prescribes learner control (p. 258). However, Merrill's is learner control over microstrategy components, whereas Reigeluth's is learner control over macrostrategy components.

objectives, suggested modifications in the objectives given, and in other ways resulted in a more integrated lesson. However, in order to provide a better opportunity for comparison with the other versions of this same subject matter, this chapter presents somewhat independent lesson fragments corresponding to each of the objectives as given to the author by the editor. Since CDT is not a method but, rather, a theory, we also took this opportunity to use a different instructional method for each lesson segment. An integrated lesson would not have used such a wide variety of methods and delivery systems.

Each lesson segment is preceded by a statement of the objective as it was given to the author. The objective is classified on the performance/content matrix of CDT. The objective is followed by a brief description of the method/delivery system used for the segment. Then follows a set of prototype displays of the lesson segment. The presentation contains marginal notes that refer to the prescriptions and comments in the third section of this paper.

LESSON SEGMENT 1

Objective: Remember Instance-Fact

"Students will be able to state from memory the three significant events in the history of the microscope."

Instructional Method: Flash Cards

The CDT prescriptions for teaching Remember-Instance-Fact Objectives could be implemented in many ways. Fragment 1 suggests that the student drill using flash cards. One part of each association is placed on one side of the card and the associated information on the other. The student is instructed to look at the first side and recall the information on the reverse side before turning the card to check the correct answer feedback. The student is further advised to repeat the process until a criterion of no errors and immediate recall is achieved.

---

[1]   SEGMENT 1: SIGNIFICANT EVENTS IN THE HISTORY OF
THE MICROSCOPE

There are several important events in the history of the microscope. You will be required to remember each of these events.

[2]   1. What was probably the first magnifying glass?
Ans: A glass globe filled with water.
2. Who probably used the first magnifying glass?
Ans: Engravers.
3. When was this first magnifying glass used?
Ans: About 3,000 years ago.

4. When were the first solid glass lenses used?
   Ans: Late 1200s.
5. Who developed the first compound microscope?
   Ans: Zacharias Janssen.
6. When was the first compound microscope developed?
   Ans: About 1590.

LEARNING TIP

[3]   Use the following cards for drill.
[4]   Look at the front and say the information on the back.
[5]   Shuffle the cards and try again.
[6]   Repeat until you make no mistakes and your answers are immediate.

FRONT	BACK
First magnifying glass What?	Glass globe filled with water.
First Magnifying glass When?	3000 years ago Approx. 1000 BC
First Magnifying glass Who?	Used by Engravers
First solid glass lens. When?	Late 1200's AD
First compound microscope, when?	About 1590 AD
First compound microscope, who?	Zacharias Janssen

LESSON PREFACE:
SEGMENT 2

Objective: Use-Concept

"Students will be able to classify previously unencountered lenses as to whether or not they are convex lenses."

Instructional Method: Expository Workbook

The CDT prescriptions for teaching Use-Concept Objectives could be implemented in many ways, including discovery, conversational tutorial, or expository. We have selected a straightforward expository workbook method that starts by presenting a reference example followed by the definition. The definition is followed by some elaboration. Next follows a section consisting of several matched example-nonexample pairs. Each pair is accompanied by attention-focusing help. The example section is followed by practice that asks the student to classify drawings of lenses as to whether or not they are convex. The practice is followed by helped feedback.

SEGMENT 2: CONVEX LENSES

Introduction

[7] This segment will teach you to identify convex lenses. Study the reference example and the key idea; then study the examples that follow. Finally, practice classifying convex lenses by completing the study problems.

[8] **Reference Example**

Fig. 7.7 illustrates a convex lens.

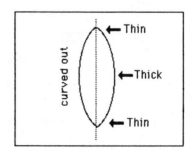

FIG. 7.7

Key Idea

[9]
[10]

All conuex lenses haue two characteristics:

1. at least one side is curued out,

2. thick middle and thin edges.

FIG. 7.8

212

*Study the reference example and key idea (Figs. 7.7 and 7.8) until you are
sure you understand the difference between **convex** and **concave**; then turn
to the next page and study the examples.*

END OF PAGE

[7] Helpful Information

The term *convex* means curved or rounded like the outside of a ball. You
should be careful to distinguish it from the term *concave,* which also means
curved or rounded, but like the inside of a ball. Fig. 7.9 shows the difference
between **convex** and **concave**.

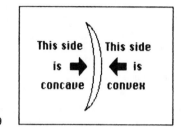

FIG. 7.9

[9] Examples

[11]   This is a convex lens.   This is not a convex lens.

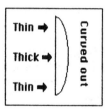   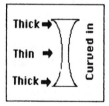

[12]

FIG. 7.10

Note: Note:
- one side curved out   - both sides curved in
- thick in the middle   - thin in the middle
- thin at the edges   - thick at the edges

END OF PAGE

[13] More Examples

This is a convex lens.   This is not a convex lens.

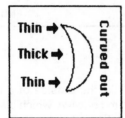   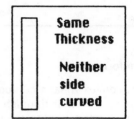

FIG. 7.11

Note: Note:
- one side curved out   - neither side curved
- thicker in the middle   - same thickness
- thinner at the edges
- left side is concave
- right side is convex

Study the examples until you are sure you can identify convex lenses, then turn to the study problems and test your knowledge.

[9] Study Problems

[12] Following are several practice problems that ask you to distinguish convex lenses from other types of lenses. Read each question carefully, and then write your answer in the space provided.

LEARNING TIP: These questions are like those you will be required to answer on the quiz for this segment. If you get lazy and sneak a peek at the answer section before you have written your answer, you may not be able to remember the information during the actual quiz.

Problem 1: You may recall from segment one that water-filled glass globes were the first magnifying glasses. Would they be classified as a convex lens? Explain your answer.

Yes   No _____

_____

END OF PAGE

214

Problem 2: Look at the illustration in Fig. 7.12. Circle one letter corresponding to the convex lens.

[14]

[15]

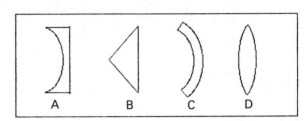

FIG. 7.12

Problem 3: Imagine a drop of water resting on a flat surface. Would it be a kind of convex lens? Explain your answer.

Yes No _____

_____

Problem 4: Look at Fig. 7.13. Circle the letter of *each* lens that is convex.

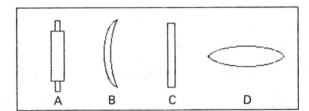

FIG. 7.13

Check your answers. When you are sure they are correct turn the page for the correct answers and explanations.

END OF PAGE

Answers for Study Problems

Problem 1: **Yes**
Water-filled globes have both characteristics of a convex lens: at least one curved surface, and the middle is thicker than the edges.

Problem 2: **D**
Only example D has both characteristics. Example C is curved out on one side but has the same thickness at both middle and ends. Example B is thick in the middle and thin on the edges, but it is not a lens because it is not curved. See Fig. 7.14.

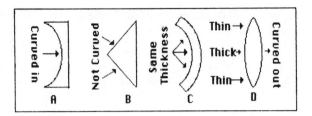

FIG. 7.14

Problem 3: **Yes**
A water droplet always has a curved surface that is thicker in the middle than at the edges. See Fig. 7.15.

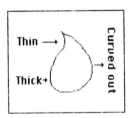

FIG. 7.15

Problem 4: **B** and **D** are convex.
[14] A & C are not convex.
Try to explain why each example is or is not convex.

If you missed any of the study problems, perhaps it would be wise to review the key ideas and examples before going to the next segment in this lesson.

LESSON PREFACE: SEGMENT 3

Objective: Remember-Generality-Concept

"Students will be able to define focal length."

Instructional Method: Printed Study Sheet

In an integrated lesson this objective would not usually be treated as an isolated lesson segment but would be integrated with a segment teaching the concept of focal length or teaching the principle of magnification. This lesson fragment is included here to illustrate the CDT prescriptions for teaching a Remember-Generality objective. The CDT prescriptions for teaching Remember-Generality-Concept could be implemented in several ways. The lesson fragment included presents a reference example followed by definitions for each of the components of the definition of focal length. A mnemonic is presented to help the student remember the meaning of the word *focus*. The student is then asked to label a diagram illustrating focal length. The definition of focal length is restated, and the student is ask to supply the words *focal point* or *focal length* as appropriate.

SEGMENT 3: FOCAL LENGTH

Introduction

One of the most important characteristics of a lens is its focal length. The illustrations and statements that follow define focal length.

[16] Reference Example

[17] The drawings in Fig. 7.16 illustrate focal length for a convex lens.

[18]

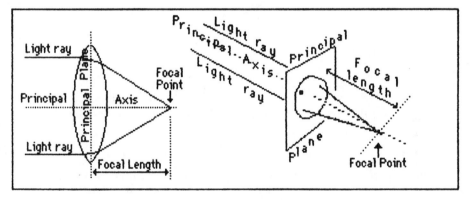

FIG. 7.16

Definition

The *principal plane* of a lens is an imaginary slice from edge to edge through the center of the lens.

The *principal axis* of a lens is an imaginary line through the center of the lens perpendicular to the principal plane of the lens.

A light ray passing through the lens on the principal axis is not bent. Light rays that are parallel to the principal axis are bent when passing through the lens. Light rays bend toward the thicker part of the lens.

The *focal point* of a convex lens is that point on the principal axis where all
[17] the light rays passing through the lens parallel to the principal axis converge or meet.

The *focal length* of a convex lens is the distance along the principal axis from the principal plane or center of the lens to the focal point. Focal length is usually measured in millimeters (mm). Hence, a 35 mm lens is a lens where the focal point is 35 mm from the center of the lens.

END OF PAGE

---

[19] Learning Tip

Focus means to come to a point. (See Fig. 7.17.)

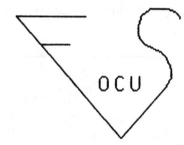

FIG. 7.17

Focal point is the distance required for light rays to come to a point.

Practice

In the diagram in Fig. 7.18 label the important characteristics of the lens. Write in the labels without looking at the diagram on the previous page. When you have finished, check your labels with those shown on the previous page.

[17]

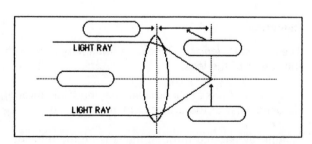

FIG. 7.18

END OF PAGE

[17] Study Problems

Fill in the blank spaces with the words *focal length* or *focal point.*

A magnifying glass is used to focus the sun's rays to a pinpoint of light on a piece of paper. The pinpoint of light is called the _____ _____. The distance from the middle of the lens to the point of light is called the

_____ _____.

A fat lens bends light rays more than a thin lens. Parallel light rays passing through a fat lens converge at a _____ _____ closer to the lens than do parallel light rays passing through a thin lens. The fat lens has a shorter _____ _____ than the thin lens.

[20] Answers to Study Problems

DON'T LOOK at the answers until you fill in the blanks.

The first answer in each paragraph is focal point; the second in each is focal length. The middle of the lens is the same as the center where the principal axis passes through the principal plane. Sun rays are parallel rays of light that bend to form a bright spot at the focal point. The thickness of a convex lens determines the distance of the focal point from the center of the lens.

LESSON PREFACE: SEGMENT 4

Objective: Use-Principle

"Students will explain or predict what effect different convex lenses will have on light rays. Students will explain the way in which the curvature of a lens influences both the magnification and the focal length of different lenses."

Instructional Method:
Computer Simulation/Conversational Tutorial

The CDT prescriptions for teaching use-principles could be implemented in many ways, including discovery, simulation, conversational tutorial, or expository tutorial. We have selected a combination simulation/conversational tutorial method using a computer presentation. We combined the two objectives into a single presentation because we felt that they both required understanding of the same principles. The student is first presented a simulation that enables him or her to change the curvature of a lens and observe the corresponding

219

changes on the image produced. This simulation serves as a set of reference examples to which the subsequent conversational tutorial refers. The student is asked questions about the simulation designed to lead to the statement of the principle. The student is then presented with different situations requiring predictions about the image produced by different lenses and lens combinations. Feedback is provided by allowing the student to see via simulations whether or not the predictions were accurate.

Segment 4: Focal Length and Magnification

This segment is presented in the form of computer-assisted instruction. Space and the limitations of the printed page prevent a complete presentation; hence only representative displays are illustrated. See Fig. 7.19.

Following the introduction the student is immediately presented a simulation to illustrate the principle being taught (see Figs. 7.20 and 7.21). The simulation is preceded by a brief explanation frame not shown here.

The student can experiment with the curvature of the lens using the arrow keys. As the curvature is increased, the focal point moves closer to the lens and the focal length gets shorter as shown by the display in Fig. 7.21.

The simulation is followed by a conversational tutorial (shown in Figs. 7.22 and 7.23) presenting the generalities associated with the principles of focal length and refraction.

The first two displays (shown in Figs. 7.22 and 7.23) direct the student to think about the simulation that was just experienced. If the student is right in his or her observations, the program acknowledges the input and enables the student to continue to the next frame of the tutorial or to return to the simulation. If the student is not correct in the observation, he or she is advised to return to the

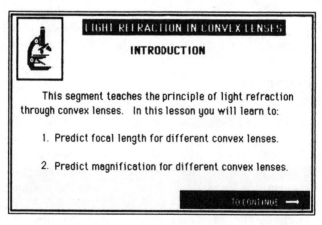

FIG. 7.19

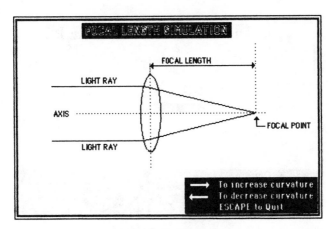

FIG. 7.20

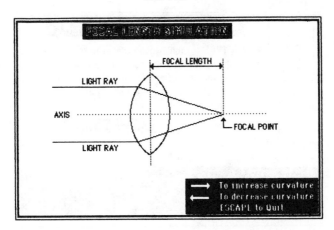

FIG. 7.21

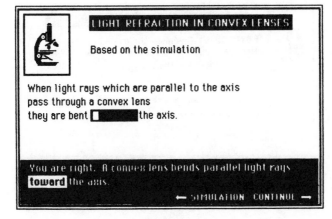

FIG. 7.22

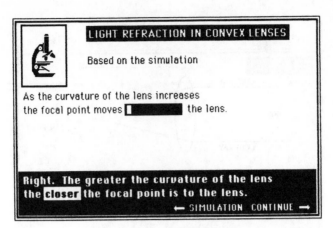

FIG. 7.23

[24]

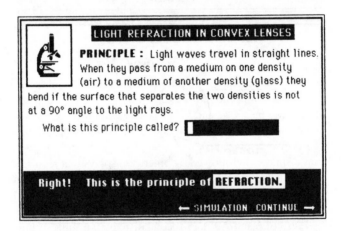

FIG. 7.24

[24]

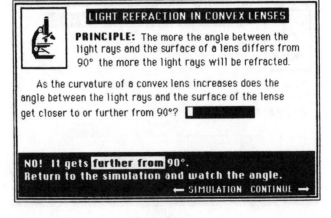

FIG. 7.25

222

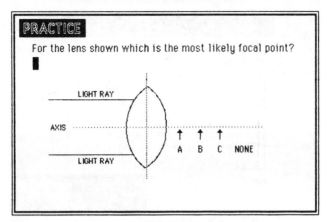

FIG. 7.26

simulation. The student retains control and can return to the simulation or continue the tutorial.

After a series of such displays that quiz the student about observations made while using the simulation, the tutorial then presents more formal statements of the generalities (see Figs. 7.24 and 7.25). These displays are also accompanied by questions that serve to direct the student's attention and cause him or her to process the information presented.

The tutorial displays are followed by practice displays that require the student to predict the focal length of different lenses. When the student answers the question, he or she is provided with RIGHT or WRONG and then the display draws the light rays to the appropriate focal point to confirm the student's response (see Figs. 7.26 and 7.27). A second display (not shown) shows the light rays in dashed lines drawn after the student's response.

[25]

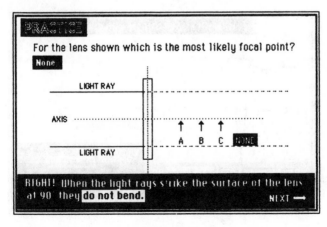

FIG. 7.27

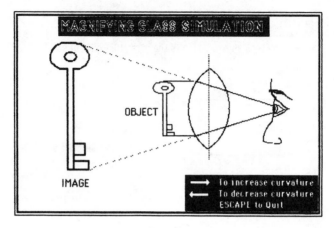

FIG. 7.28

We have presented only part of the segment here. The other parts demonstrate the effect of the lens on magnification. The format of these other segment parts is
[26] similar to the first. The student is presented a simulation allowing the manipulation of the lens curvature and observing the effect on a magnified object. Three such simulation displays are presented in Figs. 7.28, 7.29, and 7.30. After each the student is presented a conversational tutorial leading to a formal statement of the principles involved. After each tutorial the student is presented practice items asking him or her to predict the relative size of objects as seen through each of the various lens systems.

Each subsequent simulation presents a slightly more complex arrangement of convex lenses. The microscope simulation (see Fig. 7.29) involves two convex

[27]

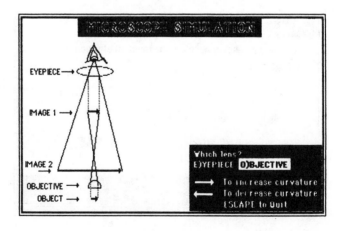

FIG. 7.29

224

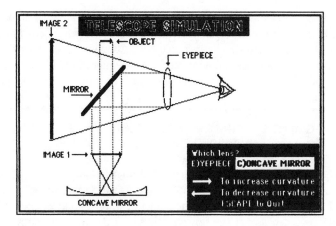

[28]

[29]

FIG. 7.30

lenses working together. The tutorial will help the student observe that the eyepiece magnifies the image resulting from the objective. The student can change curvature for either lens.

The telescope simulation (see Fig. 7.30) complicates the situation further by introducing two kinds of mirrors into the system. The student must first be led to understand that a concave mirror acts like a convex lens. The student must also recognize that an object seen reflected by a 45° mirror is as if the object were behind the mirror. The simulation and the tutorial will help the student see these modifications.

LESSON PREFACE: SEGMENT 5

Objective: Use-Procedure

"Students will be able to use a previously unencountered optical microscope properly."

Instructional Method: Video Disc

Demonstrations for Use-Procedure objectives that follow CDT prescriptions can involve a wide variety of instructional techniques. Because the lesson fragment included must be presented on the printed page, it is demonstrated using a story board. Representative frames of the presentation are steps of the procedure frozen in time. The actual presentation would consist of either a film strip, slides, or computer screens using a series of still pictures. If resources are available the pictures could be video sequences on a VCR or an interactive video disc. We

225

have described part of an interative video disc sequence. The major steps of the process are first illustrated to provide the big picture. Then a series of pictures and captions explain each step in the procedure. Adequate practice for this skill is not possible using only the demonstration; subsequent practice would be provided in a laboratory where the student has access to equipment of the type being demonstrated.

SEGMENT 5: USING THE MICROSCOPE—A SPECIFICATION FOR A VIDEO DISC DEMONSTRATION

There are two parts to the lesson on using the microscope. Part 1 is a video disc demonstration that shows the student how to use the microscope. The unique feature of the demonstration is that the student can repeat any step or substep as many times as is necessary. The flowchart in Fig. 7.31 shows the structure of this video disc demonstration. The numbers and letters (1a) refer to the section of the script that corresponds to the procedure identified in the diagram.

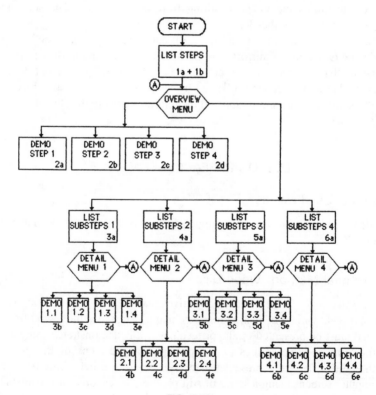

FIG. 7.31

The following segment of a script corresponds to this structure diagram and provides more detail concerning this demonstration. Note the following characteristics of the demonstration: The demo first lists the steps for the student. The overview menu allows the student to view a short action segment corresponding to each step (see Fig. 7.32). The overviews can be viewed in any order and as many times as the student wishes. Selecting "☐ Details" from the menu takes the student to a detail menu for that step which first lists the steps and then allows the student to view a detailed demonstration for each substep in any order and as many times as necessary. Selecting "☐ Overview" returns the student to the Overview menu.

Part 1:   Script for Microscope Demonstration

1a. Introduction

(Music)

{Overview menu is on the screen. Picture shows microscope.}

[30]

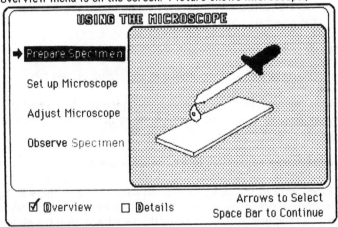

FIG. 7.32.   Screen display for video disk demonstration. (Overview menu is on the screen. Picture shows microscope.)

NAR: In this segment of the course we will demonstrate how to use a simple optical microscope. You can view this demonstration at your own pace. To repeat a given section, press the arrow keys to select the step. (Highlight the directions **Arrows to Select** on the screen.) To move to the selected part of the demonstration, press the *space* bar. (Highlight the directions **Space Bar to Continue** on the screen.) If the overview box is selected when you press the space bar, you will see an overview of the step. If the details box is selected when you press the space bar, you will be shown the substeps involved in the step which is selected. It is usually wise to view the overview before you view the details for a step. You may repeat any part of the demonstration by selecting the step using the arrow keys and pressing the space bar. When you are ready to begin, please press the space bar.

[31]   *1b. List the Steps*

(Music)

> **NAR:** There are four major steps in using a microscope.
> {Highlight step name **1. PREPARE SPECIMEN.** A still picture represents the step.}
> First, you must prepare the slide. The slide will contain the specimen we wish to view under the microscope. {short pause}
> {Highlight **2. SET UP MICROSCOPE** with still picture.} Second, you must set up the microscope by mounting the slide and adjusting the light. {short pause}
> {Highlight **3. ADJUST MICROSCOPE** with still picture.} Third, you must adjust the microscope so that the specimen is in focus. {short pause}
> {Highlight **4. OBSERVE SPECIMEN** with still picture.} Fourth, you may now observe the specimen. {short pause}

[31]   *2a. DEMO of Step 1*

[32] {Picture of assistant with microscope and apparatus on the table.}

NAR: This is my assistant, Eric. He will demonstrate the use of the microscope for us. Eric will show us each of the major steps in the use of the microscope.

{Highlight the name of the step **PREPARE SPECIMEN.**}

{In the picture area of the screen a motion sequence will show Eric get the glass slide from the case, wash the glass slide, get the sample of pond water to be used, use the eyedropper to place the pond water on the slide, spread the top with the cover glass, and slip the cover glass in place.}

NAR: {Synchronize narration with demonstration.} First, Eric will show us how to prepare a slide. He first washes the slide to remove any foreign matter and allows it to air dry. {Pause to allow action sequence to be completed.} He then places a drop of pond water on the slide containing the specimen we want to observe. {Pause as necessary.} The specimen is spread thin and covered with the cover glass. {Pause as necessary.} We will show you the details of each of these steps later in this demonstration. {Pause.} {Demonstration to freeze frame as Eric turns toward the microscope with slide in hand.}

2b. DEMO of Step 2

{Highlight the name of the step, **SET UP MICROSCOPE.**}

{In the picture area of the screen a motion sequence will show Eric get the microscope, carefully clean the lenses with lens paper, position the scope for easy viewing, adjust the mirror so that the light is directed into the objective, carefully place the slide on the stage of the microscope.}

NAR: {Synchronize narration with demonstration.} Next Eric demonstrates how to set up the microscope. The lenses should be carefully cleaned with lens paper. {Pause.} The microscope is positioned for easy viewing with the arm toward him. {Pause.} He then adjusts the light. Adjusting the light is one of the most important steps because without proper adjustment he will be unable to see the specimen. {Pause.} He now places the slide carefully on the stage of the microscope to avoid disturbing the adjustment of the light. {Pause.} {Demonstration to freeze frame with Eric getting ready to adjust microscope.}

2c. DEMO of Step 3

{Highlight the name of the step, **ADJUST MICROSCOPE.**}

{In the picture area of the screen a motion sequence will show Eric select the lowest magnification objective, use the coarse adjustment to lower the objective almost to the cover glass while observing from the side, then, while looking through the eyepiece, use the fine adjustment to bring the specimen into focus.}

NAR: {Synchronize narration with demonstration.} Now Eric is ready to make the final adjustments so that he can observe the specimen. First, he selects the proper obejctive, in this case the one with the lowest power of magnification. {Pause.} Then, using the coarse adjustment knob, he carefully lowers the objective down until it almost touches the cover glass. {Pause.} While looking through the eyepiece, Eric now uses the fine adjustment knob to bring the specimen into focus. {Pause.} He is now ready to make observations of the specimen. {Pause.} {Demonstration to freeze frame with Eric moving forward to look into the eyepiece of the microscope.}

2d. DEMO of Step 4

{Highlight the name of the step, **OBSERVE specimen.**}

{In the picture area of the screen a motion sequence will show Eric look through the eyepiece of the microscope. The picture will change to show what Eric is seeing. Then Eric will look at a picture in the textbook and make notes on a pad about the specimen he is observing. This observe-the-specimen, look-at-the-textbook, and write-notes sequence will be repeated three times before the sequence stops.}

NAR: {Narration in sync with demonstration.} Eric is now ready to use the microscope to observe the specimen. He looks through the eyepiece. {Pause.} The screen now shows what Eric sees in the drop of pond water. {Pause.} Eric has been assigned to draw pictures of all the different organisms he observes. He is making sketches and comparing them with the illustrations in the textbook to try to see if he can identify the different forms of organisms. {Pause.} {Demonstration to freeze frame with Eric looking through the eyepiece.}

3a. STEP ONE (PREPARE specimen) Substeps

{Highlight step name, **PREPARE specimen**}.

[34]

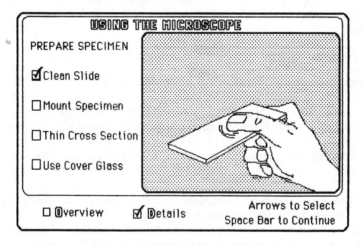

FIG. 7.33

{Still picture shows closeup of table, including jar of pond water, box of slides, cover glasses.}.

NAR: Eric and I will now show you the first step in more detail so that you will know exactly what to do when you get to the laboratory. You will recall from the overview that the first step is to prepare the specimen. In this demonstration our specimen will be small organisms present in some stagnant pond water that was previously collected in this jar. {Still picture shows closeup of the jar in the context of the table shown in the previous picture.}

Preparing the specimen requires several substeps:

- {Highlight first substep, **Clean Slide.**}
  {Show still picture of Eric washing slide.}

[35] The first substep is to be sure that our slide is clean so that our specimen won't be contaminated by organisms already on the slide. {Pause.}

- {Highlight second substep, **Place specimen on Slide.**}
  {Show still picture of eyedropper placing drop on slide.}
  Next we must place the specimen on the slide. In the demonstration we will place a drop of pond water on the slide. {Pause.}
- {Highlight third substep, **Provide Thin Cross-Section.**}
  {Show still picture of drop spread thin by cover glass.}
  In order to see the specimen, it must be very thin. The cover glass is used to spread the drop into a thin film on the slide. {Pause.}
- {Highlight fourth substep, **Protect with Cover Glass.**}
  {Show still picture of cover glass in place on slide.}
  The cover glass serves to protect the specimen and to protect the lens in the objective of the microscope. {Pause}

3b. Step One, Substep 1: Clean Slide

{Highlight first substep, **Clean Slide.**}

{Action sequence will show Eric remove slide from slide tray, wash the slide, very carefully rubbing it between his thumb and forefinger, rinsing it with very hot water while holding it by the edges, and placing it in the rack to air dry. All of the photography will be closeup of the slide and his hands, whereas the previous overview was from back further.}

NAR: {Narration in sync with the presentation.} It is very important to use a clean slide. If the slide is not clean we may be observing organisms or **[36]** material that were already on the slide rather than those that come from the specimen. Eric is demonstrating the procedure we will use to clean the slide in our laboratory. Note that he scrubs the slide carefully between his thumb and his forefinger to remove any material that may cling to the glass. Also note that he is using a disinfectant soap that will destroy most microorganisms that may be on the slide. After he scrubs the slide with the disinfectant soap, he than rinses it very carefully with very hot water while holding the slide by the edges to avoid placing fingerprints or organisms from his fingers on the clean slide. He then places the slide in the rack to air dry. If he were to use a cloth to dry the slide, he would be likely to place material or organisms from the drying cloth on the slide.

{Action sequence showing someone else in a lab coat placing microscope slides in a sterilizer.}

[35] In laboratories where accurate observation is very important, the slides are sterilized after they are thoroughly washed. The sterilization process heats the surface of the slides, killing any microorganisms that may still be present. **[37]** For our purposes sterilization is not necessary, and we will merely wash our slides very carefully as was demonstrated by Eric.

3c. Step One, Substep 2: Mount Specimen

{Highlight second substep, **Mount specimen.**}

{Action sequence showing Eric carefully removing the lid from the jar of pond water and using the eyedropper to place a single drop of the liquid on the slide.}

NAR: In our demonstration we will be observing organisms present in stagnant pond water. The jar of pond water was previously gathered from a nearby pond that is rich in algae and other life forms. Eric carefully places a single drop of the pond water on the slide.

{Action sequence showing someone other than Eric placing various kinds of samples on a slide.}

Many different kinds of specimen can be observed under a microscope. Some of these represent thin slices of tissue from animals or plants, {Action sequence illustrates tissue slices.}. Other specimens are crystal structure, best observed by grinding the specimen to be observed to a fine powder. {Shows the grinding of a mineral to a powder and being placed on the slide.} Oftentimes it is necessary to stain the specimen with special dyes in order to observe its shape or structure. {Shows technician placing dye on a specimen.} The preparation of specimens for observation under a microscope is a special branch of science all by itself. For our introduction we will merely use simple techniques such as the drop of pond water which we have illustrated.[1]

Part 2

[38]
[35] After the video disc demonstration the student is allowed to experiment with an actual microscope in the laboratory. This is a series of laboratory exercises that really involve backward chaining. That is, the student first does only the last step, the previous steps having already been completed by the lab assistant. Each successive exercise adds the previous step until finally the student does all of the steps necessary to using a microscope.

The ideal way to use the video disc demonstration and the laboratory is to integrate the two as follows. First the student sees the overview (1a, 1b, 2a through 2d). Then the student views the detailed presentation in 6a through 6e concerning how to observe through the microscope (see Fig. 7.34). Then the student goes to the lab and completes the first lab exercise, requiring only observation through a previously set up microscope. The next experi-

---

[1]The script continues for other substeps. Space prevents the inclusion of the entire script here.

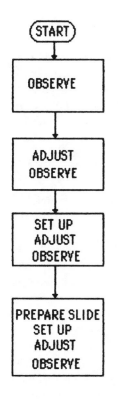

1. Microscope is all set up with slide in place. Student is asked to observe and draw what is seen.

2. Microscope is set up with slide in place but student must first adjust the objective and then observe and draw what is seen.

3. Slide is prepared but student must set up the microscope, place the slide on the stage, adjust the microscope, observe and draw what is seen.

4. Student must prepare the slide. After the slide is prepared student must set up the microscope, place the slide on the stage, adjust the microscope, observe the slide and draw what is seen.

FIG. 7.34

ment would be to view the demonstration 5a through 5e and to review parts of 6 that might be unclear. Then do the second laboratory exercise, and so on. Thus the demonstration and lab experience are more integrated. Unfortunately, most school situations may make such an arrangement difficult or impossible.

When the student gets to step 1, preparing slides, there should be opportunity to work with different kinds of specimens and to prepare a variety of types of slides for observation. If the class is in biology, mineralogy, or general science, then these additional practice experiences could be integrated as part of the remaining curriculum rather than as special exercises in the use of the microscope. After this demonstration and initial practice, the microscope should be integrated into the curriculum as a tool, thus providing the variety and additional practice necessary.

COMMENTS

For each type of objective Component Display Theory provides a set of prescriptions for consistent and adequate instruction. We have used these prescriptions in preparing the lesson segments presented. The following section lists the prescriptions used in the preparation of each lesson segment, together with specific comments as to how the prescription applies to the lesson segment included.

Segment 1—
Significant Events: Remember-Instance-Fact

1. The presentation should consist of an **expository instance** (''example''— *Eeg*) followed by an **inquisitory instance** (''practice''—*Ieg*) where the practice instance is the same as the example instance (see Fig. 7.3).

[*NOTE:* The first page of the sample lesson, which lists the six events that the student is to remember, is a set of six *Eegs*. The second page of the lesson, which contains the flash cards for use in student practice, is a corresponding set of the six *Iegs.*]

2. Each instance should consist of an **arbitrary association** of a symbol-symbol, object-symbol, event-symbol, object-event, object-object, etc. (see Fig. 7.4).

[*NOTE:* The six facts to be memorized involve the association of dates (events) with objects or people (objects) with inventions (objects). Each of these associations is arbitrary in the sense that there is no generality that can be used to derive the association.]

3. Feedback for each *Ieg* should consist of **correct answer** information (see Fig. 7.5).

[*NOTE:* The back of each flash card provides correct answer information for the student.]

4. Subsequent practice trials should present the set of pairs to be associated in **random order** (see Fig. 7.6).

[*NOTE:* Shuffling the flash cards provides random order.]

5. The entire set of associations should be learned without error (See Fig. 7.6).

[*NOTE:* The students are instructed to practice with the flash cards until they make no mistakes. It should be noted that when one is memorizing facts, a criterion of less than 100% is not meaningful. Either you need to know a particular association or you do not. It is like learning only 24 of the letters of the alphabet—which two is it unnecessary to know? If less than 100% is okay, then one wonders if it is necessary to learn any of the facts.]

6. In practice mode (*Ieg*), given one item of the pair, the student should be able to provide the associated item without delay (see Fig. 7.6).

(*NOTE:* The students are instructed to provide the answer immediately. Although problem solving requires time, associations should require minimal processing time.)

Segment 2—Convex Lenses: Use-Concept

7. The presentation should consist of an expository generality ("rule"—*EG*) followed by a set of expository instances ("examples"—*Eegs*) consisting of several different examples, followed by a set of previously unencountered inquisitory instances ("practice"—*Iegs*) consisting of several additional instances different from the instances used for *Eegs* (see Fig. 7.3).

[*NOTE:* The generality or definition of the concept "convex lens" is presented by the key idea appearing in the box. A set of examples, somewhat different from each other, are presented and labeled EXAMPLES. The STUDY PROBLEMS present yet another set of instances requiring the student to classify those that are convex lenses and those that are not.]

8. The definition (*EG*) should be elaborated by way of **secondary presentation forms** that provide attention-focusing information (EG'_h) to help the student identify the relevant attributes and to help the student recall prerequisite information that should have already been learned. The definition should also be **restated** or represented via some different mode, such as a graphic, chart, or diagram (see Fig. 7.5).

[*NOTE:* The reference example serves as one form of alternative representation of the definition. The notes on the diagram indicating the thickness of the lens and the direction of curvature are attention-focusing devices to help the student identify the critical characteristics of a convex lens. The helpful information is another attempt to present the generality in a slightly different way and thus clarify the meaning for the student.]

9. The expository generality (*EG*) should consist of a definition of the concept. The definition should include identification of the superordinate class, the relevant attributes that distinguish instances of this concept from coordinate concepts within the same superordinate class, and the relationship of these attributes to one another. Each of the examples (*Eegs*) should be a **specific object, event,** or **symbol** from the class, or a **representation** of a specific object, event, or symbol from the class. If a representation is used, it must **include all of the relevant attributes** as defined by *EG*. Each of the practice instances (*Iegs*) should also be a specific object, event, or symbol from the class, or a suitable representation that includes all of the relevant attributes. Further, the practice instances (*Iegs*) should be **different from the examples** (*Eegs*) (see Fig. 7.4).

[*NOTE:* The superordinate concept for the definition is "lens." The coordinate concepts are "different kinds of lenses." Hence, the relevant attributes are those that distinguish one kind of lens from another, in this case the nature of the curved surface and the direction of the curve. Instances for both *Eeg* and *Ieg* are drawings (representations) of lenses rather than actual lenses. The lesson would be improved if the student had the opportunity to see and classify some actual lenses. The drawings do illustrate the critical attributes—curvature and thickness—thus enabling the student to make appropriate classifications. The down side is that the drawings exclude many of the irrelevant characteristics that would be present if actual lenses were used. Thus, classifying diagrams may be easier than classifying actual lenses. The practice items are somewhat different from the examples requiring the student to do more than merely remember specific instances.]

10. Each of the primary presentations (PPFs) should be **isolated** from surrounding text and related information so that the main ideas and illustrations of these ideas are easily identified by the student (see Fig. 7.6).

[*NOTE:* Several techniques are used to isolate the primary presentation forms in this lesson. First, labels—REFERENCE EXAMPLE, KEY IDEA, HELPFUL INFORMATION, EXAMPLES, STUDY PROBLEMS, ANSWERS FOR STUDY PROBLEMS—are used to call attention to the different sections. Second, the key idea is separated from the text by a box drawn around the definition.]

11. The examples (*Eegs*) should also be elaborated by **secondary presentation forms** (SPFs) that provide attention-focusing information (sometimes called *prompting*) linking the specific attributes of the examples to the labels for these attributes contained in the definition. The amount of this helping information should be **faded** or gradually decreased during the later stages of the presentation. Different examples should also be presented using **alternative modes of representation** (see Figs. 7.5. and 7.6).

[*NOTE:* Examples contain arrows and labels to call attention to the relevant attributes. The relevant attributes, or lack of relevant attributes, of a particular example or nonexample are listed below the diagram. There is little fading of this prompting during the example presentation. The lesson would be strengthened if examples without this additional information were also presented. When attention-focusing information is immediately available, students tend to rely on this information before they study the examples long enough. This gives them the illusion of understanding when in fact they still need to put forth more mental effort. The fading of attention-focusing information promotes this increased mental effort. This lesson is weak in this respect. The divergence of representation would be better if actual lenses were used.]

12. Instances that are presented in *Eegs* should be matched to potentially confusing nonexamples from coordinate concepts within the same superordinate concept. This procedure assists the student to discriminate members of the class from nonmembers. This matching procedure should be used early in the presentation but **faded** during the later stages of the presentation. Matching should **not**

be used during practice *legs*. Both instances and noninstances should be presented for student classification, but they should be presented one by one in a random order to minimize unintentional prompts (see Fig. 7.6).

[*NOTE:* In the example presentation each example is paired with a similar nonexample. This matching assists the student in discriminating relevant from irrelevant characteristics.]

13. Subsequent instances in both *Eegs* and *Iegs* should be **divergent** from one another so that the student is exposed to the variety of instances that can be included in the concept class. This procedure assists the student to generalize to all members of the concept class (see Fig. 7.6).

[*NOTE:* There is some divergence in that several different kinds of lenses are represented. Within the limits of using only a limited number of representation forms, we have used considerable divergence in convex lenses.]

14. The practice instances (*Iegs*) should be presented using a **variety of representation** modes. Student responses should be followed by SPFs in the form of **feedback** that provides attention-focusing information that shows the student why the instance belongs to the concept class under consideration. This attention-focusing help should **not be used prior to the student's response,** and the amount of information provided should be **faded** during the later stages of practice. When help is not faded, students become help-dependent and do not try as hard as they might before responding because they know that not only the correct answer but also an explanation will follow (see Figs. 7.5 and 7.6).

[*NOTE:* The Study Problems do provide some variety in the representation of the instances used. In addition to the diagrams there are descriptions of glass-filled globes and drops of water. This divergence of representation would be better if there were actual lenses for the student to classify. There is some attempt to limit the amount of attention-focusing information in the feedback, but it may not provide enough unassisted practice.]

15. In both the example (*Eegs*) and practice (*Iegs*) stages of the instruction, the instances used should represent a **range of difficulty.** This prescription assures exposure to the variety of instances the student is likely to encounter following the instruction (see Fig. 7.6).

[*NOTE:* In practice the recognition of a drop of water as a convex lens is a more difficult example than the drawings that have been used in the example section. More complex concepts require even greater range of difficulty.]

Segment 3—
Focal Length: Remember-Generality-Concept

16. The presentation should consist of an **expository generality** (*EG*) followed by a single **reference example** (*Eeg*) followed by **practice in paraphrasing** the generality (*IG.P*) (see Fig. 7.3).

[*NOTE:* The reference example (*Eeg*) is presented first, followed by a list of definitions (*EG*), followed by Practice and Study Problems (*IG*) that require the student to recognize the paraphrase of the definition.]

17. The generality (*EG*) should consist of a **definition** of the concept that includes identification of the superordinate class, the relevant attributes that distinguish instances of this concept from coordinate concepts within the same superordinate class, and the relationship of these attributes to one another. The reference example (*Eeg*) should represent a **typical illustration** of the concept that clearly shows the relevant attributes. Practice (*IG.p*) should provide opportunity for the student to **recognize the definition** stated in two or more different ways (see Fig. 7.4).

[*NOTE:* The reference example presents alternative views of a convex lens showing the light rays, the primary axis and primary plane, and clearly indicating the focal length and focal point. The definition describes in words the principal plane, principal axis, focal point, and focal length. The superordinate concept for principal plane is "imaginary slice," the relevant attribute is "location through the center of the lens." For principal axis the superordinate concept is "imaginary line," the relevant attribute is "location perpendicular to the principal plane." For focal point the superordinate concept is "point" and the relevant attribute is "the point at which the light rays converge." For focal length the superordinate concept is "distance," the relevant attributes are "the two locations of the principal plane" and "the focal point defining the ends of the distance." Notice that practice enables the student to label each of these concepts on the diagram and to use the terms in statements of the definitions.]

18. The presentation of the reference examples (*Eeg*) should be accompanied by **attention-focusing help** (*Eeg'h*) clearly indicating each of the critical attributes. Students tend to remember examples more easily than verbal statements, and this reference example will probably be used by the student to reconstruct the definition (see Fig. 7.5).

[*NOTE:* The arrows and words in the diagram illustrating focal point and focal length provide attention-focusing information for the student.]

19. The presentation of the generality should be accompanied by a **mnemonic aid** (*EG'mn*) that facilitates the student's ability to remember the critical attributes (see Fig. 7.5).

[*NOTE:* The word FOCUS is written in a fancy script to try to help the student remember that it means to come to a point. This is an attempt at a mnemonic aid.]

20. Practice (*IG*) should be followed by **correct answer feedback** (*FB'ca,h*) that indicates to the student the synonyms involved (see Fig. 7.5).

[*NOTE:* Correct-answer feedback is provided in two ways. For the diagram students are instructed to look back at the original reference example. For the short-answer questions students are provided with the correct labels for each question. The feedback would be improved if it was not available until after the students had responded.]

4. Segment 4—
Refraction Through a Lens: Use-Principle

21. The presentation should consist of a **statement of the proposition** (*EG*) followed by a set of **expository examples** (*Eegs*) consisting of several different explanations of specific applications, followed by application **practice** (*Iegs*) consisting of several additional instances that require the student to explain or predict relationships (see Fig. 7.3).

[*NOTE:* The simulation presented here varies somewhat from a traditional Rule, Example, Practice format but is still consistent with CDT. The expository generality (*EG*) is represented by the conversational tutorial represented in the sample lesson by Figs. 7.22 through 7.24. The rhetorical questions asked on each of these displays do not constitute practice. They are merely attention-focusing devices to get the student to pay attention to critical aspects of the simulation. Asking a question does not make a primary presentation practice. It is okay to ask questions on expository generality or expository example displays. This point is often a misunderstanding about CDT. The examples (*Eegs*) are provided by the simulation, shown by Figs. 7.20 and 7.21. By being given the ability to manipulate the display, the student can actually provide for himself or herself a number of examples. In a sense these examples are matched, inasmuch as only the relevant attribute changes from one to the next. Practice (*Iegs*) is provided by a series of questions shown by Figs. 7.26 and 7.27.]

22. The illustrative explanations (*Eegs*) should be elaborated by secondary presentation forms (*Eeg'h*) that provide **attention-focusing information** clearly indicating the causal or correlational relationships between the component concepts. This helping information should be **faded,** that is, generally decreased, during the later stages of the presentation. Different explanations should be presented using **alternative forms** of representation (*Eeg'r*) (see Figs. 7.5 and 7.6).

[*NOTE:* Attention-focusing information is provided in the simulations by arrows and the dynamics of the simulation itself. The student can see the rays bend when changes are made in the thickness of the lens. In practice with the other lens systems, the student is asked to make predictions first prior to manipulating the simulation. This change of order in events increases the amount of mental effort the student must put forth. The instruction would be even more adequate if the system prevented the student from using the additional simulations before he or she made predictions. The representation forms used are all very similar. Perhaps photographs of real lens systems would provide a good alternative representation for the ideas presented.]

23. The proposition (EG) should be elaborated by means of secondary presentation forms $(EG'h)$ that provide **attention-focusing information** that helps the student visualize the relationships between the component concepts. Additional secondary presentations should also review **prerequisite information,** such as definitions or examples of the component concepts $(EG'p)$. The proposition should also be restated or represented via some **alternate mode** $(EG'r)$, such as a graph, chart, or diagram (see Fig. 7.5).

[*NOTE:* Attention-focusing information for the generality consists of rhetorical questions designed to get the student to attend to the relevant parts of the simulation in preparation for observing the action of the principle. The lesson does not review prerequisite information as completely as may be necessary. However, previously learned concepts are reviewed as part of the rhetorical questions presented in the expository generality phase of the instruction. The proposition is represented both formally in statements and by the reference example simulation provided.]

24. The expository generality (EG) should consist of a proposition identifying the principle. This statement of the proposition should clearly indicate the **component concepts** of which it is comprised and the **causal or correlational relationships** between these concepts. Each of the illustrative explanations $(Eegs)$ should consist of a **specific situation** involving the principle. If some form of representation is used, it must include adequate **representation of each of the component concepts** involved. Each of the practice applications $(Iegs)$ should also consist of specific situations or adequate representations of specific situations involving the principle. Further, the practice applications $(Iegs)$ should be **different** from the illustrative explanations $(Eegs)$ (see Fig. 7.4).

[*NOTE:* The formal statement of the principle appears in Figs. 7.24 and 7.25. The component concepts are light rays, a surface between two media of different densities, and the angle at which the rays strike the surface. The causal relationship is between the angle of incidence and the amount of bend in the light rays. The examples represented by Figs. 7.20 and 7.21 contain all of the relevant attributes and the capability for the student to manipulate these parameters and observe the effect on the angle of bend for the light rays. Divergent practice items are provided by having the student predict the occurrence of change in the various lens systems before checking these predictions by using the simulation (see Figs. 7.28, 7.29, and 7.30).]

25. The practice applications $(Iegs)$ should also use a **variety of representation** modes $(Ieg'r)$. Student predictions should be followed by feedback $(FB'h)$ that provides **attention-focusing information** clearly indicating the causal or correlational relationships that the student should have identified as part of the prediction. This attention-focusing help should not be used prior to the student's

response. The elaboration should also be faded during the later stages of practice (see Figs. 7.5 and 7.6).

[*NOTE:* The practice provides for predictions using a variety of lens systems, but the representation form itself is very similar, using schematic diagrams. The feedback is allowing the student to check the predictions by manipulating the simulations. This feedback contains all of the attention-focusing devices of the original presentation.]

26. Each of the primary presentations (*EG, Eegs,* and *Iegs*) should be **isolated** from surrounding text and related information so that the main ideas and key points of the explanations are easily identified by the student (see Fig. 7.6).

[*NOTE:* Isolation is provided by labels indicating the principle and practice. The examples and subsequent practice are less carefully isolated but could be in requiring the students to make predictions and clearly indicating that this is necessary before they can use the simulation to check their work.]

27. Subsequent instances for both the examples (*Eegs*) and practice (*Iegs*) should be **divergent** from one another so that the student is exposed to a variety of situations to which the principle is applicable. This prescription facilitates generalization to subsequent events or situations that are explained by the principle being taught (see Fig. 7.6).

[*NOTE:* Divergence occurs when different lens systems are used for subsequent examples. Each requires some modification in the application of the principle.]

28. In both the explanation (*Eegs*) and practice (*Iegs*) phases of the instruction, the situations selected for illustration should represent a **wide range of difficulty.** That is, in some situations the application of the principle should be more obvious, while in others the application should be more subtle. This prescription increases the student's ability to apply the principle to a wide variety of situations following the instruction (see Fig. 7.6).

(*NOTE:* The simulations increase in difficulty by introducing more and more complex lens systems. Each simulation is more difficult than the last.)

29. Illustrative explanations presented in *Eegs* should include explanations of **common misconceptions.** The student should be shown where the principle does not work or situations to which the principle does not apply. This procedure assists the student to be discriminating in the application of the principle to subsequent situations. In later stages of the presentation and in practice the student should be asked to identify inappropriate applications of the principle. Practice that asks the student to predict a given situation is better than having the student choose between an appropriate and inappropriate application or prediction (see Fig. 7.6).

[*NOTE:* This lesson does not implement this principle. Perhaps showing the student some of the common mistakes in reasoning about the bending of light rays would be useful.]

Segment 5—
Use an Optical Microscope: Use-Procedure

30. The presentation should consist of a general **description of the process** (*EG*), followed by **demonstrations** with specific objects (*Eegs*), followed by opportunities for the **student to demonstrate** the procedure with a similar but different object and/or materials (*Ieg*) (see Fig. 7.3).

[*NOTE:* The description of the process is represented by Fig. 7.32 and script 1b, which shows each of the major steps. At the next level down this same procedure is followed by representing the steps within a major step as a list (see script 3a). The demonstrations show each of the major steps (script 2a, 2b, 2c, and 2d), and later demonstrations show each of the substeps within each of the major steps (script 3b, 3c, etc.). This lesson uses elaboration theory, as described in Chapter 8, by presenting the major steps first and then elaborating the detail. Finally, using backward chaining, the student is asked to demonstrate his or her ability to use the microscope (see part 2).]

31. The generality (*EG*) should consist of a description of the process that identifies the **outcome** that will result from following the procedure, indicates each of the **steps** and their **order of execution,** and indicates each of the **decisions** required and the resulting **branches** (steps) following the various alternatives from these decisions. The demonstrations (*Eegs*) should show how to perform each of the steps and how to make appropriate decisions. If the demonstration is a representation rather than hands-on, this representation must be sure to **clearly illustrate each of the steps,** the **proper sequence** for execution, and the **expected consequence** of each step. The practice demonstration (*Iegs*) should enable the student to execute each of the steps. If possible this execution should be using objects and materials involved or simulation of such objects and materials. If the procedure being taught will be used with a **variety** of objects and materials, the student should have an opportunity to practice with the variety of different objects and/or materials (see Fig. 7.4).

[*NOTE:* Script 1b presents the steps at the main level, script 3a illustrates generality for substeps. Scripts 2a through 2d demonstrate the major steps; script 3b, 3c, etc. demonstrate the substeps. Part 2 enables the student to execute each of the main and substeps.]

32. The description of the process (*EG*) should be elaborated by secondary presentation forms that **help the student remember** the individual steps and the sequence required for execution (*EG'mn*). When decisions involve previously learned concepts or facts, the secondary presentations should review generalities and/or instances of these **prerequisite ideas** (*EG'p*). If possible, the procedure should be described and illustrated via some chart, diagram, picture, or other illustration to present at least two **alternative representations** of the process (see Fig. 7.5).

[*NOTE:* Arrows, voice over, an assistant on the screen all provide the attention focusing required. Some prerequisite ideas are intrdouced as part of the script.]

33. The demonstrations (*Eegs*) should also be elaborated by secondary presentation forms that clearly identify each step as it is being executed (*Eeg'h*). This information should **focus the student's attention** on the decisions required and the consequences of these decisions. A second demonstration should **fade** this attention-focusing information, requiring the student to attend more closely to the task (see Figs. 7.5 and 7.6).

[*NOTE:* The narration and video clearly focus the student's attention on the relevant aspects of the procedure. The practice fades much of this detailed attention focusing.]

34. The description of the process should be concise and to the point. Critical steps and actions should be clearly **separated** from elaborative information (see Fig. 7.6).

[*NOTE:*The title slides and text on screen provide the necessary isolation of critical parts of the procedure. Single-word labels for each of the steps enable the student to remember the most important aspect of each step.]

35. If the real world, where the procedure will be used, involves different types of equipment and materials, then the student should see a **variety** of equipment demonstrated and should have the opportunity to practice on a variety of equipment (see Fig. 7.5).

[*NOTE:* If different microscopes are not available, at least a variety of specimens could be examined requiring different preparation of slides, different objectives for viewing, etc.]

36. During the demonstration the student should be shown **common incorrect ways** to perform the steps or make the required decisions. These incorrect paths should be clearly labeled and the student given sufficient warning to avoid these incorrect procedures. Clearly identifying and illustrating incorrect paths helps the student avoid such mistakes during his or her own practice (see Fig. 7.6).

[*NOTE:* This prescription has not been implemented as well as it might be. During the demonstration some cautions may be very appropriate: for example, getting a fingerprint on the slide by not handling it by the edges, damaging a slide by using the coarse adjustment knob while looking through the scope, or not getting the light focused correctly. Showing these common mistakes and adding a caution will help the student avoid them.]

37. If the process involves both simple and more complex means of execution, the **range** of such operations should be illustrated during the demonstrations and the student should have an opportunity to practice both the straightforward and the more complex forms of the procedure (see Fig. 7.6).

[*NOTE:* The range of procedures is illustrated during the demonstration to show the student sterilization procedures, various ways to prepare a specimen, etc. Even though the student will not be required to use these more advanced procedures, they are illustrated to show him or her the range of possibilities. Some range of activity is included in this lesson, but the real range of activity will come as the microscope is used during the course.]

38. Opportunities for the student to demonstrate the process (*legs*) should include **several tries** using a **variety** of equipment and materials (*leg'r*). During the early practice tries, **correct-answer feedback** (*FB'ca,h*) should be immediate and precise, indicating to the student steps omitted, steps performed correctly, decisions omitted or incorrect, etc. Later stages of practice should let the consequences of the student's actions provide the feedback concerning adequate performance (see Fig. 7.5).

[*NOTE:* Limitations in equipment available would probably limit the variety of experience that could be provided. In this case the student may use the same microscope but could certainly have a variety of experience with different slides and specimens.]

ACKNOWLEDGMENT

I would like to acknowledge the contributions of Eric Von Hurst to the writing of this chapter. Eric wrote an early draft that was used for our presentation at the 1982 AERA convention. The current version is a significant revision of this earlier draft.

REFERENCES

Merrill, M. David. (1983) Component display theory. In C. M. Reigeluth (Ed.), *Instructional design theories and models: An overview of their current status.*

8 Lesson Blueprints Based on the Elaboration Theory of Instruction

Charles M. Reigeluth
Syracuse University

FOREWORD

History

This theory was first developed by Reigeluth and Merrill to extend Merrill's Component Display Theory to the macro level, that is, to provide prescriptions for selecting, sequencing, synthesizing, and summarizing instructional content. Its development was guided by a dissatisfaction with Gagné's hierarchical, parts-to-whole sequence and by the metaphor of the "zoom lens" as an alternative. Careful analysis revealed that the sequences proposed by Ausubel, Bruner, Scandura, Paul Merrill, Don Norman, and others were all consistent with the zoom-lens metaphor. The development of the theory proceeded by analyzing the differences among these sequencing strategies, identifying the situations for which each was most appropriate to use, and extending, modifying, and operationalizing the optimal strategy for each situation. Like the Component Display Theory, this theory is indicative of the highly integrative, multiperspectived approach to prescriptive theory construction that is greatly needed at this point in the development of our knowledge about instruction.

Unique Contributions

Given that the sequencing strategies prescribed by this theory largely preexisted the theory, the major contribution of this theory is probably the integration of the various kinds of elaborative sequencing strategies into an internally consistent set of prescriptions that were all guided by the goal of building stable cognitive

245

structures in a meaningful, subsumptive (Ausubel), or assimilative (Mayer) way. Another contribution is the considerable effort that has gone into operationalizing each of these sequencing strategies so as to provide detailed guidance for instructional designers.

However, one of the three sequencing strategies, the one based on principles (used in this chapter), entailed considerably more creative modification and extension. Another of them, the one based on procedural content, was also modified to a simplifying-assumptions approach from the shortest-path approach.

Furthermore, the Elaboration Theory was perhaps the first to place any emphasis on strategies to synthesize the instructional content, that is, to explicitly teach the interrelationships within the content. Finally, this theory may be the only one that specifically allows for some learner control over the selection and sequencing of the content.

Similarities

As with Merrill's Component Display Theory, the integrative roots of the Elaboration Theory have resulted in many prescriptions being similar to those of other instructional theories. The simplifying-assumptions approach for the procedure-based elaboration sequence is quite similar to (and was derived from) Scandura's shortest-path approach. The general-to-detailed approach for the concept-based elaboration sequence is quite similar to (and was derived from) Ausubel's progressive-differentiation sequence. And the prescription for systematic review is similar to (though more detailed than) the Gagné-Briggs prescription for enhancing retention (Event 9). These and other similarities are identified with Editor's Notes.

Issues to Think About

Are there any other useful kinds of simple-to-complex sequences besides the three prescribed by Elaboration Theory? Are there any other important kinds of relationships to synthesize? Gagné's hierarchical sequence has been integrated into all three of the Elaboration Theory's sequencing strategies, but should Landa's and Scandura's prescriptions for the selection of content also be integrated? If so, how? Finally, given the lack of empirical research support for most of the Elaboration Theory's prescriptions, how much confidence can we have in its validity?

STUDY QUESTIONS

1. What is the difference between summarizing and epitomizing?
2. What is a simple-to-complex sequence based on concepts?
3. What is a simple-to-complex sequence based on procedures?

4. What is a simple-to-complex sequence based on principles?
5. What kinds of synthesizers are prescribed, and how do they differ from each other?
6. What characteristics should a summarizer have?
7. When and how often should summary and synthesis occur?
8. What is the most important basis for deciding how long a lesson should be?

C.M.R.

INTRODUCTION

The purpose of the Reigeluth-Merrill Elaboration Theory of Instruction (Reigeluth, 1979; Reigeluth, Merrill, M. D., Wilson, B. G., & Spiller, R. T., 1978; Reigeluth & Stein, 1983) is to make life easier for instructional designers by integrating current knowledge about what the overall structure and sequence of a course or curriculum should be like. The Elaboration Theory presently prescribes seven major strategy components:

1. An elaborative sequence for the main structure of a course (and curriculum).
2. A variety of prescriptions for sequencing within individual lessons of a course (including a learning-prerequisite sequence).
3. Summarizers.
4. Synthesizers.
5. Analogies.
6. Cognitive strategy activators.
7. A learner-control format.

Elaborative Sequence

The most important prescription of the Elaboration Theory is the use of a special kind of simple-to-complex sequence. There are many possible varieties of simple-to-complex sequences, some of which have better effects on learning than others. Gagné's (1985) learning-prerequisite sequence (see chapter 2 of this book), Bruner's (1960) spiral sequence, Ausubel's (1968) subsumptive sequence, Norman's (1973) web sequence, and the shortest-path sequence (P. F. Merrill, 1980; Scandura, 1973) are all kinds of simple-to-complex sequences. The elaboration approach to sequencing integrates and builds upon all of these sequencing strategies. Both an analysis of the structure of knowledge and an understanding of learning theories and cognitive processes have been used to design the elaborative sequence.

The Elaboration Theory's instructional sequence is much like the following approach to studying a picture through the zoom lens of a camera. A person starts with a wide-angle view, allowing him or her to see the major parts of the picture and the major relationships among the parts, but without any detail. Once the person zooms in on a part of the picture, the person is able to see more about each of the major subparts. After studying those subparts and their interrelationships, the person can then zoom back out to the wide-angle view to review the other parts of the whole picture and to review the context of that one part within the whole picture. Continuing in this "zooming in" pattern, the person gradually progresses to the level of detail and breadth desired.

Similarly, the Elaboration Theory starts the instruction with a special kind of overview containing the simplest and most fundamental ideas, called the "epitome" (because it epitomizes the content). Then, subsequent lessons add complexity or detail to a part or aspect of the overview in layers (called "elaborations"). Each lesson also reviews content and teaches relationships between the most recently presented ideas and those presented earlier. This pattern of elaboration followed by summary and synthesis continues until the desired level of complexity has been reached. The elaborative sequence can allow considerable freedom for the learner to select which part to zoom in on next and how far to zoom in on each one of the major ideas.

The elaborative sequence has two major features: The earlier ideas *epitomize* rather than summarize the ideas that follow; and the sequence is based on a *single* content orientation (Reigeluth & Stein, 1983). To epitomize is to present a few of the most fundamental and representative ideas at a concrete, application (or skill) level (Reigeluth, 1979). Then subsequent lessons add complexity or detail to one part or aspect of the overview in layers (elaborations).* The nature of the elaborations will differ depending on the content orientation: whether the instruction should focus primarily on "what" (concepts), "how" (procedures), or "why" (principles). Careful analysis has shown that virtually every course holds one of these three to be more important than the other two. Hence, the Elaboration Theory proposes that the nature of the simple-to-complex sequence must differ depending on the kind of content that is considered to be most important to the goals of the instruction.

In carefully reviewing the sequencing strategies of Bruner, Ausubel, P. F. Merrill, and others, Reigeluth and M. D. Merrill found that each of these strategies used a simple-to-complex sequence. However, each of those sequences

---

*This kind of macro-level sequencing is very different from the few theories in this book that address macro-level sequencing at all, with the exception that Scandura's sequence based on the complexity of paths through a rule (p. 164) is very similar to one of the three kinds of elaboration sequences described later in this Introduction.

was elaborating on a different dimension. That is, Bruner used *principles,* while P. F. Merrill utilized *procedures,* and *concepts* were the primary target of Ausubel's sequence. In all the work that has been done on sequencing, elaborations based on concepts, principles, and procedures are the only three we have found, although additional ones may be identified in the future. This finding is consistent with M. D. Merrill's (Merrill & Wood, 1974; Merrill, 1983) identification of just three content types for generalizable knowledge. Therefore, the Elaboration Theory proposed three different ways of elaborating, based on those three content types:

Conceptual Elaboration.   If the goals of a course are primarily conceptual in nature, as is usually the case in an introductory biology course, then the elaborative sequence should follow the process of meaningful assimilation of *concepts* to memory (Ausubel, 1968; Mayer, 1977). First, according to Elaboration Theory (Reigeluth & Darwazeh, 1982), you analyze and organize the concepts into conceptual structures, which show their superordinate, coordinate, and subordinate relationships. Then you design the instructional sequence by selecting the most important, comprehensive, and fundamental conceptual structure and sequencing its concepts from the top down (i.e., from the most general and inclusive concepts to progressively more detailed and less inclusive concepts.* Finally, other concepts and other types of content, including learning prerequisites (Gagné, 1968), must be "fleshed" onto that "skeleton" of a sequence at the point where each is most relevant. Details of this sequencing strategy are described by Reigeluth and Darwazeh (1982). The result is a "blueprint" for the course similar to that shown in Fig. 8.1.

Procedural Elaboration.   On the other hand, the goals of your course might be primarily procedural (addressing the "how"), as in an English composition course. In this case, the elaboration sequence should follow the optimal process of *procedural* skill acquisition. Your first activity as a designer is to identify the simplest possible version of the task (usually equivalent to the shortest "path" through the procedure in P. F. Merrill's 1980 path analysis methodology)† and to identify the "simplifying assumptions" that define that simplest version. Your next task is to design the instructional sequence by gradually relaxing the simplifying assumptions in the order of most important, comprehensive, and fundamental ones first, such that progressively more complex paths are taught. Then

---

*Although this sequence goes from the top down in a "conceptual structure," whereas Gagné's hierarchical sequence goes from the bottom up in a learning hierarchy (which on the surface looks much like a conceptual structure), both sequences go from simple to complex, and the elaboration sequence is consistent with (i.e., does not in any way violate the principles of) the hierarchical sequence.

†This is similar to Scandura's sequence that starts the instruction with the simplest path through a rule and proceeds to teach progressively more complex paths one at a time (p. 164).

250

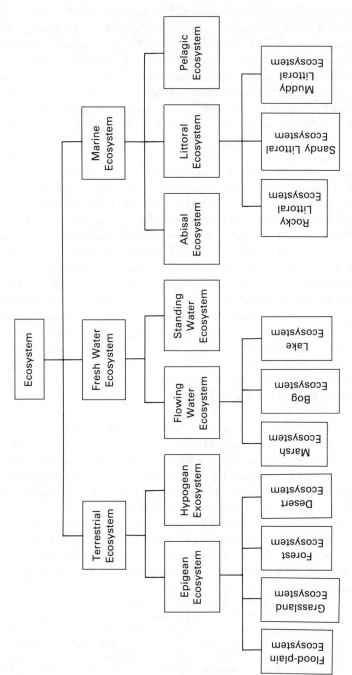

FIGURE 8.1a   A kinds-conceptual structure for a conceptual blueprint.

the other types of content, including concepts, principles, learning prerequisites, and remember-level information, are "plugged into" that sequence at the point where each is most relevant. Details of this sequencing strategy are described by Reigeluth and Rodgers (1980). The result is a "blueprint" for the course similar to that shown in Fig. 8.2.

Theoretical Elaboration. The final possibility is that the goals of your course are primarily theoretical (addressing the "why"), as in an introductory economics course. In this case, the elaboration sequence follows the psychological process of developing an understanding of natural processes (primarily causes and effects), which is usually similar to the order of the historical discovery of such knowledge. After identifying the breadth and depth of principles that should be taught, you design the instructional sequence by asking the question, "What principle(s) would you teach if you had the learners for only one hour?" and ". . . one more hour?" and so on. This process continues until all the principles have been arranged in a sequence that progresses from the most basic and observable principles to the most detailed, complex, and restricted principles (see Comments 1, 2, 4–9, 11, 12, and 15). During this process, it is often helpful to look at an earlier principle and ask "Why?" "Which way?" "How much?" or "What else?" to identify more complex principles that elaborate on the earlier one (see Comments 16, 17, and 19). Other types of content are then plugged into that sequence at the point where each is most relevant (see Comments 20 and 23). The result is a "blueprint" for the course similar to that shown in the next section of this chapter.

Within-Lesson Sequence

Next, you need to design a sequence for all content *within* each lesson (see Comment 24). The Elaboration Theory offers several guidelines here:

1. For a conceptual organization present the easiest, most familiar organizing concepts first, for a procedural organization present the steps in the order of their performance,* and for a theoretical organization present the simplest organizing content first (see Comments 3, 10, 13, and 28).
2. Usually put supporting content immediately after the organizing content to which it is most closely related (see Comments 27 and 30).
3. Put each learning prerequisite immediately before the content for which it is prerequisite (see Comments 26, 29, and 32).†

---

*This is a "forward-chaining" sequence, and Landa's "snowball principle" is also a forward-chaining sequence (p. 122).

†This is Gagné's notion of learning prerequisite (p. 22), which is also prescribed by Gropper (p. 58). However, here it is used on a much narrower scale of sequencing—within approximately a one-hour unit of instruction.

Lesson	Level	Elaborates on lesson	Conceptual Organizing Content	Supporting Content				
				Conceptual	Theoretical	Procedural	Learning Prerequisites	Verbal Information
1	Epitome	—	Ecosystem	Abiotic environment Biotic component Food chain Producer Consumer	Population is controlled by food supply and predators The biotic component is dependent upon the abiotic environment	How to identify food chains in an ecosystem	System Environment Predator	Approximate ratio of prey to its predators
2	1	1	Terrestrial ecosystem Fresh water ecosystem Marine ecosystem	Adaptation —physical —behavioral Community	Adaptations help the animal to survive in its ecosystem. Water cycle O_2-CO_2 cycle Material cycle	How to create a composte heap	Terrestrial Marine Evaporation Condensation Water vapor Decomposer	The most common adaptations for each of the three kinds of ecosystems
3	2	2	Epigean (above-ground) ecosystem Hypogean (subterranean) ecosystem	Soil components Kinds of organisms that live in these kinds of ecosystems Kinds of soil	Adaptations and how they help survival in each ecosystem	How to observe life in hypogean ecosystems	Subterranean	The most common hypogean food chains The most common adaptations for hypogean

4	2	2	Standing-water ecosystem Flowing-water ecosystem	:	:	:	:	:
5	2	2	Littoral ecosystem Pelagic ecosystem Abysal ecosystem	:	:	:	:	:
6	3	3	Flood-plain ecosystem Grassland ecosystem Forest ecosystem Desert ecosystem	Kinds of climate Kinds of animals that live in these kinds of ecosystems	Seasonal changes Effects of people on each of these ecosystems	How to help preserve each of these kinds of ecosystems	Pollution Conservation Extinction Endangered	The most common food chains for each of these kinds of ecosystems The most common adaptations for each
7	3	4	Marsh ecosystem Bog ecosystem Lake ecosystem	:	:	:	:	:
8	3	5	Rocky littoral ecosystem Sandy littoral ecosystem Muddy littoral ecosystem	:	:	:	:	:
:								

FIG. 8.1b Part of a conceptual blueprint.

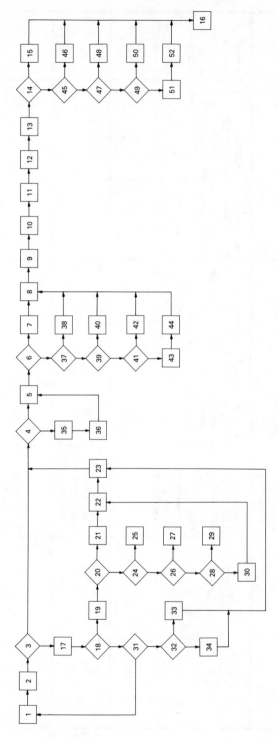

FIG. 8.2a. Flowchart for the procedural blueprint.

Lesson	Level	Elab's on	Organizing Content	Simplifying Conditions
1	Epitome	--	1 Identify "given" substance. 2 Identify "to find" substance. 5 Identify units of "given" substance. 7 Use 1 mole per atomic formula unit or molecular mass as conversion factor. 8 Convert to moles of "given" substance. 9 Identify coefficient of "given" substance. 10 Identify coefficient of "to find" substance. 11 Set up mole ratio. 12 Find moles of "to find" substance. 13 Identify "to find" required units. 15 Use atomic, molecular, or formula unit mass per 1 mole as conversion factor. 16 Check the solution.	A A chemical equation is given (cuts steps 3, 17-34). B The equation is balanced (cuts steps 4, 35-36). C "Given" unit is grams (cuts steps 6, 37-44). D "To find" unit is grams (cuts steps 14, 45-52).
2	1	Lesson 1	3 Decide if a chemical equation is given. 17 Identify reactants and products. 19 Identify type of chemical compound based on composition 21 Classify compound as binary molecular. 22 Use rules of chemical nomenclature to write the chemical formula for each reactant. 23 Place reactants on left side and products on right side of yield symbol in chemical equation.	Relax condition A (adds steps 3, 17-34). E Names of reactants and products are given (cuts steps 18, 31-34). F Compound is composed of 2 nonmetals (cuts steps 20, 24-30).
3	1	Lesson 1	4 Decide if the equation is balanced. 35 Determine number of each element on both sides of equation. 36 Assign stoichiometric coefficients to each reactant and product to make each element on reactant side equal to each element on product side.	Relax condition B (adds steps 4, 35-36).

FIG. 8.2b.   Part of a procedural blueprint. None of the supporting content is shown.

4	1	Lesson 1	6 Decide if "given" unit is grams. 38 Use 1 mole per 6.02 x 10 atoms, molecules, or formula units as converstion factor. 14 Decide if "to find" unit is grams. 46 (Same as step 38)	Relax conditions C & D (or H, I and/or J, depending on lessons taught). G Unit is a no. of atoms, molecules, or formula units.
5	2	Lesson 2	18 Decide if names of reactants and products are given. 31 Decide if analytical data are given for reactants and products. 32 Decide if molecular weight is given. 33 Find empirical formula. 34 Find molecular formula.	Relax condition E (adds steps 18, 31-34).
6	2	Lesson 2	20, 24, 25, 26, 27, 28, 29, 30.	Relax condition F (adds steps 20, 24-30
7	1	Lesson 1	37, 40, 45, 48	Relax conditions C & D (or G, I, and/or J, depending on lessons taught). H Unit is volume of solution.
8	1	Lesson 1	39, 42, 47, 50	Relax conditions C & D (or G, H, and/or J, depending on lessons taught). I Unit is volume of a gas at STP
9	1	Lesson 1	41, 43, 44, 49, 51, 52	Relax conditions C & D (or G, H, and/or I, depending on lessons taught). J Unit is volume of a gas not at STP.

FIG. 8.2b. (Continued)

4. Group coordinate concepts together (see Comment 31).

5. Teach a principle (meaningful understanding of processes) before a related procedure (see the Lesson Outline on page 270).

Other macrostrategy components are integrated into the lesson sequence, such as summarizers, synthesizers, analogies, cognitive-strategy activators, macrolevel motivational components, and macrolevel learner-control options (see Reigeluth & Stein, 1983).

Summarizers

A summarizer is a strategy component used to systematically review what has been learned (Reigeluth & Stein, 1983). It provides (a) a concise statement of each idea or fact that has been taught; (b) a typical, easy-to-remember example; and (c) some diagnostic, self-test practice items for each idea. *Lesson* (internal) summarizers usually appear at the end of each lesson (see Comments 33 and 35–42), whereas "set" (unit) summarizers summarize all of the ideas and facts that have been taught so far in an entire set of lessons (see Comment 43). A "set" of lessons (or unit) is all those lessons that elaborate directly on a single lesson.*

Synthesizers

A synthesizer is used to interrelate and integrate ideas. It is intended to (a) provide the learner with a valuable kind of knowledge; (b) facilitate a deeper understanding of the individual ideas; (c) increase the meaningfulness and motivational appeal of the instruction (Ausubel, 1968; Keller, 1983); and (d) increase retention. The Elaboration Theory presently prescribes three types of synthesizers, each of which interrelates ideas of a single content type (Reigeluth & Stein, 1983): conceptual (see Comment 33), procedural (see Comment 40), and theoretical (see Comment 38). As with summarizers, these may be *lesson* (for a single lesson) or *set* (for a whole unit) synthesizers. Furthermore, it is possible to provide contextual synthesis at the beginning of a lesson (see Comment 25) or post synthesis at the end of a lesson or unit (see Comment 35).†

Analogies

An analogy takes new information and relates it to a more familiar and hence more meaningful context of organized knowledge that the learner already possesses (Ortony, 1979; Verbrugge & McCarrell, 1977). It reminds the learner of

---

*Gagné-Briggs's theory is the only other one in this book that explicitly prescribes review as an instructional strategy (p. 21).

†Synthesis appears in several forms in several other theories in this book (e.g., Landa's "snowball principle," p. 122).

something more concrete within the learner's experience in order to prepare him or her for understanding a more abstract, complex type of idea (Curtis & Reigeluth, 1984; Reigeluth, 1983).*

Cognitive-Strategy Activators

A cognitive-strategy activator, which activates the learner's use of a "generic skill," can be used for any content area. It may be *embedded* into the instruction, as is the case when a mnemonic or analogy is presented, or it may be *detached,* as is the case when the learner is only provided with the directions to use a previously learned cognitive strategy (Rigney, 1978), such as "think up an analogy" or "try to come up with a mnemonic."†

Learner Control

Learner control may offer the learner options for the selection and sequencing of his or her content and instructional strategies, and thereby control over how he or she will study and learn (M. D. Merrill, 1983, 1984; Reigeluth & Stein, 1983). Learner control of *content* offers selection of any lesson for which the learner has already acquired the prerequisites (see Comment 22), whereas learner control of *instructional strategies* offers selection of the type, order, and number of such microstrategy components as examples, practice items, and alternative representations (see Chapter 7), and type and timing of such macrostrategy components as summarizers, synthesizers, and analogies (see Comment 35).‡

In summary, the Elaboration Theory prescribes the following strategy components:

1. An elaborative sequence of lessons (either conceptual, procedural, or theoretical).
2. A within-lesson sequence for each lesson, including any necessary learning-prerequisite sequences.
3. A summarizer for each lesson.
4. A synthesizer for each lesson.
5. Analogies as needed.
6. Cognitive-strategy activators as needed.
7. Learner control to the extent appropriate.

---

*Analogies are also prescribed by Keller (see companion volume) as a motivational strategy component.

†This kind of prescription is overlooked by most other theories.

‡This is the same as Merrill's "learner control" (p. 209), except that it applies to control over macro-level strategy components whereas Merrill's applies to control over micro-level strategy components.

LESSON PREFACE

The Elaboration Theory of Instruction provides prescriptions for structuring and sequencing courses or even a whole curricula, but it provides no guidance for teaching those bits of knowledge and individual skills that comprise the course or curriculum. The latter guidance must be sought from a theory that deals with prescriptions such as those proposed by Merrill or Collins and Stevens. Such theories are completely compatible with and complementary to this theory.

Because the Elaboration Theory provides no guidance as to how to teach each individual skill or piece of knowledge, it is not beneficial to present a completed lesson to illustrate the theory. Rather, the following pages present *outlines* of several related lessons in a curriculum. The outlines illustrate for a specific set of subject matter most of the Elaboration Theory's prescriptions without the distracting lesson details that are beyond the scope of the Elaboration Theory.

The lesson outlines in this chapter include only those parts of a science curriculum that are in some way related to the six objectives used throughout this book:

1. Students will be able to classify previously unencountered lenses as to whether or not they are convex lenses.
2. Students will be able to define focal length.
3. Students will be able to explain or predict what effect different convex lenses will have on light rays.
4. Students will be able to explain the way in which the curvature of a lens influences both the magnification and the focal length of different lenses.
5. Students will be able to state from memory the three significant events in the history of the microscope.
6. Students will be able to use a previously unencountered optical microscope properly.

Step 1

The first decision that was made in creating the outlines for the instruction was to decide whether the simple-to-complex sequence should be based on conceptual knowledge (*what* are the important classes of things), procedural knowledge (*how* does a person accomplish certain things), or theoretical knowledge (*why* do certain processes occur). Given that the objectives emphasize an understanding of the behavior of light (a dynamic natural process) more than classes of things (concepts) or means to achieve ends (procedures), a theoretical organization was selected.

Simple-to-complex sequencing occurs on a number of different levels. We have found it useful to think in terms of the following levels:

ELEMENTS SEQUENCED	APPROXIMATE INSTRUCTIONAL TIME	APPROXIMATE SCHOOL TIME
Individual ideas within a lesson	1 hour	1 day
Lessons within a unit	5 hours	1–2 weeks
Units within a module	25 hours	1–2 months
Modules within a course	150 hours	1 year
Courses within a curriculum	varies	varies

It seemed that theoretical knowledge (natural processes) was the most important kind at all of these levels.

However, it is quite common for different types of content to be used as the basis for the simple-to-complex sequencing at different levels. For example, a biology course could be comprised of modules that are sequenced based on *concepts*, such as an introductory module on "life," followed by modules on "plant life" and "animal life," followed by "mammals," "reptiles," "birds," and so on. Each such module could then be comprised of units that are sequenced based on *principles* that relate to that concept, such as the effects of climate, habitat, predators, etc. on the evolution of its physical characteristics, social behavior, diet, etc. Then each such unit could be comprised of lessons that are sequenced based on *procedures* or rules that relate to that principle, such as steps that the animal follows in mating, hunting, nesting, or even steps that the student follows in dissecting, and so forth.

Step 2

Given that a theoretical organization was chosen, the next task was to select and sequence all the theoretical content that should be taught in the curriculum. After "brainstorming" to list all the principles (usually statements of causes or effects), we needed to arrange them into a simple-to-complex sequence. We started by listing the most obvious ones (in this case, the principles specified by the objectives) and then began to "epitomize"; that is, to look for the simplest principle or principles that are among the most basic, observable, and representative of the whole set of principles for the curriculum. Several useful heuristics for doing this include: (a) ask a subject-matter expert (SME) what principle he or she would teach if it was possible to teach only one; and (b) ask an SME to identify what principles were discovered earlier. These techniques result in the identification of progressively simpler principles—principles in which fewer things happen but the things that do happen are the "essence" (i.e., the most important and observable aspects) of the larger set of principles.

Using these techniques, we found three major ways of simplifying an understanding of what happens to light when it passes through a convex lens.

1. Type of lens.

The first dimension for simplifying is related to the convex lens. The behavior of light as it passes through a *concave lens* (as opposed to a convex one) is simpler, because there is no focal point and hence there is no effect of the image being inverted beyond the focal point while being normal before the focal point. The behavior of light as it passes through a *prism* is simpler still, because there are no curved surfaces and hence all light rays of the same frequency remain parallel after passing through it. The behavior of light as it passes through *plane glass* is even less complex, because both surfaces are parallel and hence all rays end up going in the same direction as before they passed through the glass. And finally, the behavior of light as it merely passes from *one medium into another* (as opposed to going both into and out of a medium) is still less complex, because there is only one surface instead of two and hence only one change in the direction of the light rays instead of two.

2. Reflection.

A second dimension for simplifying what happens to light is that what happens when it is *reflected* is simpler than what happens when it is refracted. When it is refracted, light changes velocity and direction, whereas when it is reflected, it just changes direction. Also, the change in direction is precise and intuitive: the angle of reflection equals the angle of incidence; whereas when it is refracted, the change in direction depends on several factors, including the density of the medium and the sharpness of the angle of incidence.

3. Waves/Particles.

A third dimension for simplifying is that light behaves like *waves* in some ways and like *particles* in others. Hence, understanding the behavior of waves alone or of particles alone is simpler, and understanding the behavior of particles alone is the simplest, because waves have such behaviors as interference, which are related to their wavelength and amplitude, while particles do not.

Step 3

After we simplified to the level of student entering knowledge, we needed to make sure that we had gone far enough in the opposite direction: that we had identified all of the more complex principles that the students should learn in the course or curriculum. Several useful heuristics for identifying more complex principles include: (a) asking "What else happens?"; and (b) asking such questions as "Why?" "Which way?" and "How much?" Each of these is illustrated in the lesson outlines and commented upon below.

Remaining Steps

Finally, we allocated supporting content to each elaboration, completing the selection of all content; we allocated all content to individual lessons; and we sequenced the content within each lesson.

As a final comment, it should be known that, in violation of Elaboration Theory procedures, we did not have a subject-matter expert (SME) to work with in the design of this blueprint. Had an SME been available, the same Elaboration Theory prescriptions that we used here would have resulted in a better product and one with which science education experts would find fewer shortcomings and points of disagreement. Although this blueprint is not one that we would want to implement without further consultation and revision, it does nevertheless, in its present form, still serve as a good illustration of the prescriptions of the Elaboration Theory.

LESSON: COURSE OUTLINES

[1]
Module 1: General Science
(Approx. Sixth Grade[1])

Unit 1: Earth Science

. . .

Unit 2: Biology

. . .

Unit 3: Chemistry

. . .

Unit 4: Physics

[2]   *Lesson 1: How Particles Behave*

Use balls on a flat table to teach the following (expository or discovery approach may be used):

[3]   a. *Linear Movement.* They move in a straight line, unless acted upon by something.
b. *Reflection.* They bounce off a surface.

---

[1]The grade levels are completely arbitrary (they could have been eighth, ninth, and tenth), and so in fact are the divisions (modules, units, lessons). The specific pattern shown here was selected becaue it seemed viable for interspersing this content with the rest of a typical high school curriculum. But a course tailored for an interested adult might enable him or her to study these three courses in order during a single year.

[2]It is doubtful that any of the basic sciences (Earth Science, Biology, Chemistry, Physics) can be viewed as a more complex iteration of any other basic science; any relationships among them are insufficient to warrant arranging them in an elaborative sequence. Hence, their order is arbitrary with respect to Elaboration Theory criteria.

c. Something like *Refraction.* They change direction and speed when the inclination of the surface is changed.

d. *Absorption.* They stop (lose their energy) when they collide into styrofoam.

[4]   *Lesson 2: How Waves Behave*

Waves in a water tank:

a. *Rectilinear Movement.* They move in a straight line perpendicular to the wave, unless acted upon by something.

b. *Reflection.* They bounce off a surface.

c. Similar to *Refraction.* They change direction and speed when the density of the fluid changes and when the depth of the fluid changes.

d. *Interference.* When two waves cross, the trough of one cancels out the crest of the other, and the troughs and crests of one magnify the troughs and crests, respectively, of the other.

e. *Transmission.* They require a medium in which to move.

f. *Absorption.* They stop (lose their energy) when they collide into a "soft" or steeply inclined surface.

[5]   *Lesson 3: How Light Behaves*

A pencil of light:
   (the simplest case of each of the following behaviors is taught in such a way that students can predict what light will do in those cases).

a. *Linear Movement.* Light moves in a straight line unless acted upon by something. (Demonstration of a pencil of light).

b. *Reflection.* Light bounces off things. (Demonstration of a pencil of light on a plane mirror.)

[6]   c. *Refraction.* Light bends as it passes from one medium to another. "When light goes from one medium to another, it bends." (Demonstration of a stick or pencil of light in water.)

d. *Diffraction.* When light bends, some of its parts bend more than others, causing those parts to separate from each other. (Demonstration of a pencil of light through a prism onto a surface.)

[7]   e. *Interference.* When two light waves cross, the trough of one cancels out the crest of the other, and the troughs and crests of one magnify the toughs and crests, respectively, of the other. (Demonstration of light through two slits onto a surface that is moved away from the slit.)

f. *Transmission.* Light requires no medium in which to move.

g. *Absorption.* Light stops (loses its energy) when it strikes a black surface.

Unit 1: Particles

. . .

Unit 2: Waves

. . .

[8]   Unit 3: Light

Lesson 1: Linear Movement and Transmission

    . . .

Lesson 2: Reflection

a. Effects of a plane mirror on light and image
[9]   • image is reversed (L ⟨-⟩ R)
        • rays bounce but remain parallel to each other
b. Effects of a convex mirror on light and image
        • no image
        • rays disperse
[10] c. Effects of a concave mirror on light and image
        • smaller image before 2FL (Focal Length), enlarged image after 2FL
        • normal image before FL, inverted image after FL
        • rays converge to a point, then disperse

[11]   *Lesson 3: Refraction*

[12] a. Effects when light passes from one medium into another
        • apparent position and size of image usually change
        • rays bend but remain parallel to each other
b. Effects when light passes from one medium into and out of another
[13]   • plane glass
            image remains the same
            rays continue in same direction and parallel to each other
        • prism
            image remains the same
            apparent location of the image is different
            rays go off in a different direction but are basically parallel to each
            other
            white light is broken into colors (diffraction)
        • concave lens
            no image
            rays disperse
        • convex lens
[14]   an image is formed at a plane beyond FL

264

smaller image if before 2FL, enlarged image if after 2FL
normal image if before FL, inverted image if after FL
parallel rays converge at a Focal Point (FP), then disperse
rays from the same point on the object converge at a point beyond the FP, then disperse

Lesson 4: Diffraction

Lesson 5: Interference

Lesson 6: Absorption

[15]   **Module 17: Light (Approx. Twelfth Grade)**

Unit 1: Rectilinear Propagation and Transmission
. . .
Unit 2: Reflection
. . .
Unit 3: Refraction

[16]   *Lesson 1: Into a Medium*

What else happens?

[17]
a. A portion of each ray is reflected off the surface, while the rest is
   refracted into the new medium.
b. The sharper the angle between the ray and the surface, the more of
   each ray that is reflected and the less that is refracted.
c. When the angle is equal to or sharper than the critical angle, all of the
   ray is reflected.

Why, which way, and how much do light rays bend at the interface?

d. The higher the optical density, the lower the speed of the light.

[18]
e. If they pass into a denser medium, the light rays bend toward the
   normal.
f. The greater the difference in optical density between two media, the
   more the light rays bend.

g. Index of refraction (n) $= \dfrac{c_i}{c_r} = \dfrac{\sin i}{\sin r}$

h. Relationship between critical angle and index of refraction: $\sin i_c = \dfrac{1}{n}$

Why and which way does the apparent size of the object change?

    i. When the rays be. d, they change their distance from each other.

    j. When the rays bend toward the normal, they become farther apart.

Why does the change in the apparent size of the object differ with the angle of the surface?

    k. The more slanted the surface, the more the light rays bend from their initial direction.

[19]   *Lesson 2: Into and Out of Plane Glass*

Principles a–k in Lesson 1 remain of importance, but we can also add:

Why do rays continue in the same direction and remain basically parallel?

    a. (Lesson 1e) If they pass into a denser medium, the light rays bend toward the normal.

    b. If they pass into a less dense medium, the light rays bend away from the normal.

    c. On entering glass, rays bend toward the normal by a certain amount, and on leaving the glass they bend away from the normal by the same amount.

    d. Since the entering and exiting surfaces are parallel, the normals are parallel, and hence the rays are returned to their original direction.

[19]   *Lesson 3: Into and Out of a Prism*

Principles a–k in Lesson 1 remain of importance, but we can also add:

Why do rays change direction but remain basically parallel?

    a. (Lesson 2a) If they pass into a denser medium, the light rays bend toward the normal.

    b. (Lesson 2b) If they pass into a less dense medium, the light rays bend away from the normal.

    c. (Lesson 2c) On entering glass, rays bend toward the normal by a certain amount, and on leaving the glass they bend away from the normal by the same amount.

    d. Since the entering and exiting surfaces are not parallel, the normals are not parallel, and hence the rays are not returned to their original direction.

[19]   *Lesson 4: Into and Out of a Concave Lens*

Principles a–k in Lesson 1 remain of importance, but we can also add:

Why and which way do rays disperse (diverge)?

a. (Lesson 3a) If they pass into a denser medium, the light rays bend toward the normal.

b. (Lesson 3b) If they pass into a less dense medium, the light rays bend away from the normal.

c. (Lesson 3c) On entering glass, rays bend toward the normal by a certain amount, and on leaving the glass they bend away from the normal by the same amount.

d. (Lesson 3d) Since the entering and exiting surfaces are not parallel, the normals are not parallel, and hence the ray is not returned to its original direction.

e. Since the difference in angle between the two normals increases with distance from the center of the lens, the amount that rays change their direction increases with distance from the center of the lens.

f. The more curved the lens, the more sharply the rays disperse.

[19] *Lesson 5: Into and Out of a Convex Lens*

Principles a–k in Lesson 1 remain of importance, but we can also add:

Why, which way, and how much do rays converge to a point, cross, and then disperse?

a. (Lesson 4a) If they pass into a denser medium, the light rays bend toward the normal.

b. (Lesson 4b) If they pass into a less dense medium, the light rays bend away from the normal.

c. (Lesson 4c) On entering glass, rays bend toward the normal by a certain amount, and on leaving the glass they bend away from the normal by the same amount.

d. (Lesson 4d) Since the entering and exiting surfaces are not parallel, the normals are not parallel, and hence the ray is not returned to its original direction.

e. (Lesson 4e) Since the difference in angle between the two normals increases with distance from the center of the lens, the amount that rays change their direction increases with distance from the center of the lens.

f. The more curved the lens, the more sharply the rays converge. The image will therefore be larger as long as it is beyond the focal length. Also, the focal length will be shorter.

g. Relationship between object size and distance and image size and distance: $s_o/s_i = d_o/d_i$.

h. Relationship between object distance, image distance, and focal length:

$$\frac{1}{d_o} + \frac{1}{d_i} = \frac{1}{F}.$$

Course Unit Lesson	Elab's on	Organizing Content*	Simplifying/ Elaborating Conditions	Supporting Content			
				Concepts	Procedures	Learning Prerequisites**	Information
1 4 1 **[21]**	—	Linear Movement Reflection (Refraction) Absorption	Particles	...	...	...	...
1 4 2 **[22]**	1 4 1	Rectilinear Movement Reflection (Refraction) Interference Transmission Absorption	Waves	...	...	...	...
1 4 3	1 4 1 1 4 2	Linear Movement Reflection Refraction Diffraction Interference Transmission Absorption	Light Plane surface Reflection & re-fraction	...	...	...	...
5 1 1 ...	1 4 1	...	...	...	...	...	...
5 2 1 ...	1 4 2	...	...	...	...	...	...
5 3 1	1 4 3	...	...	...	...	...	...
5 3 2	1 4 3	Effects of -plane mirror -convex mirror -concave mirror	Light Reflection All surface types	...	...	...	...
5 3 3	1 4 3 5 3 2	Effects of -1 plane surface -plane glass	Light Refraction All surface types	Kinds of optical instruments (telescope, mi-	How to use a microscope. 6 How to use a telescope.	Apparent location Apparent size Apparent position	Object Medium Common uses of prisms

Objective #	Prerequisites	-prism -concave lens convex lens 3	croscope, binoculars, camera lens, etc.). Critical angle Kinds of concave lenses. Kinds of convex lenses.		Plane glass Prism Concave lens Convex lens 1 Image Eye piece Coarse adjustment knob Fine adjustment knob	Common uses of concave lens and convex lens Focal length 2 Focal point History of lenses and optical instruments 5 How lenses are made
5 3 4	1 4 3 / 5 3 3	...	...	...	...	...
5 3 5	1 4 3 / 5 3 4	...	...	...	...	...
5 3 6	1 4 3	...	...	...	...	...
17 1 1 / ...	5 3 1	...	...	...	...	...
17 2 1 / ...	5 3 2	...	...	...	...	...
17 3 1	5 3 3	(See listing in outline)	Light Refraction How much? What else? Why? Which way? 1 plane surface		...	...
17 3 2	5 3 3	(See listing)	Same except: -plane glass		...	...
...	...		...	...	...	...

*See lesson outline for details   # indicates objective # specified for this book.   **Only unmastered prerequisites are listed. Objective 4 is taught in Lesson 3.3.5 (f).

FIG. 8.3. A partial curriculum blueprint showing the simple-to-complex sequence of principles, along with supporting content for one lesson in the curriculum.

COURSE BLUEPRINTS

[20] The Course Outlines just presented show only the organizing content (principles) and sequence. Clearly, other kinds of content are also important, and they are shown together with the organizing content in Course Blueprints (see Fig. 8.3). Because these blueprints were developed for illustrative purposes only and without the help of a subject-matter expert, the supporting content is included for only one of the lessons. It would ordinarily be included for all lessons.

[21]

[24]   LESSON OUTLINE

Within-Lesson Sequence for:

Module 5: Physics
Unit 3: Light
Lesson 3: Refraction

[25] *Initial synthesizer:* context and demos of most important causes and effects.
Context: State that refraction is but one aspect of the behavior of light. Very briefly review each of the behaviors: linear movement and transmission, reflection, refraction, diffraction, interference, and absorption. State that this lesson will explore just refraction.
Demonstrations: What happens to an object when seen

- from a different medium?
- through plane glass?
- through a prism?
- through a concave lens?
- through a convex lens?

[26]   1a. Teach prerequisite concepts (for 1b) at remember level: object, medium, apparent location, apparent size, apparent position.
   b. Teach principle at application (skill) level: When an object in one *medium* is seen from another, its apparent location and size change, but its apparent position remains unchanged. The greater the angle of the surface, the more the object's apparent size changes.

[27]   c. Teach supporting concept at application (skill) level: critical angle.
   d. Teach principle at application level: When light passes from one *me-*
[28]   *dium* into another, its rays bend at the surface but remain parallel to each other.
   2a. Prerequisite concept (for 2b and 2c) at application level: plane glass.
   b. Principle at application level: When an object is seen through *plane*

270

glass, its apparent location, apparent size, and apparent position remain unchanged.

   c. Principle at application level: When light passes into and out of *plane glass,* its rays continue in the same direction and remain parallel to each other.

[29]   3a. Prerequisite concept (for 3b and 3c) at application level: prism.

   b. Principle at application level: When an object is seen through a *prism,* its apparent location changes, but its apparent size and apparent position remain unchanged. Some colored outlines may appear.

   c. Principle at application level: When light passes into and out of a *prism,* its rays change direction but remain basically parallel to each other. Also, while light is broken into colors.

[30]   d. Supporting information (remember level): Common uses of prisms.

[31]   4a. Prerequisite concepts (for 4b, 4c, 5b, and 5c) at application level: Concave lens, convex lens, image.

   b. Principle at application level: When an object is seen through a *concave lens,* it has no clear image.

   c. Principle at application level: When light passes into and out of a *concave lens,* its rays disperse (spread out).

   d. Supporting information (at remember level): Common uses of concave and convex lenses.

[32]   e. Supporting concepts at application level: Kinds of concave lenses (plano, concavo, convexo), kinds of convex lenses (plano, concavo, convexo). Present a conceptual synthesizer-summarizer after teaching all of these concepts (see Fig. 8.4 for an example).

   5a. Prerequisite concepts (for 5b and 5c) at remember level: focal length (FL), focal point (FP).

   b. Principle at application level: When an object is seen through a *convex lens,* its image
     • is formed at a plane beyond FP
     • is smaller than the object when it is formed closer than 2 FL.
     • is the same size as the object when it is formed at 2 FL.
     • is larger than the object when it is formed farther than 2 FL.
     • is normal when it is formed closer than FP.
     • is inverted when it is formed farther than FP.

[34]   c. Principles at application level: When parallel light rays pass into and out of a *convex lens,* they converge to a point at FP, where they cross and then disperse. When rays from the same point on the object pass through a *convex lens,* they converge to a point beyond the focal point and then cross and disperse.

   d. Supporting concepts at application level: Kinds of instruments that use convex lenses (microscope, telescope, binoculars, cameras, etc.)

How to read this chart: Each box contains a concept that is a _kind_ of what's directly above it.

Example: Concave lens is one of two kinds of lens.
What is the other kind of lens?
What are the three kinds of concave lenses?

[33]

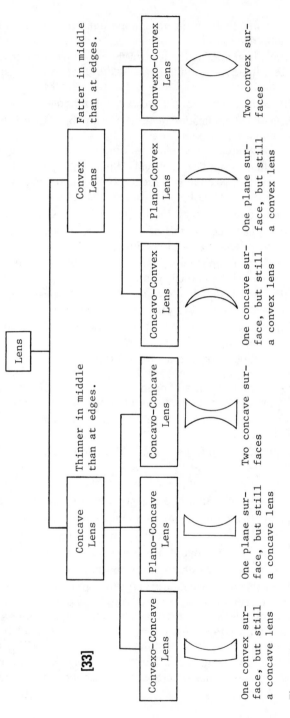

The correct answers to the above questions are on p. 73.

FIG. 8.4. A combination summarizer—synthesizer for related concepts.

   e. Prerequisite concepts (for 5f) at remember level: Eyepiece, coarse adjustment knob, fine adjustment knob.

   f. Supporting procedures at application level: How to use a microscope properly, how to use a telescope properly.

   g. Supporting information at remember level: Significant events in the history of lenses and optical instruments.

   h. Supporting information at remember level: How lenses are made.

Summarize, including theoretical synthesizer. (This part of the lesson is further illustrated next.)

**LESSON SUMMARIZER AND SYNTHESIZER
FOR LESSON 5.3.3**

[35]

Review

Terms to Remember

The following are the concepts you should remember:
(Prototypical illustrations of the concepts would appear as in Fig. 8.5.)

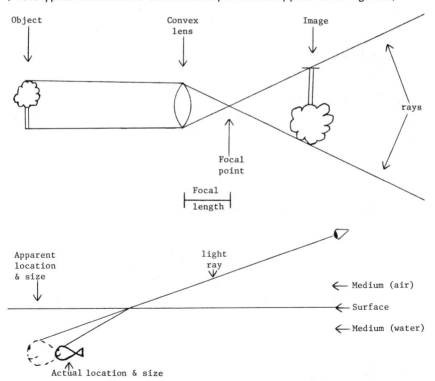

FIG. 8.5

Directions:

1. Cover the right side of this page with a piece of paper.
2. Try to state the definition of the first term.
3. Move the paper down just enough to see if your definition was right.
4. Do the same for each remaining term.

[37]

1. Object	something which is viewed or projected.
2. Medium	a substance through which light can pass.
3. Apparent location	where the object appears to be.
.	
.	
.	
6. Critical angle	all of the light is reflected.
.	
.	
.	
13. Convex lens	fatter in middle.
.	
.	
.	
17. Convexo-concave lens	one convex surface but still thinner in middle.

Principles to Remember

(Prototypical illustrations of the five sets of principles would be placed here. For example:)

1. . . .
.
.
.

5. Effects of a *convex lens.*

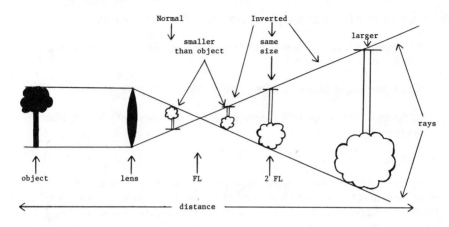

FIG. 8.6

Self-test

Directions:

1. Cover the two right-hand columns below with a piece of paper, leaving the column headings visible.
2. Try to answer the questions.
3. Move the paper down just enough to see if your answer was right.
4. Do the same for each remaining principle.

[39]

WHEN LIGHT DOES THIS:	WHAT HAPPENS TO ITS IMAGE?	WHAT HAPPENS TO ITS RAYS?
1. passes into another medium	apparent location and size change a bit.	they bend but remain basically parallel.
2. passes through plane glass	is unchanged.	are unchanged.
.		
.		
.		
5. passes through a convex lens	is a point at FL. is small when closer than 2 FL. is large when farther than 2 FL. is inverted when farther than FL.	they converge at FL, cross, and disperse.

275

[40] To use a microscope properly, remember to do the following:

(Diagram of a microscope with numbered steps and arrows pointing to appropriate parts of microscope.)

To use a telescope properly, remember to do the following:

(Diagram of a telescope with numbered steps and arrows pointing to appropriate parts of telescope.)

Self-test

[41] Imagine that you have a microscope and a specimen in front of you. Close your eyes and go over in your mind the steps that you would follow to use the microscope to look at the specimen. Try to picture exactly what you would do for each step.
Then open to this page to check whether you missed any steps or did any of them in the wrong order.

(Same for telescope)

Facts to Review

You should remember the following information:

1. Glass globe with water	magnifying glass	engravers 3,000 years ago.
2. Glass lenses	magnifying	late 1200's A.D.
3. Compound microscope	Zacharias Janssen, Dutch spectacle maker.	1590 A.D.

[42] *Self-test*

1. Use a piece of paper to cover all but one column.
2. Try to remember each item in the other column.
3. Then change columns.

[43]

[44] _____

COMMENTS

1. With respect to elaborative sequencing of modules in a course, there is a module to elaborate on each unit in Module 1. For example, Module 5 elaborates on the Physics Unit in Module 1 (see Fig. 8.7). There is also a module to elaborate on each unit in Module 5. For example, Module 17 expands on the Light Unit in Module 5 (also see Fig. 8.7). Similarly, what was taught in a single lesson in Module 1 ("How Light Behaves") receives a full unit (a set of lessons) in Module 5 (Unit 3, Lessons 1–6). And what was taught in a single lesson in Module 5 ("Refraction") receives a full unit in Module 17 (Unit 3, Lessons 1–5). Elaborations would, of course, continue beyond the few levels shown in Fig. 8.7. It should be noted that some lessons at virtually any level of elaboration may not have other lessons that elaborate further on them. This outline does not show what courses the modules would be grouped into for reasons explained in footnote 1.

2. This is the epitome lesson. With respect to elaborative sequencing of lessons in a unit, only the three lessons most closely related to the lesson objectives for this book are outlined in this unit. One can readily see that Lessons 1 and 2 both provide more concrete and less complex versions of fundamentally the same principles as those taught in Lesson 3 on the behavior of light. Lesson 1 is the simplest, "epitome" version because particles can be seen and touched, and they have fewer behaviors. Lesson 2 is the first level of elaboration because

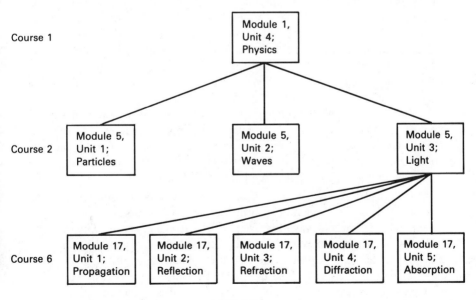

FIG. 8.7

wave behavior is considerably more complex than that of particles. Lesson 3 is the second level of elaboration because light behaves like particles in some ways and like waves in others. Hence, Lesson 3 elaborates on Lesson 2 as well as directly on Lesson 1. Also, light particles cannot be touched and light waves cannot be seen, making the behavior of light still more difficult to understand than that of either particles alone or waves alone. It should be clear that the simple-to-complex sequence of the three lessons is based on the particle-wave-light dimension discussed in the Lesson Preface.

3. This section illustrates elaborative sequencing of individual ideas within a lesson. The principles that have been allocated to Lesson 1 are a simplification on *all three* dimensions of elaboration mentioned in the Preface to Lesson Outlines: refraction-reflection, light-wave-particle, and convex-concave-prism-etc. The Elaboration Theory prescribes that the sequence should expand on the most important and most representative dimension first. In this case, we decided that knowledge of the variety of behaviors (e.g., linear movement, reflection, refraction) is more important and more representative of the whole domain of knowledge than their distinct applications to waves and light. (However, it might be appropriate to make it clear to students from the beginning that waves and light do behave very similarly to particles, and that the students will learn more about them later in the module.) The remaining dimension (convex-concave-prism-etc.) requires prior elaboration of the particle-wave-light dimension and hence would be the last dimension for elaboration.

Therefore, with respect to sequencing of individual ideas within a lesson, the principles within the lesson are presented in a simple-to-complex sequence based on the refraction-reflection dimension: reflection is taught before something similar to refraction, and the principle of linear movement is even simpler than, and hence taught before, reflection. As a result, Lesson 1 deals only with the behavior of particles, such as rubber balls or billiard balls, meaning that this lesson is, as a whole, a simplification based on the particle-wave-light dimension discussed earlier.

Please keep in mind that only principles are shown here, and that various kinds of "supporting content" (i.e., related concepts, procedures, and information, including Gagné-type learning prerequisites) are later plugged into this "organizing" sequence at the most appropriate point. Such a complete sequence of ideas within a lesson is illustrated later in this chapter.

4. Lesson 2 is a level-1 elaboration because it elaborates on the epitome (Lesson 1). It begins elaborating on the second most important dimension of elaboration: the particle-wave-light dimension. It elaborates on Lesson 1 by dealing with the way *waves* behave rather than with the way particles behave. It is more complex than Lesson 1, first because it entails more principles, such as those relating to interference and transmission, and second because the similar principles are usually more complex, such as rectilinear movement of waves being more complex than simple linear movement of particles. The behavior of

waves is taught before the behavior of light because it is simpler (see next comment).

5. Lesson 3 is a level-2 elaboration because it elaborates on Lesson 2 (and, incidentally, also directly on Lesson 1). It further elaborates the same dimension as did Lesson 2 (particle-wave-light). The additional principle is diffraction (although one could argue that refraction is also a new principle). And the principles that are similar to those in Lesson 2 are also more complex for light, such as the way it moves, which is a combination of particle movement and wave movement. This lesson is also more difficult because it is less concrete: you cannot touch the particles of light nor see the individual light waves.

6. Notice that the introduction to refraction in this lesson is at the very simplest level of the third dimension of elaboration: the convex lens–concave lens–prism–etc. dimension. The same is true for all of the other principles in this lesson.

7. Notice that one form of systematic review is built in by cycling back (as in Bruner's "spiral curriculum") to what are basically the same principles in a new, more complex application or context. For those who believe that "process" is an important part of the curriculum, this sequence leads students through the same process of discovery of similarities that characterized the historical development of the discipline. This kind of sequence is perhaps even more important for a discovery approach to instruction, such as that advocated by Bruner or by Collins and Stevens (see chapter 6). However, it also shows that an expository mode can give students some of the excitement of, and feel for, the process of discovery. Chapter 7 of Lindsay and Norman (1977) also illustrates such an expository treatment of the process of discovery. This kind of sequence is equally useful and exciting in the social sciences and humanities. And of course the systematic review function of this kind of sequence should not be underrated.

8. This unit elaborates on Lesson 3 of Module 1 ("How Light Behaves"). A comparison of the contents of this module with the Unit on Physics in the previous module illustrates how the "epitome" principles in the first can be elaborated upon in the second module. Specifically, there is a unit that elaborates on each of the three lessons in Module 1; and there is a lesson that elaborates on each principle that was taught in the earlier module (reflection-refraction, etc.).

9. This principle is basically a review of the principle that was taught under reflection in Lesson 3 of Module 1. It is elaborated a little bit by pointing out that the light rays remain parallel to each other and that the image is reversed. Many students may have realized this already, but it had not been explicitly stated or demonstrated as such previously. This lesson is a level-3 elaboration because it elaborates on a level-2 elaboration (Lesson 3 of Module 1).

10. These next two principles elaborate on the first one (and therefore on the corresponding principle from Module 1) by introducing complexity from the

third dimension of elaboration (convex-concave-etc.) as it applies to reflection. Notice how, in effect, each principle in Lessons 2 and 3 is comprised of a special case (e.g., plane mirrors, convex mirrors, concave mirrors), each of which results in different effects on the behavior of light within that category of behavior (e.g., reflection). The behavior of light is more complex when it is reflected off a **convex mirror,** because the rays are no longer parallel and the image is enlarged. The behavior is even more complex when light is reflected off a **concave mirror,** because the rays converge to a focal point and the image is inverted after the focal point and changes size with distance from the mirror.

11. With respect to sequencing *lessons,* notice that Lessons 2 and 3 have much in common. For example, the effects of a concave mirror are very similar to the effects of a convex lens. However, reflection off a mirror is simpler to understand because there is only one surface that matters, whereas with refraction by a lens there are two, nonparallel surfaces that one must consider. Also, when light is reflected, it just changes direction, whereas when light is refracted, it changes velocity and direction. Furthermore, the change in direction is precise and intuitive with a mirror: The angle of reflection equals the angle of incidence; whereas when it is refracted, the change in direction depends on several factors, including the density of the medium and the sharpness of the angle of incidence.

12. Again, this principle is basically a review of the principle that was taught under refraction in Lesson 3 of Module 1. As with the first principle in Lesson 2, it is elaborated slightly. Notice that each set of principles is comprised of two principles: one that describes the effect of something on the image of an object and one that describes its effect on the direction and relative position of the individual rays. The latter is a more complex elaboration on the former because (a) it explains why the image is affected the way it is; (b) there are many rays that often undergo various changes, and it is difficult to show all the changes that the multitude of rays undergo; and (c) the image is more concrete than the rays—it can be seen.

13. These principles progressively elaborate on the first in this lesson by introducing complexity from the third dimension of elaboration as it applies to refraction, just as was the case for Lesson 2 of this module. What happens to light when it passes *from one medium into another* is less complicated than what happens when it passes *into and out of* a medium because in the former situation there is only one surface at which the light rays bend, whereas in the latter there are two surfaces. *Plane glass* is simpler than a *prism* because the former's two surfaces are parallel. A *prism* is simpler than a *concave lens* because both of its surfaces are straight, whereas the concave lens has at least one curved surface. And finally, a *concave lens* is simpler than a *convex lens* because the latter focuses rays to a point and inverts the image of an object.

14. These principles and the various concepts and information associated with them represent the majority of the objectives established for this book (see Comment 34 for details).

15. With respect to sequencing *modules,* this module illustrates a second level of elaboration because it elaborates directly on the principles in the first level of elaboration, the Physics module. Each unit in this module elaborates on a lesson in the unit on light in Module 5, and each lesson in this module elaborates on one of the specific cases from Module 5 (see Fig. 8.7). This need not necessarily be the case. It would not be uncommon for each lesson here to elaborate on some characteristic that cuts across many or all of the cases from the earlier elaboration.

16. This lesson elaborates on the first principle in Lesson 3 of Module 5. In fact, each lesson in this unit elaborates on a different level of the third dimension of elaboration in that earlier lesson: into a medium, plane glass, prism, concave lens, and convex lens. Therefore, each of these lessons serves to review a part of what was learned in Lesson 3 of Module 5. Notice that each lesson elaborates on the earlier principle or principles by presenting principles that answer the questions, "Which way?" and "How much?" Directionality and quantification are two of the most common ways of elaborating on simple principles, but answering the questions "What else happens?" and "Why?" are also very common.

17. Most of the principles that answer "What else happens?" "Why?" "Which way?" and "How much?" are common to all of the types of lenses and whatnot that cause light to refract. Therefore, this first lesson is considerably longer than any of the others in this unit, but its principles are continually reviewed as they are applied to different situations (lenses, etc.) in the following lessons.

18. Continuing our earlier discussion of compatibility with both discovery and expository approaches to instruction, it should be evident that this lesson lends itself well to a project or "episode" approach such as that advocated by Bruner (1960). Given the level of knowledge that the students already have about the behavior of light as it refracts, it would not be too difficult for them to discover many of these principles (with a little bit of help and guidance). Bruner's notion of discovery-oriented episodes that have a clear beginning, middle, and end could easily be extended to expository episodes if discovery is inappropriate (i.e., time is short or students have already learned how to discover principles).

19. It can readily be seen that each of these progressively more complex situations (lenses, etc.) requires progressively more principles to explain the behavior of light at a similar level of understanding.

20. After identifying and listing all the principles that should be taught in each lesson of each course in the curriculum, the Elaboration Theory indicates that supporting content should be identified for each lesson. When this activity is complete, you will have selected *all* of the content that is to be taught, and you will have allocated *all* of that content to lessons and sequenced *all* of those lessons. Although it is not necessary to break down the supporting content into "concepts," "procedures," "learning prerequisites," and "information," we

have found it helpful for reducing the chances of the designer overlooking important supporting content. "Information" refers to all of the remember level in M. D. Merrill's (1983) taxonomy or all of Gagné's (1977) verbal information. The other three types of supporting content are Merrill's use-a-generality level or Gagne's intellectual skills. "Learning prerequisites" are listed separately to remind the instructional designer to identify such prerequisites not only for the organizing content but also for both of the first two types of supporting content.

21. One of the additional benefits of this kind of sequence is its clear communication of the adage, "The more you learn, the more you realize how little you know." It raises questions, broadens horizons, stimulates thought, and creates realizations that might not otherwise have surfaced. It truly helps to create a meaningful understanding of the sort that Ausubel, Bruner, and Dewey all advocated but did not clearly operationalize.

22. Because many lessons elaborate on two lessons at the same time in this curriculum, the degree of learner control over selection and sequence of content is more limited than usual. However, many options could (should) still be provided to learners. After mastering Lesson 1.4.1, the learner could choose between 1.4.2 and 5.1.1. Similarly, after 1.4.3 has been mastered, the learner could choose between 5.1.1 (and perhaps 5.1.2, 5.1.3, etc.), 5.2.1 (and perhaps 5.2.2, 5.2.3, etc.), 5.3.1, and 5.3.6, depending on his or her interest in the various aspects of particles, waves, or light. And after all of the 5.3's have been mastered, the learner could be allowed to choose among *any* of the lessons in Module 17. Of course, it is not necessary to wait until all of the 5.3's are mastered before selecting various lessons in Module 17; 17.1.1 can be selected as soon as 5.3.1 has been mastered.

23. Notice that the supporting concepts are all learned as concept classification tasks (the use-a-generality level). In contrast, two concepts are listed under "Information" because concept classification is not their desired learning outcome—rather, meaningful understanding (remember-paraphrased in M. D. Merrill's taxonomy) is desired. The same applies to the procedures; note that "How lenses are made" is a procedure listed under "Information."

24. After allocating all the content to lessons and sequencing those lessons, the designer should plan the sequence for all content *within* each lesson. This Lesson Blueprint illustrates sequencing of individual ideas within one of the lessons in the Course Blueprints. This is the most detailed level for which the Elaboration Theory has prescriptions. This level of sequencing is usually designed *after* all of the lessons in a course have been sequenced because revisions are often made on earlier parts of the overall sequence while one is working on the later parts of it.

The Elaboration Theory does not make any prescriptions relating to discovery versus expository, inquiry versus noninquiry, educational game versus nongame, individualized resources versus lecture versus discussion versus tutoring versus group activities. Nor does it make any prescriptions relating to sequencing examples or practice items, selecting media, or using management strategies. The Elaboration Theory is highly compatible with all of these alternatives, and these are all important kinds of prescriptions that should be included in any truly comprehensive theory of instruction. On a recent project, the author was able to complete some initial work on such integration of prescriptions (Reigeluth, Doughty, Sari, Powell, Frey, & Sweeney, 1982).

For example, for a public high school audience, motivation is a major concern. Hence, it would probably be beneficial to use some form of inquiry (see chapter 5). Inquiry, as distinct from discovery, would begin the instruction with a major question, such as "How can you create a projected image that is inverted and twice as large as the object?" Then the following instruction, which could be either expository or discovery, would be directed toward answering that question. It might also be beneficial to use a discovery approach occasionally, but probably not too frequently due to time limitations. Much of the practice could occur through especially designed educational games (preferably computer games) that require the student to predict effects of certain lenses on light rays or to discover the causes of certain light ray patterns. Lasers and space wars might make one exciting context for such educational games.

The purpose of this discussion is to clearly identify important aspects of instruction that the Elaboration Theory does not include. It should be noted that we are not aware of any such methods with which the Elaboration Theory cannot or should not be used.

25. The initial synthesizer is really a lot more than a synthesizer. It provides external synthesis (relating the lesson content to the "larger picture") and facilitates some measure of internal synthesis (interrelating the organizing content that is to be taught in this lesson). The **external synthesis** takes the form of a statement of context that (a) reviews the organizing content that was taught in the lesson upon which this lesson elaborates and (b) explains which aspect of that organizing content is being investigated in this lesson. The **internal synthesis** provides some advance indication of the *interrelationships* among the ideas that are to be taught: how they relate to each other. But those interrelationships are not explicitly taught at this point. As with virtually everything else, analysis must precede synthesis; and therefore explicit internal synthesis must wait until the student has analyzed and understood each element (each principle).

But if it does not explicitly teach the important interrelationships, what does it do? In the case of both principles and procedures, *demonstrations* are generally the most effective way to show those interrelationships. But if the organizing content had been concepts, then something like the combination summerizer-synthesizer shown in Fig. 8.4 would generally be best. In addition, besides indicating important interrelationships, a demonstration is ideal for serving a variety of other purposes that an initial presentation should serve: It provides a concrete presentation of the *objectives* of the lesson and something in the way of a *preview* of the organizing content, and it stimulates *interest* in the content of the lesson. Research has shown that objectives are often of little value to learners. This is probably because objectives are usually too abstract to communicate meaningfully to learners. Therefore, the Elaboration Theory proposes use of a concrete demonstration of the most important (terminal) capabilities that the learner will acquire from the lesson, to overcome this problem while still accomplishing the basic purpose of an objective. And it simultaneously serves the preview, motivational, and synthesis functions mentioned earlier.

26. 1b on this page is the first principle to be taught in this lesson. However, all of its unmastered prerequisites (1a) must be taught first. These prerequisites were identified by performing a standard Gagné-type hierarchical analysis on the principle.

27. Nonprerequisite supporting content (information, concepts, and procedures) for the first principle (1b) is taught immediately after the principle (see 1c). The one exception to this rule is that highly related concepts should always be taught together. For example, kinds of convex and concave lenses are best learned together because they are coordinate concepts (see Comment 31).

28. As was indicated in the Course Outlines, another version of the principle is now presented (1d) that describes what happens to the light rays rather than what happens to the image of an object. This sequence is based on the observation → deduction process of the development of knowledge (changes in the image are observed, but the behavior of the rays is deduced), which is also a concrete → abstract sequence of instruction.

29. Again, the principles are immediately preceded by their unmastered prerequisites.

30. Again, nonprerequisite supporting content immediately follows its most relevant organizing content.

31. Even though "convex lens" is not a prerequisite concept for the principle of 4b, it is taught here because it is the only coordinate concept that concave lens has: every lens is either concave or convex. Therefore, to learn concave lens, the students simultaneously learn convex lens, and they might as well learn its label while they are at it.

32. If there were any learning prerequisites for this supporting content, they would immediately precede the particular supporting concept for which they were prerequisite.

33. This conceptual synthesizer-summarizer is intended to make sure that the concepts are organized in a proper and stable manner in the student's memory. The brighter students may not need it, but the slower students may even need some extra explanation to be able to benefit from it. Notice that, unlike most synthesizer-summarizers, this one is not at the end of the lesson. It is placed here because all of the content that it contains has already been taught at this point.

This summarizer-synthesizer illustrates a number of important characteristics. First, a summarizer should present a *concise generality* for each idea (in this case, concepts). A concise generality should contain just enough critical words to stimulate recall of the generality. In this summarizer the concise generalities are either placed beside or below the corresponding concept box. Secondly, a summarizer should usually provide a *prototypical example,* preferably in visual form. Line drawings are ideal for concepts. All critical attributes should be visible. Thirdly, a synthesizer should show simply, and with a minimum of words, the major *relationships* among the ideas. In this case, it should show which concepts are kinds of which other concepts. Fourthly, a summarizer-synthesizer should encourage active processing of the relationships and should also provide an opportunity for low-risk *self-test* (see the questions at the top of the page), complete with the availability of immediate feedback (see the statement at the bottom of the page). To prevent premature "peeking" at the answer and to ensure that the student in fact responds to the questions, computer-based instruction is ideal. This is but one of many forms that a summarizer-synthesizer could take, but the four basic components should be present in all forms.

34. The prerequisite concepts (5a), the principle (5c), the supporting procedure (5f), and the supporting information (5g) represent four of the objectives established for the lessons in this book (numbers 2, 3, 6, and 5, respectively). Objective 1 is taught in 4a just above, and objective 4 is taught in Module 3, Unit 3, Lesson 5, Topic f.

35. This lesson (internal) summarizer-synthesizer illustrates a number of characteristics. As in the conceptual summarizer-synthesizer, this one contains *concise generalities,* but the generalities are arranged in such a way that they can be used expositorily as a summary or inquisitorily as a *self-test* (practice). Preferably, they will be used both ways. This synthesizer-summarizer also contains a *prototypical example* of each generality, in this case line drawings again. All of these characteristics are provided for concepts, principles, and procedures. Because many of the concepts are prerequisites for the principles, they are reviewed first. Finally, the information is reviewed. In a learner-controlled system, the learner would be able to access the summarizer-synthesizer on demand at any time during, and perhaps even before or after, the lesson.

36. These are prototypical examples of the concepts. Only a few are illustrated here; the remaining ones would also be included so that all concepts that were introduced in this lesson would be reviewed.

37. These serve either as generalities (definitions) for the same concepts or as practice on the generalities, depending on whether or not the student peeks at the right side of the page. In computer-based instruction, this can be controlled, preferably in a way that only requires a covert response before the right side is shown. It is often good to include some practice on instances, also (that is, practice in classifying new examples and nonexamples of the concepts). Note

that the generalities (on the right side) are reduced to a few key words, because their purpose is to trigger recall of acquired knowledge rather than to create new understanding.

38. This is a theoretical synthesizer as well as a summarizer. There is one drawing for each of the five pairs of principles. The first set of principles can easily be integrated with each of the remaining four (i.e., the process in the first is a part of the processes in the remaining four), so they can be explicitly integrated. However, the remaining four can only be compared and contrasted; they cannot be explicitly synthesized with a theoretical synthesizer because they are not parts of the same process (causal chain).

The theoretical synthesizer in Fig. 8.6 uses a prototypical example to show the causal relationship between distance of the image and both the image's position (normal or inverted) and size. Furthermore, the enlarged circle shows how the principles for "into a medium" fit in with the principles for a convex lens. Although this theoretical synthesizer does not use the arrows and boxes that characterize many theoretical synthesizers, it explicitly communicates the inter-relatedness of the processes (the chain of causes and effects). A dynamic demonstration on computer or video disk would be even better, because a process (cause-effect) is being illustrated.

39. As with the concepts, these serve either as generalities or as practice on the generalities. Practice on instances could also be included.

40. This is a procedural synthesizer. It shows the order of the many steps that make up the complete performance of the task. For more complicated procedures, a flow diagram would probably be better than just a listing of the numbered steps. In either case, relating the steps (generality) to a picture or drawing of a microscope (prototypical example) is important.

41. Again, the student could be asked to use the procedure on a new (previously unencountered) microscope, but most students probably would not take the time to do it.

42. Again, a computer would be ideal for making sure that the learner does the active cognitive processing called for in this self-test.

43. A unit (set) summarizer-synthesizer (often referred to as an *expanded epitome*) would contain all the same elements as this one. The only difference is the scope of the content being summarized and synthesized; it would include all of the content from all of the lessons that elaborate directly on a single lesson.

44. Many examples of analogies are available elsewhere (see, e.g., Curtis & Reigeluth, 1984), and examples of cognitive strategy activators were provided in the introduction to this chapter. Therefore, because of space limitations, examples of these two strategy components are not provided here.

REFERENCES

Ausubel, D. P. (1968). *Educational psychology: A cognitive view.* New York: Holt, Rinehart & Winston.

Bruner, J. S. (1960). *The process of education.* New York: Random House.

Collins, A., & Stevens, A. L. (1983). A cognitive theory of inquiry teaching. In C. M. Reigeluth (Ed.), *Instructional-design theories and models: An overview of their current status.* Hillsdale, NJ: Lawrence Erlbaum Associates.

Curtis, R. V., & Reigeluth, C. M. (1984). The use of analogies in written text. *Instructional Science, 13,* 99–117.

Gagné, R. M. (1968). Learning hierarchies. *Educational Psychologist, 6,* 1–6.

Gagné, R. M. (1977). *The conditions of learning* (3rd ed.) New York: Holt, Rinehart & Winston.

Gagné, R. M. (1985). *The conditions of learning and theory of instruction* (4th ed.) New York: Holt, Rinehart & Winston.

Keller, J. M. (1983). Motivational design of instruction. In C. M. Reigeluth (Ed.), *Instructional-design theories and models: An overview of their current status.* Hillsdale, NJ: Lawrence Erlbaum Associates.

Lindsay, P. H., & Norman, D. A. (1977). *Human information processing: An introduction to psychology* (2nd ed.). New York: Academic Press.

Mayer, R. E. (1977). The sequencing of instruction and the concept of assimilation-to-schema. *Instructional Science, 6,* 369–388.

Merrill, M. D. (1983). Component display theory. In C. M. Reigeluth (Ed.), *Instructional-design theories and models: An overview of their current status.* Hillsdale, NJ: Lawrence Erlbaum Associates.

Merrill, M. D. (1984). What is learner control? In R. K. Bass & C. Dills (Eds.), *Instructional development: The state of the art, II.* Dubuque, IA: Kendall-Hunt Publishing Co.

Merrill, M. D., & Wood, N. D. (1974). *Instructional strategies: A preliminary taxonomy.* Columbus, OH: Ohio State University. (ERIC Document Reproduction Service No. SF 018-771)

Merrill, P. F. (1980). Analysis of a procedural task. *NSPI Journal, 19,* 11–15.

Norman, D. A. (1973). *Cognitive organization & learning* (Report Number 37). San Diego: University of California, Center for Human Information Processing.

Ortony, A. (Ed.). (1979). *Metaphor and thought.* Cambridge, England: Cambridge University Press.

Reigeluth, C. M. (1979). In search of a better way to organize instruction: The elaboration theory. *Journal of Instructional Development, 2,* 8–15.

Reigeluth, C. M. (1983). Meaningfulness and instruction: Relating what is being learned to what a student knows. *Instructional Science, 12,* 197–218.

Reigeluth, C. M., & Darwazeh, A. N. (1982). The elaboration theory's procedure for designing instruction: A conceptual approach. *Journal of Instructional Development, 5,* 22–32.

Reigeluth, C. M., Doughty, P., Sari, I. F., Powell, C. J., Frey, L., & Sweeney, J. (1982). *Extended development procedure: User's manual.* Fort Monroe, VA: U.S. Army Training and Doctrine Command.

Reigeluth, C. M., Merrill, M. D., Wilson, B. G., & Spiller, R. T. (1980). The elaboration theory of instruction: A model for structuring instruction. *Instructional Science, 9,* 125–219.

Reigeluth, C. M., & Rodgers, C. A. (1980). The elaboration theory of instruction: Prescriptions for task analysis and design. *NSPI Journal, 19,* 16–26.

Reigeluth, C. M., & Stein, F. S. (1983). The elaboration theory of instruction. In C. M. Reigeluth (Ed.), *Instructional-design theories and models: An overview of their current status.* Hillsdale, NJ: Lawrence Elrbaum Associates.

Rigney, J. W. (1978). Learning strategies: A theoretical perspective. In H. F. O'Neil, Jr. (Ed.), *Learning Strategies*. New York: Academic Press.

Sari, I. F., & Reigeluth, C. M. (1982). Writing and evaluating textbooks: Contributions from instructional theory. In D. Jonassen (Ed.), *The technology of text: Principles for structuring, designing, and displaying text*. Englewood Cliffs, NJ: Educational Technology Publications.

Scandura, J. M. (1973). *Structural learning I: Theory and research*. London/New York: Gordon & Breach Science Publishers.

Verbrugge, R. R., & McCarrell, N. S. (1977). Metaphoric comprehension: Studies in reminding and resembling. *Cognitive Psychology, 9*, 494–533.

9

An Application of the ARCS Model of Motivational Design

John M. Keller
Florida State University

Thomas W. Kopp
Miami University of Ohio

FOREWORD

History

This is another theory that arose out of the desire to integrate the current state of our knowledge into a prescriptive form that would be useful to instructional designers and teachers. It integrates prescriptions from a broad range of theoretical perspectives, including social learning theory, environmental theories, humanistic theories, and aspects of attitude theory, decision theory, attribution theory, cognitive evaluation theory, equity theory, cognitive dissonance theory, locus of control, and learned helplessness. Unlike all of the other theories in this book, this one is not intended to stand alone; its prescriptions are intended to supplement other instructional theories. Perhaps for that reason, it takes a very different form than the other theories; it prescribes individual motivational strategies in a smorgasbord fashion to meet the individual motivational requirements of the situation. Any module of instruction could require anywhere from none to all 12 of the kinds of strategies Keller has identified. Like the Component Display Theory and Elaboration Theory, this theory is also indicative of the highly integrative, multiperspectived approach to prescriptive theory construction that we need so much at this point in the development of our knowledge about instruction.

Unique Contributions

The most obvious unique contribution of this theory is that it is perhaps the first, and certainly the only one in this book, to explicitly address the use of motivational strategies. Furthermore, it has done so in an eclectic, comprehensive manner, such that it includes (or at least attempts to include) all the kinds of motivational strategies that would be useful to instructional designers. In this sense, it is not just unique, it is revolutionary—and long overdue. It opens the door to making instruction fun, not just effective.

Similarities

In spite of its revolutionary nature, there are a few similarities with prescriptions in other theories, such as the use of inquiry (Collins) and gaining attention and presenting objectives (Gagné-Briggs). Other prescriptions of Keller's serve to extend or qualify prescriptions in other theories, such as the nature of examples and feedback. These similarities are identified in the chapter with Editor's Notes.

Issues to Think About

Have any important motivational concerns been left out? And how can Keller's prescriptions best be integrated with other theories?

STUDY QUESTIONS

1. Describe each of the three kinds of strategies for gaining and maintaining attention.
2. Describe each of the three kinds of strategies for establishing the relevance of the instruction.
3. Describe each of the three kinds of strategies for building confidence in the learner.
4. Describe each of the three kinds of strategies for creating satisfaction with the instruction.
5. Describe when you should and should not use each of the three kinds of strategies for gaining and maintaining attention.
6. Describe when you should and should not use each of the three kinds of strategies for establishing the relevance of the instruction.
7. Describe when you should and should not use each of the three kinds of strategies for building confidence in the learner.
8. Describe when you should and should not use each of the three kinds of strategies for creating satisfaction with the instruction.

C.M.R.

The motivational design strategies presented in this chapter are similar to those presented by Keller (1983a), but there have been some modifications. The introductory section of this chapter contains a presentation of the categories of strategies contained in the motivational design model, and an explanation of how they are used in the instructional-design process. The motivational design model is not, by itself, an instructional-design model. It is meant to be used in conjunction with instructional-design models. Consequently, this chapter has a slightly different structure from the others in this book.

Selections have been taken from two of the other lessons presented in this book and used to illustrate various motivational strategies. Whenever possible, features have been identified within the original lesson that illustrate specific motivational strategies. In addition, modifications have been made to illustrate still other strategies. These modifications do not imply any criticism of the original lesson. They simply reflect certain assumptions we have made about the lesson's audience, and about specific strategies that might be motivational. We have also tried to use strategies that provide a fuller understanding of the motivational aspects of lessons.

Following the presentation of the motivational model in the first section of this chapter, the two lesson segments are presented in the second section, and the motivational strategy examples are referenced in numerical order. The final part of the chapter contains a commentary that explains which strategies are illustrated by the referenced parts of the lesson segments.

INTRODUCTION: OVERVIEW OF THE ARCS MODEL

The motivational model described by Keller in the companion volume to this book (Reigeluth, 1983) has remained the same with respect to the four basic categories of motivational variables and the theoretical foundation that supports them. However, the model has been changed and refined in some respects (Keller, 1983b). The names of two of the categories were changed to give them a slightly different emphasis and to create an acronym that makes the model easier to use in an applied setting. The first category has been changed from ''Interest'' to ''Attention,'' and the third category from ''Expectancy'' to ''Confidence.'' Taking the first letter of each category produces the word ARCS, and the model is now referred to as the ARCS Model.

The second change in the model is more substantive. The subcategories and strategies that represent each major category have undergone several changes. The method of deriving these subcategories and the results of field tests were reported in earlier publications (Keller, 1983b; Keller & Dodge, 1982). Based on this earlier work, and on the work of Kopp (1982, 1983), Malone (1981), McCombs (1984), and Wlodkowski (1981, 1985), further refinements were made in the strategy list (Keller & Kopp, 1985). The current strategy list, which is included in this chapter, provides a basis for prescribing the motivational strategies in the lesson segments and for organizing the commentary.

Despite the changes, the model presented in this chapter is parallel to the one presented (Keller, 1983a) in the earlier volume of this series (Reigeluth, 1983).

The four major categories are the same, except for the name changes in two cases, and the theoretical foundation for each category is the same. Two subcategories of variables have been relocated, and these changes are described later in this section.

As presently constituted, the ARCS Model has three major subcategories of strategies under each of the four major categories (Fig. 9.1). Each of the major categories will be briefly described, but readers who are familiar with the earlier model will note that the concept of familiarity (relating new instruction to what the student already knows) has been moved from "Attention" to "Relevance," and the concept of goal orientation (including "utility") has been added as a separate category under "Relevance" rather than being subsumed under need for achievement.

The following section contains both a brief explanation of each major category of motivational strategy and lists of the major strategy statements in each category. As is probably unavoidable in working with motivation, each of the strategy statements is fairly general. Discussions of this issue, together with descriptions of obstacles in working with motivation, explanations of each strategy, and supporting research were included in Keller (1979, 1983a, 1983b), and

STRATEGY	COMMENTS
Attention	
A.1 Perceptual Arousal	4, 10, 12, 14, 19, 24, 30, 46, 62
A.2 Inquiry Arousal	1, 5, 8, 18, 26, 42, 56, 70
A.3 Variability	20, 27, 54, 59
Relevance	
R.1 Familiarity	2, 13, 17, 23, 25, 47, 55, 57, 61
R.2 Goal Orientation	6, 7, 15, 28, 40, 43, 45, 50, 52, 63, 71
R.3 Motive Matching	3, 33, 37, 64
Confidence	
C.1 Expectancy for Success	9, 11, 16, 22, 32, 36, 44, 48, 49, 51, 58, 67
C.2 Challenge Setting	21, 34, 41, 65
C.3 Attribution Molding	31, 35, 53, 68
Satisfaction	
S.1 Natural Consequences	38
S.2 Positive Consequences	29, 39, 60, 66, 69
S.3 Equity	

FIG. 9.1. ARCS strategy categories.

Keller and Kopp (1985). The present chapter contains specific examples that help illustrate how each strategy can be operationalized.

Attention

This is the same as the category called "Interest" in Keller (1983a). It refers primarily to curiosity arousal as defined by Maw and Maw (1968) and Berlyne (1965). A first step in motivation is to gain and sustain the learner's attention. This is also the first step in information-processing theory, but there is a difference. Information-processing theory applies more to learning than motivation. The motivational concern is for *getting* attention. The information-processing concern is more for *directing* it to that which is to be learned.*

Strategy A.1. *Perceptual arousal.* Gain and maintain student attention by the use of novel, surprising, incongruous, or uncertain events in instruction. (See Comments 4, 10, 12, 14, 19, 24, 30, 46, 62.)

Strategy A.2. *Inquiry arousal.* Stimulate information-seeking behavior by posing, or having the learner generate, questions or a problem to solve.† (See Comments 1, 5, 8, 18, 26, 42, 56, 70.)

Strategy A.3. *Variability.* Maintain student interest by varying the elements of instruction. (See Comments 20, 27, 54, 59.)

Relevance

After having their curiosity stimulated, people will question the relevancy of the situation before they become highly motivated. When students ask, "Why should I have to study this?" they are wondering what importance the instruction has for their lives. In general, it can be more difficult to establish the relevancy of instruction than to generate attention. Unless relevancy is established externally by such things as job requirements or college admissions requirements, the instructor has to find ways of connecting the instructional objectives to important interests and motives of the learners.

Strategy R.1. *Familiarity.* Use concrete language, and use examples and concepts that are related to the learner's experience and values.‡ (See Comments 2, 13, 17, 32, 25, 47, 55, 57, 61.)

---

*Gagné-Briggs's "gain attention" (p. 17) appears to be the second of the two: directing attention to that which is to be learned.

†Collins's theory incorporates this strategy component, although more by posing than by having the learner generate questions or problems to solve.

‡This prescription specifies characteristics for a strategy component that is routinely prescribed by other theorists: examples.

Strategy R.2. *Goal Orientation*. Provide statements or examples that present the objectives and utility of the instruction, and either present goals for accomplishment or have the learner define them.* (See Comments 6, 7, 15, 28, 40, 43, 45, 50, 52, 63, 71.)

Strategy R.3. *Motive Matching*. Use teaching strategies that match the motive profiles of the students. (See Comments 3, 33, 37, 64.)

Confidence

People have often avoided pursuing an interesting and desired goal because they believed that the likelihood of achieving it was too low. A positive expectancy for success is the third requirement for motivating learners. The risk level needs to be adjusted according to the confidence levels of the learners and the type of learning objectives. Adults, like children, who are expected to learn a new skill need an opportunity to acquire and practice the skill under conditions where the psychological risks are reasonably low; that is, they need conditions where they do not have to fear loss of face or embarrassment as they try to develop the skill. In contrast, a degree of risk, or challenge, is necessary to stimulate peak performance once the learner has begun to master the new skill.

Strategy C.1. *Expectancy for Success*. Make learners aware of performance requirements and evaluative criteria. (See Comments 1, 9, 11, 16, 22, 32, 36, 44, 48, 49, 51, 58, 67.)

Strategy C.2. *Challenge Setting*. Provide multiple achievement levels that allow learners to set personal standards of accomplishment, and performance opportunities that allow them to experience success. (See Comments 21, 34, 41, 65.)

Strategy C.3. *Attribution Molding*. Provide feedback that supports student ability and effort as the determinants of success.† (See Comments 31, 35, 53, 68.)

Satisfaction

Learners can become unmotivated rather quickly if the outcomes of their efforts are inconsistent with their expectations. If the evaluation and grading system seems subjective and arbitrary, if the intrinsically motivated person is locked into

---

*This is similar to Gagné-Briggs's call for presenting the objectives to the learner (p. 17), although this prescription extends the other by calling for an indication of the utility of the objective.

†Feedback is a strategy component routinely prescribed by other theorists, but this prescription specifies a characteristic for that feedback that is unique among the theories in this book.

an externally controlled contingency system, or if the experience of the instruction simply isn't what was expected, then it will be very difficult to maintain a continuing motivation for the instruction. The instructional designer has to be concerned about the sometimes delicate balance between fostering and maintaining intrinsic motivation and the appropriate, and sometimes unavoidable, use of extrinsic reinforcements.

> Strategy S.1. *Natural Consequences.* Provide opportunities to use newly acquired knowledge or skill in a real or simulated setting. (See Comment 38.)
>
> Strategy S.2. *Positive Consequences.* Provide feedback and reinforcements that will sustain the desired behavior.* (See Comments 29, 39, 60, 66, 69.)
>
> Strategy S.3. *Equity.* Maintain consistent standards and consequences for task accomplishment. (There are no comments pertaining to this strategy.)†

Use of the ARCS Model in Instructional Design

Detailed presentations of how to use the ARCS Model in the instructional-design process were included in Keller (1982, 1983b) and Keller and Kopp (1985). Four critical events in this process are important to keep in mind. They are audience analysis, motivational objectives, strategy selection, and evaluation.‡

Audience analysis is necessary to determine how much emphasis to give to a particular area of motivation. Because an increase in the use of motivational strategies often results in an increase in the length or expense of instructional development and implementation, it is helpful to know exactly what type of motivational problem is likely to exist.

The ARCS Model provides the basis for identifying audience motivation in terms of the four major categories. For a given body of instruction, the audience might be interested and already aware of the relevance, but they might lack confidence in their ability to master the new knowledge or skills. Furthermore,

---

*This specifies still another characteristic that feedback should have.

†This, like most of the previous prescriptions, is highly unique among the theories in this book and among instructional theories in general. Nevertheless, these prescriptions are not at all incompatible with any of the theories in this book. This illustrates the need to integrate our current knowledge about instructional design into a common knowledge base—a truly comprehensive theory of instruction.

‡Note that these are not instructional strategy components; rather they are development procedures, steps that an instructional designer should follow, not specifications as to what the instruction will be like.

they might be motivated by the promise of monetary or other extrinsic benefits of acquiring the new skill, rather than by intrinsic enjoyment.

The second critical event is to prepare *motivational objectives*. These should specify the student behaviors that the instructor wishes to observe relative to motivational factors. The objectives can be cognitive, affective, or psychomoter in nature. For example, a cognitive motivational objective could state, "The students will indicate a higher expectancy for success midway through the lesson than at the beginning. Affectively, the objective might be that the students will rate the instruction as at least moderately interesting. And in the psychomotor area, the instructor might specify a physical activity that demonstrates motivated effort on the part of the students. This could be indicated by duration of attention, time on task, or duration of participation in a practice activity.

The third critical event, *strategy selection*, requires the instructor or designer to select or create language and activities that accomplish the motivational objectives. There are five guidelines (Keller, 1983b) that are helpful in this process. The motivational strategies should:

1. not take up too much time,
2. not detract from the learning objectives,
3. fall within the time and money constraints of the development and implementation phases of the instruction,
4. be acceptable to the audience, and
5. be compatible with the delivery system, including the instructor's personal style.

In our previous example, the designer would not need to devote a great deal of effort to Attention and Relevance. The goal here would be to avoid boredom and to maintain the sense of relevance that the students entered with. However, in the area of Confidence, the instructor would need to reduce anxiety and structure the learning activities carefully to support the development of positive expectancies for success. Given the extrinsic motivation of the students in this example, the instructor would need to produce the expected rewards for success, or evidence that the immediate achievement was indeed a step on the way to getting the expected reward.

The final critical event is *evaluation*. All too often in studies of motivation, only one of two variables is used to measure the success of motivational activities. The first is achievement. The reasoning is that if the students are more motivated, their achievement will improve. This is not necessarily true. Achievement can vary independently of motivation because of other psychological and environmental factors (Keller, 1979). The second common approach is to use a global measure of affect. These can be useful in determining whether the students basically liked the instruction, but they are usually too general to be useful in motivational design. It is better to have measures that are tied specifically to the motivational objectives, just as one does with learning objectives.

The procedure just described was used in the preparation of the rest of this chapter, with the exception that it has not actually been taught and formatively evaluated. There are two reasons for this. The lessons used in this chapter are segments from longer lessons. Consequently, it would not have been meaningful to try to teach them as they are. However, strategies similar to those recommended in the following pages have been used successfully by the authors and other designers and instructors. The second reason is that the authors have included, for illustrative purposes, more strategies than would probably be needed in an actual application of this lesson. We could justify this quantity of motivational strategies by assuming a low entry level of learner motivation. But even then, we would need to place this lesson into the broader course and unit of instruction before making final decisions on specifically which motivational strategies to use.

LESSON PREFACE

Segments from lessons in two of the other chapters in this book were selected for "motivational enhancements" to illustrate principles of motivational design as described in the ARCS Model. Two segments were chosen instead of one entire lesson because this allowed us to apply the motivational principles to segments that originated from different theoretical points of view. These two segments do not represent the entire range of instruction in the microscope lessons in this book, but they are sufficient to illustrate the motivational principles. To have chosen enough segments to cover the entire microscope lesson, and to have then motivationally enhanced them would have made this chapter unnecessarily long and redundant. However, we have included an introduction to the entire lesson to illustrate certain motivational possibilities in lesson introductions.

As is necessary in preparing motivational strategies for an instructional situation, we have made certain assumptions about the audience. These are not based on an actual analysis because of the hypothetical nature of the present instructional situation, but they do represent one type of audience that often receives this type of instruction. We assumed that the primary audience for this microscope instruction is high school students, most likely ninth graders, who are not in the gifted or college preparatory tracks. This material would be used in a general science or general biology class with adolescents of average intelligence.

Motivationally, these young people would tend to be moderate to high in their responsiveness to a curiosity-arousing situation. They would be moderate to low in their sense of relevance for science instruction, although they would respond if they saw some immediate utility or were stimulated by the instructional methods. They would be low to moderate in confidence, because they would not have had highly successful experiences in math or other science-type activities. Finally, they would be moderate to high in their responsiveness to both motivational and corrective feedback, especially if the instruction and criteria for evaluation were at levels that helped them succeed in their work.

The motivational strategies in the segments were selected judiciously to enhance the original structure and purpose of the segments. Whenever possible, we have used elements in the original segments that were motivational in nature. As we have mentioned, our revisions do not imply any criticism of the original versions. Our revisions are based on the preceding assumptions about the intended audience for the microscope lesson, which may be different from those of the original authors of these segments. We have also attempted to illustrate as many motivational principles as feasible given the scope of this instruction, the limitations of this medium, and our desire to not change the basic instructional design approach in each segment.

We have not attempted to overload the segments purely for the sake of displaying a great variety of motivational strategies but, rather, to follow a basic principle within the ARCS Model, which is that the motivational strategies should not overshadow the primary instructional objectives. Consequently, there are no games, simulations, or extensive motivational illustrations (which are expensive to create and publish) given the rather simple and limited scope of instruction represented by the learning objectives.

In the remainder of this part of the chapter, we have included an introduction to the microscope lesson, a revised version of Segment 2 from Merrill's lesson, and a revised version of Segment 3 from Gropper's lesson. The comment numbers in the left margin are referenced to the comments in Part 3, and are listed with the appropriate strategy statements in Part 1. The "Introduction to the Microscope" lesson follows.

LESSON:
INTRODUCTION TO THE MICROSCOPE

[1]   Suppose you found yourself facing this situation in your science class:

[2]   You are given three things: two glasses of water that appear identical
[3]   to the naked eye, and a microscope. Your task is simple. Drink all of the
water in one of the glasses. However, be warned that while one of the
glasses is filled with pure spring water, the other has been taken from a
pond polluted with nasty, microscopic bacteria.

[4]

[5] The challenge: Can you use the microscope effectively enough to insure that your reward will be cool and refreshing, and not vile and nauseating

[6] This situation is not one that you are likely to encounter, but it is not too different from ones that people who work in public health, hospitals, and scientific laboratories face every day. They have to be able to tell the difference between dangerous and safe substances.

[7] In this lesson you will learn how a microscope works. This is the first step in learning how to use a microscope. You will use the microscope several times in this class. You will also learn things about magnification and lenses that apply to all magnifying glasses and microscopes. You might find some in-

[8] teresting applications of this in your home and when you go camping. For example, do you know how to start a fire with the crystal (the glass top) of a

[9] wristwatch? By the time you finish this lesson, you will know the answer.

Contents

Look at the picture of the microscope in Fig. 9.2. It shows the six parts of this lesson and how they are related to the parts of the microscope, its uses, and its history.

[10]

[11]

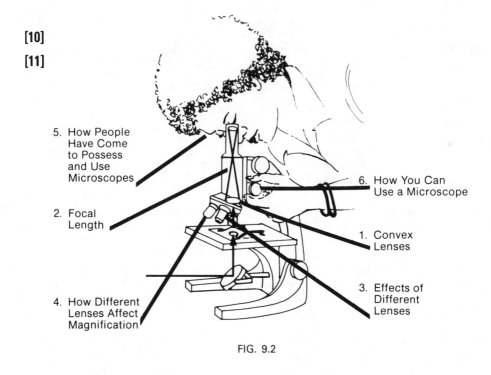

5. How People
   Have Come
   to Possess
   and Use
   Microscopes

6. How You Can
   Use a Microscope

2. Focal
   Length

1. Convex
   Lenses

3. Effects of
   Different
   Lenses

4. How Different
   Lenses Affect
   Magnification

FIG. 9.2

[12]

THROUGH THICK AND THIN
WITH CONVEX LENSES[1]

Introduction

[13] Before Anton Leeuwenhoek and others were ever able to build their early
microscopes to see "tiny beasties" swimming in drops of water, they had to
[14] be able to identify *convex* lenses, the one type of lens that they knew could
make small objects look larger. The methods they used to tell convex lenses
from other lenses are still used today. This lesson will provide you with
[15] descriptions, examples, and practice that will help you become an ace identifier of convex lenses. As a matter of fact, most students who finish this lesson
solve three or four of the study problems at the end without any difficulty at
[16] all.

---

[1]Based on "Segment 2: Convex Lenses" from Merrill.

Reference Example

[17] The convex lens that you see in Fig. 9.3 has been removed from a microscope
so we can examine its characteristics. Check the three clues to identifying
[18] convex lenses as we look at a side view of the lens.

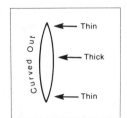

Note:
    It is thick in the middle
    It is thin at the edges
    At least one side is curved out

FIG. 9.3

Key Ideas

Identifying any convex lens boils down to a simple rhyme:

[19]   Thin, thick, thin,
         With a bulge within

because all convex lenses have:

[20]   1. Thin edges surrounding a thicker middle.
         2. At least one side curved outward.

         Repeat the rhyme in your mind until you can easily remember the words
[21] and how they describe the characteristics of convex lenses.

         After some more helpful information in the next section, the rest of the
lesson contains examples and study problems that will test your ability to tell
convex lenses from other types of lenses, and from things that are sometimes confused with convex lenses.

Helpful Information

[22] There is another term that is often confused with *convex,* but it is easy to
remember how to tell them apart. The term *convex* means curved or rounded
like the outside of a ball or circle. The term *concave* also means curved or
rounded, but like the *inside* of a ball, circle or *cave.* If you remember that
concave curves always curve in, like a *cave,* then you can remember that
convex does the opposite: it curves out.

[24]

[25]

This side

is

concave

(like a cave)

This side

is

convex

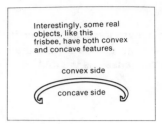

FIG. 9.4

Examples

[26] Some examples of lenses are shown in Fig. 9.5. You can test yourself as you
[27] go along by putting your hand over the notes under each example. Then, see
[28] if you can tell whether it is convex or concave, and give the reasons why.

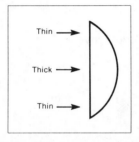

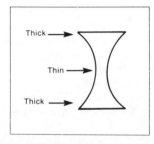

[29]

Note: This is a convex lens
    one side curved out
    thick in middle
    thin at edges

Note: This is not a convex lens
    both sides curved in
    thin in middle
    thick at edges

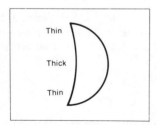

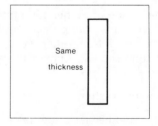

Note: This is a convex lens
    one side curved out
    thicker in middle
    thinner at edges
    left side concave
    right side convex

Note: This is not a convex lens
    neither side curved
    same thickness

FIG. 9.5 Examples of lenses.

[30]

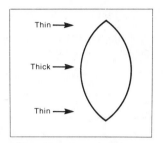
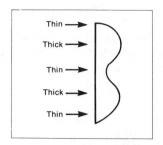

Note: This is a convex lens
both sides curved out
thick in middle
thin at edges

Note: This is not a convex lens
one side flat
one side curved in and out
thinner in middle

FIG. 9.5. (*Continued*)

[31] Study the examples until you are sure you can identify convex lenses, and explain why each one is or is not convex. Then turn to the study problems and test your knowledge. If you have applied yourself to these examples and explanations, then you should do well on the study problems.

Study Problems

Following are several practice problems that will ask you to distinguish convex lenses from other types of lenses. Read each question carefully and then write your answer in the space provided.

[32]
[33]
[34] *Learning Tip.* These questions are like those you will be required to answer on the quiz for this segment. Try to answer them from memory without peeking back at the previous sections. If you can do it, you are ready to take the quiz. How many of the problems do you think you will get right on the first try?

[35]
[36] If you do have trouble with any of these problems, complete as many as you can without help, *then* go back to the KEY IDEA and EXAMPLES sections to review. Remember, if you carefully study these sections, your chances for success are good. Most students who successfully complete this segment are able to get at least three of the four problems on the quiz correct. When you are finished, you may check your answers and fill in your scorecard to see how well you did.

[37]   Problem 1.   Scorecard: Correct _____ Incorrect _____

You may recall from segment one that water-filled glass globes were the first magnifying glasses. Would they be classified as a convex lens? Explain your answer.

Yes   No _____

_____.

Problem 2.   Scorecard: Correct _____ Incorrect _____

Look at the following illustration. Circle one letter corresponding to the convex lens.

a   b   c   d

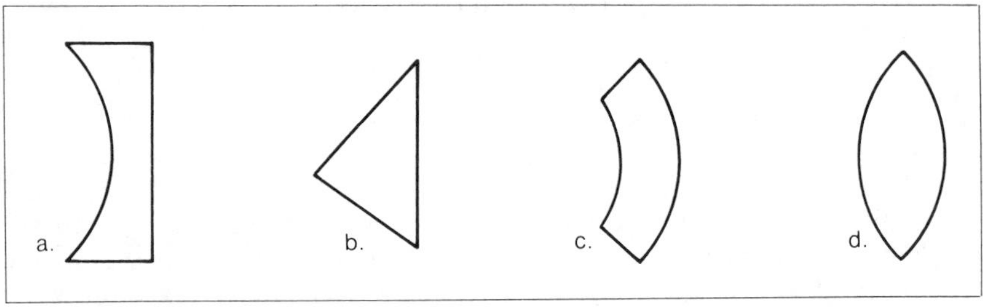

Problem 3.   Scorecard: Correct _____ Incorrect _____

Imagine a drop of water resting on a flat surface. Would it be a kind of convex lens? Explain your answer.

Yes   No _____

_____.

Problem 4.   .   Scorecard: Correct _____ Incorrect _____

Look at the following illustrations. Circle the letter of each lens that is convex.

a   b   c   d

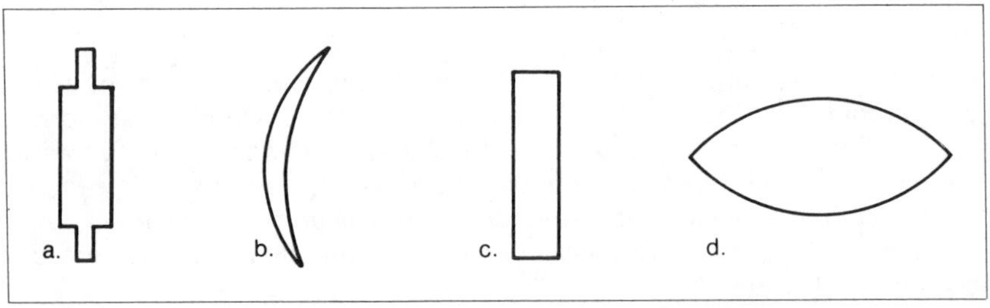

Results.   Scorecard: Total Correct _____ Incorrect _____

Double-check your own answers. When you are finished, turn the page for the correct answers and explanations.

[38] *For Those Who Wish a Further Challenge.* Outdoor survival manuals carried by people adventuring in hot, remote climates describe a way to make a simple convex lens that can be used to start fires. The manuals say to (a) pry off the domelike crystal of your wristwatch; (b) turn it upside down like a shallow cup; (c) fill it to the brim with water; then (d) use it to concentrate the sun's rays on dry tinder until smoke and hopefully flame appear.

Using the rules and information in this lesson, describe how this process makes a convex lens. You may draw an illustration if you wish.

_____

_____

_____

_____

_____

_____

Answers for Study Questions

[39] Problem 1   **Yes**

Water-filled globes have both characteristics of a convex lens: at least one curved surface, and the middle is thicker than the edges.

Problem 2   **d**

Only example d has both characteristics of a convex lens. Example c is curved out on one side but has the same thickness at both middle and ends. Example b is thick in the middle and thin on the edges but it is not a lens because it is not curved. See the following illustration.

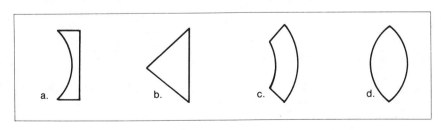

Problem 3 **Yes**

A water droplet always has a curved surface that is thicker in the middle than at the edges. See the illustration.

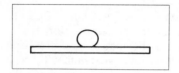

Problem 4 **b and d** are convex: **a and c** are not. Try to explain why each example is or is not convex.

[40] Again, understanding the characteristics of convex lenses is very important in understanding how microscopes work, but if you worked through this lesson with care, you should be well prepared to go on to the next lesson. If [41] you missed any of the study problems, or are still not too confident about convex lenses, it is worth the time to review the lesson until you do feel well prepared.

[42]   HOW TO PREDICT WHAT WILL HAPPEN TO LIGHT RAYS
[43]   WHEN THEY GO THROUGH A CONVEX LENS

[44] (Based on "Section 3: Predicting What Will Happen to Light Rays When They Go Through a Lens" from Gropper.)

Introduction

When you used a microscope, this is what happened (refer to Fig. 9.6): (1) the light rays from the mirror hit the specimen and were reflected off of it: (2) the [45] rays then passed through the lens; (3) the lens changed the direction in which the light rays went; (4) the change in direction made the specimen look bigger; and (5) when you looked into the lens you saw the enlarged or magnified specimen.

[48] This section will help you predict what happens to light when it goes through a convex lens by showing you how lenses change the *direction* of light.

Purpose

This section will show you how to:

• predict what direction and distance light rays will be bent when they
[49]   pass through a convex lens;

306

[46]

[47]

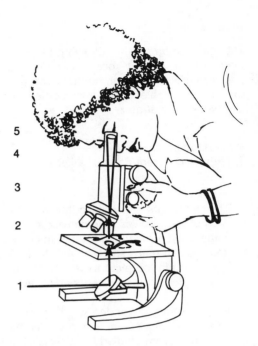

5

4

3

2

1

FIG. 9.6

- predict how the thickness of a lens will affect how much a lens will change the direction of light rays; and

[50]
- define an important term used to describe the light bending power of lenses: *focal length.*

Learning Hints

Look for information that will help you to answer the following questions:

- How can you tell the difference between what happens to light rays that go through the middle of a lens and those that go through the edges of a lens?

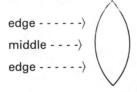

[51]
edge - - - - - -⟩

middle - - - -⟩

edge - - - - - -⟩

- How can you decide which size lens will change the direction of light rays the most and which the least?
- How do you define "focal length?"

Assignment

The information on the following pages explains and illustrates what happens to light when it goes through convex lenses. Read these information
[52] pages carefully, and then do the accompanying exercises. If you understand the exercise problems and answer them correctly, you should have no prob-
[53] lem with the final quiz.

What Happens to Light Rays
That Enter Different Parts of a Lens

The comments below describe what happens to the light rays in each of the pictures. The convex lens used in the following examples could be in a magnifying glass instead of a microscope. Any time you want to make small objects look bigger, convex lenses are used. The object in the pictures is a small nail that we would like a closer look at. Read the comments and then look at the pictures.

Why, you might wonder, would someone want a closer look at a small nail? One example is provided by an eighth grader who, for a
[54] science project, studied the effects of different kinds of chemicals on
[55] the metal in nails. A microscope helped him see the rust and
[56] patterns of erosion. He drew these patterns on poster board for
[57] everyone to see, and he won a prize!

1. Light rays from the sun or from an electric light bulb hit the nail (a). Then, the light rays are reflected from the nail in many directions (b).

2. The reflected light rays enter the convex lens. They enter the lens at many points: (c) the middle; (d) the top; and (e) the bottom.

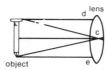

3. The lens changes the direction of the light rays. The light going through the top of the lens is bent down (f). The light going through the bottom is bent up (g). The light slanting down continues to slant down

(h). The light slanting up continues to slant up (i). Notice that the rays going through the center (j) of the lens do *not* bend.

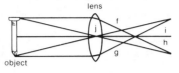

[58]   4. The image you see at the other end of the lens (k) is upside down and larger than the original nail.

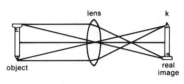

Exercise

1. What will happen to the light rays that enter at the top (a) of the lens shown below? What will happen to the light rays that enter at the bottom (b) of the same lens?

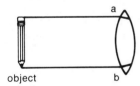

The light rays at the *top* will bend _____.

direction

The light rays at the *bottom* will bend _____.

direction

2. *Draw in* on the picture below what will happen to the light rays that enter the lens at the top (a) and what will happen to the light rays that enter the lens at the bottom (b).

[59]

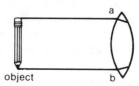

1. What will happen to the light rays that enter at the *top* (a) of the lens shown below and at the *bottom* (b) of the same lens?

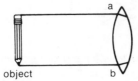

object   b

The light rays at the top will bend <u>DOWN</u>.
direction

The light rays at the bottom will bend <u>UP</u>.
direction.

2. *Draw in* on the picture below what will happen to the light rays that enter the lens at the *top* (a) and what will happen to the light rays that enter the lens at the *bottom* (b).

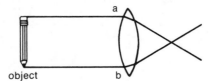

object   b

How the Width of a Lens Affects the Bending of Light Rays

---

1. Look at the three lenses below. Lens (a) on the left is the widest. Lens (c) on the right is the narrowest. Lens (b) in the middle is in between (in width).

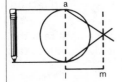 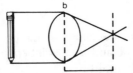 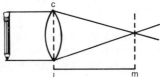

2. Read the following points about what happens to light rays when they pass through *any* lens—no matter how wide or narrow it is:
   - Light rays passing through the top and bottom of *any* lens bend.
   - The light rays at the top bend down; and the light rays at the bottom bend up.
   - Notice that the "down" rays and the "up" rays cross (intersect) on the other side of the lens—at (m).

3. How does the width of a lens affects *how much* the light rays bend?
   - The widest lens (a) made the light rays bend the most; notice

---

that the light rays *cross over* much *closer* to the lens than in the other two examples.

- The narrowest lens (c) made the light rays bend the least; notice that the light rays cross over the farthest away from the lens.

4. Remember the following general points about how the width of a lens affects the bending of light rays:
   - The *wider* a lens is, the *more* it will bend light rays; and the *more* bending there is, the *closer* to the lens will the light rays cross over (intersect).
   - The *narrower* a lens is, the *less* it will bend light rays; and the *less* bending there is, the *farther* away from the lens will the light rays cross over.

5. You're ready now to find out what the distance from the center of a lens (l) to the crossover point (m) is called: FOCAL LENGTH.

[61] 6. If you want an easy way to remember the effect of lens thickness on focal length, compare lenses to people. Picture a short, thick person and a tall (long) thin one. A thick convex lens bends the light rays short, and a thin convex lens bends them long.

Exercise

[62] This is an exercise, but try taking it like a quiz to test your understanding. Answer each question without looking back (or ahead!). Then score your
[63] results. Can you get at least 6 of the 8 possible points?

After scoring your exercise, study any parts you missed until you are confident that you understand them.

Points

_____ 1. (1 point) Look at the drawings on the previous page and then answer the question. (The distance between (l) and (m) is called the "focal length" of a lens.)
Which lens has the *longest* focal length?
_____a _____b _____c

_____ 2. (1 point) The reason *that* lens has the longest focal length is because it bent the light rays the _____most _____least.

_____ 3. (1 point) The lens that bent the light rays the *most* is lens:
_____a _____b _____c

_____ 4. (1 point) Because that lens bent the light rays the least its focal length will be the _____longest _____shortest.

_____ 5. (3 points) Explain how the width of a lens affects the focal length of a lens. Use the following three ideas in your explanation: (a) the thickness of a lens; (b) the amount of bending of light rays; and (c) "focal length."

[64] _____ 6. (1 point) Define what is meant by "focal length."

_____ Total Points. Did you get 6 or more?

[65] Yes? Congratulations! If you missed any, then figure out why you made a mistake. As soon as you understand your errors, then continue on.

[66]
[67] No? Study the instruction for the ones you missed. If you have any problems, then get some help from a teacher or another student. As soon as it "clicks," and you understand what the answers are, then you are ready to smile and continue on.

[68] Before you continue: Once you understand this material, you can be assured it's because you have the ability and you have tried! There is no luck or magic here. When you are ready, go ahead and take the quiz.

Answers to Exercise

1. Look at the drawings on the previous page and then answer this question:
   The distance between (l) and (m) is called the "focal length" of a lens. Which lens has the *longest* focal length? _____a _____b _X_c

2. The reason *that* lens has the longest focal length is because it bent the light rays the _____most _X_least.

[69] 3. The lens that bent the light rays the *most* is lens: _X_a _____b _____c

4. Because that lens bent the light rays the least its focal length will be the _____longest _X_shortest.

5. Explain how the width of a lens affects the focal length of a lens. Use the following ideas in your explanation: (a) the width of a lens; (b) the amount of bending of light rays; and (c) "focal length".

   THE WIDER THE LENS, THE MORE IT BENDS LIGHT RAYS; THE MORE IT BENDS THE RAYS, THE SHORTER THE FOCAL LENGTH WILL BE.

6. Define what is meant by "focal length."

   FOCAL LENGTH MEANS: THE DISTANCE BETWEEN THE CENTER OF THE LENS AND THE PLACE WHERE THE LIGHT RAYS CROSS OVER (INTERSECT).

Comment: Microscopes use combinations of lenses so effectively to bend light that they are able to make even the tiniest objects large enough to see. Now that you have learned how convex lenses bend light, you will understand what you are doing when you make focusing adjustments on an actual microscope.

[70]
[71]

COMMENTS

The comments in this section are in sequence. Each comment is followed by its ARCS strategy reference.

1. The opening sentence of the lesson presents a problematic situation. It raises a question in the learner's mind as to what the "situation" is going to be. (A.2 Inquiry Arousal)

2. Even though this problem is not one that the students are likely to encounter, it is one that they can relate to in terms of everyday experience. (R.1 Familiarity)

3. The problem description combined with the challenge statement help stimulate the need for achievement by defining a goal, a standard, and a moderate level of risk. (R.3 Motive Matching)

4. The picture is the first thing on the page that many readers will notice. The puzzled expressions on the children's faces are somewhat surprising and unexpected in a lesson of this type, and they generate a sense of uncertainty about what is the problem. (A.1 Perceptual Arousal)

5. The "challenge" statement is worded to stimulate inquiry arousal in the learner. (A.2 Inquiry Arousal)

6. By referring to people who have to use the microscope in their everyday work to make important decisions similar to the one in the example, students are helped to see the relevance of this lesson. (R.2 Goal Orientation)

7. This paragraph opens with a description of the relevance of the material in this lesson to the general task of learning how to use a microscope. (R.2 Goal Orientation)

8. This additional question promotes inquiry arousal by asking the learner a question related to magnification but refers to an everyday object rather than a microscope. This statement might also contribute to the perceived relevance (R.1.) of this lesson. (A.2 Inquiry Arousal)

9. This paragraph tells the learner what to expect to learn from the lesson with respect to both the main topic of the lesson and an incidental example (the wristwatch example). This helps the learner have confidence that there is something specific to be learned here. (C.1 Expectancy for Success)

10. Having the titles of each segment keyed to the illustration is an unusual way of presenting the content and is likely to stimulate more than the usual amount of attention to the lesson's contents. (A.1 Perceptual Arousal)

11. The illustration helps improve learner confidence by relating the abstract segment titles to a concrete image of the object of their study. (C.1 Expectancy for Success)

12. The original title, "Convex Lenses," clearly identified the lesson, but because titles occupy such a visually and conceptually strategic position in a

lesson, we revised it to add more of a novelty quality. ''Through Thick and Thin with Convex Lenses'' is not only a pun on the phrase ''thick and thin''; it also provides some valuable learning cues for the student. (A.1 Perceptual Arousal)

13. The use of a specific person's name, personal pronouns, and an example that the students can visualize helps the students relate to this lesson as a relevant human experience. (R.1 Familiarity)

14. In the opening paragraph, we have added unusual language (e.g., ''tiny beasties'') to help capture student interest. (A.1 Perceptual Arousal)

15. This sentence, stated in personal terms, helps the learner set a personal goal (''become an ace identifier of convex lenses'') that represents the lesson's primary objective. (R.2 Goal Orientation)

16. Providing a normative standard can help the student set a reasonable level of challenge. (C.1 Expectancy for Success)

17. The description of the convex lens as part of a microscope helps the students see it as an important part of a familiar object. An illustration could portray this even better, but would probably not be worth the space and expense for this simple point. (R.1 Familiarity)

18. By inserting the sentence beginning, ''Check the three clues . . . ,'' we are posing a problem for the learner to solve, albeit a low-level one, and helping stimulate the student's interest in seeking specific information. It also assists learning by clarifying the idea of viewing lenses in cross-section, a critical concept in describing and analyzing lenses. (A.2 Inquiry Arousal)

19. Mnemonic devices have obvious value as memory aids. Motivationally, they can serve the learner as well. This simple couplet uses novel word sounds, visual language, and of course, the ''dose of surprise that rhyming supplies'' to equip the learner with an interesting and memorable learning tool. (A.1 Perceptual Arousal)

20. The variation in format (margin width, text vs. illustration, white space) and type style on this and many of the subsequent pages contributes to sustaining learner attention. (A.3 Variability)

21. Simple exercises such as this one provide an immediate sense of accomplishment and help the learner establish a sense of confidence in his or her ability to learn the material. Exercises that are moderately challenging and provide immediate feedback can contribute in a similar way to the development of confidence. (C.2 Challenge Setting)

22. Helping the learner recognize and avoid obstacles to success also helps increase confidence. (C.1 Expectancy for Success)

23. Associating the unfamiliar term *convex* with familiar objects, and contrasting it with *concave,* with its built-in mnemonic, helps make *convex* a more familiar, relevant, and memorable word. (R.1 Familiarity)

24. A frisbee is not an object that a student would expect in a microscope

lesson. This unexpected object helps get student attention and also assists in teaching the two concepts of convex and concave by providing still another association with a familiar object. (A.1 Perceptual Arousal)

25. In addition to its interest value (Comment 24), the frisbee is a familiar object and has the same effect described in the previous example. (R.1 Familiarity)

26. This exercise presents a problem and requires the learner to search his or her memory from the previous instruction, or the information following each illustration, to solve the problem. (A.2 Inquiry Arousal)

27. Varying the response format helps maintain the stimulation level of the lesson. (A.3 Variability)

28. The student is stimulated to set a personal goal and to try to accomplish it. (R.2 Goal Orientation)

29. Immediate feedback is provided if the learner chose to set a personal challenge as suggested in the instructions for this exercise. The knowledge of results promotes learning by confirming correct responses and correcting wrong ones, but it also has a motivational effect in that it allows the achievement-motivated person to get a measure of success. (S.2 Positive Consequences)

30. This nonexample of a convex lens, although legitimate, is somewhat bizarre compared to the others and would stimulate an extra measure of attention. (A.2 Perceptual Arousal)

31. This statement (''If you have applied yourself . . .'') illustrates how esteem-building, attributional comments can be inserted into a lesson. However, you should *never* include this type of comment in a lesson unless you know for sure that the learners have the ability to succeed, which means that they will succeed if they have exerted effort in their study of the lesson. (C.3 Attribution Molding)

32. This comment has been restated in a positive fashion, in contrast to a negatively oriented statement in the original (e.g., if you peek, then you might not succeed later) in order to bolster confidence by pointing out that a current success is likely to lead to a future success because the required performance is basically the same. (C.1 Expectancy for Success)

33. Asking the learner to set a goal (''How many . . . ?''), and providing a salient feedback and scoring system help motivate the need for achievement. Because it is optional, it is nonthreatening for people who do not want to exercise the achievement motive. (R.3 Motive Matching)

34. In addition to stimulating the need to achieve (see Comment 33), this instruction allows the learner to set a goal that will allow him or her to have good personal feelings if the goal is achieved. (C.2 Challenge Setting)

35. This is another statement designed to help the student develop internal attributions for success. (C.3 Attribution Molding)

36. This gives the student a standard that helps him or her understand the challenge level in the segment. (C.1 Expectancy for Success)

37. Students with a high need for achievement will appreciate a salient method of keeping track of their accomplishment. (R.3 Motive Matching)

38. This exercise provides the intrinsically motivated learner with an opportunity to use his or her newly acquired knowledge. Furthermore, one of the best indicators of students' motivation is their inclination to freely re-engage in similar learning activities at a later date. No one is required to deal with this little problem-solving task, but those who do may feel rewarded by the high inherent interest level of the scenario. Furthermore, the teacher can subtly determine the motivation level of this lesson by informally polling students as to their reaction to this optional exercise. (S.1 Natural Consequences)

39. Having the answers immediately available allows the student to be immediately rewarded for successful responses (and bolsters confidence by supporting the expectation that effort leads to success). This comment is true only if the items are moderately challenging (if the answers are self-evident, then the feedback is somewhat redundant), and if students who do exert effort correctly answer most of the questions. The second condition is similar to the caution included in Comment 31. (S.2 Positive Consequences)

40. It is an inefficient use of design and learning time to start the motivation process all over again when we go onto the next lesson. Using passages of this kind provides a motivational bridge to the next lesson in the unit. This sentence helps relate the utility of the present lesson as preparation for the next one and contributes to the continuing motivation of the student. (R.2 Goal Orientation)

41. The learner is encouraged to set a personal level of challenge that is appropriate for himself or herself and not to continue until it is achieved. (C.2 Challenge Setting)

42. The "how to" title of this lesson segment helps stimulate an information-seeking attitude in the learner. (A.2 Inquiry Arousal)

43. Furthermore "how to" titles can be effective in creating in the learner the prospect of a useful, relevant payoff. (R.2 Goal Orientation)

44. The word *convex* has been added to the title to help tie this segment to the others in the lesson, reinforcing the student's confidence that careful study of the previous lesson segments can in fact be instrumental in achieving continued success in other parts of the microscope lesson as well. (C.1 Expectancy for Success)

45. This sequence of steps is an effective way to introduce the lesson, especially as it establishes the relevance of understanding the light-bending qualities of lenses in relation to the workings of a microscope. (R.2 Goal Orientation)

46. This illustration has a degree of novelty because it is the first one in the

two lesson segments that shows a person doing something with a microscope. (A.1 Perceptual Arousal)

47. The person using the microscope provides a familiar scene that the students can relate to, whether or not they have actually looked through a microscope themselves. (R.1 Familiarity)

48. The nicely motivating title has promised one thing, and by slightly changing this passage to remain parallel with it (i.e., referring to convex lenses rather than lenses in general), we cause the passage to build on the lesson's promise rather than causing the learner to think some other characteristic of lenses and light is about to be explained. This consistency adds subtle support to a growing level of learner confidence with respect to expectancy for success. (C.1 Expectancy for Success)

49. The original formulation of the first part of the purpose statement was identical with the title of this segment. We have changed the wording to be more specific and show that this is just one part of the lesson. In the second part of the purpose statement we changed the word *width* to *thickness* to be consistent with earlier descriptions of the lenses. Motivationally, these changes help avoid confusion and maintain learner expectancy for success. (C.1 Expectancy for Success)

50. We have revised this statement, inasmuch as it represents one of the original six objectives, to make it the same length as the others and give more of an image of importance to make its relevance equivalent to the others. (R.2 Goal Orientation)

51. Even highly motivated students find it hard to stay motivated when terms in a lesson confuse them. In this situation, it might help some students maintain their confidence if we include an illustration to make it clear that the middle and edges (we changed *end* in the original to *edge*) of a lens refer to a cross-sectional view. (C.1 Expectancy for Success)

52. This expanded assignment statement provides a straightforward explanation of the relevance, in terms of utility, of the following pages of the lesson. (R.2 Goal Orientation)

53. This statement helps build an expectancy that success will be due to personal effort. Again a caution. Do not say this unless you have validated the instructional materials. It is best if you can give an approximate figure such as, "In our tests, 80% of the students who got the exercises correct without looking at the answers passed the quiz." (C.3 Attribution Molding)

54. Note how this page changes from mostly text on the previous page to mostly illustrations. The progressive buildup in the illustrations also creates visual interest. (A.3 Variability)

55. We have replaced the stick in the original lesson with a nail, because it is concrete, familiar, and lends itself to the problem-solving scenario of our want-

ing to take a closer look at it with the lens of a magnifying glass. (R.1 Familiarity)

56. This and the previous lesson segments have been about convex lenses and microscopes. Now magnifying glasses are introduced, which stimulates a question about their relationship to the previous topics. In this example, the inquiry arousal is quickly resolved by the next sentence ("A microscope helped him . . ."). (A.2 Inquiry Arousal)

57. The anecdote portrays a familiar type of situation from a science class and provides a meaningful scenario for taking a closer look at nails. (R.1 Familiarity)

58. Several small changes were made to this page to help students know for sure if they understand the material, thus keeping confidence high. First, we substituted a nail for a stick so that the learner can confirm that the object is inverted by looking at the diagram. This is an example of providing the clearest possible feedback to keep the learner sailing through the instruction and not running aground over incidental impediments. Second, we made the image in Part 3 visibly larger than the original to emphasize the concept of magnification. Finally, we changed "real image" in Part 3 to "image" to avoid the introduction of an unexplained and possibly confusing term. This particular set of examples helps illustrate the close interplay between learning and motivational strategies that can sometimes occur. (C.1 Expectancy for Success)

59. The act of drawing an answer to a question is an effective form of active responding that provides an interesting variation in response mode. (A.3 Variability)

60. As in the earlier lesson segment, the immediate availability of feedback is an important source of satisfaction to the achievement-motivated learner who is not sure if all his/her answers are correct. (S.2 Positive Consequences)

61. The imagery in this analogy provides familiar objects (short, thick people and tall, thin people) that the students can relate to the unfamiliar lens and focal length combinations. (R.1 Familiarity)

62. The student is encouraged to treat the exercise like an informal quiz. This is an unexpected event because it has not been done previously, and should help stimulate a higher level of attention than the exercise otherwise would. (A.1 Perceptual Arousal)

63. These instructions help the student set a personal goal to accomplish in the exercise. (R.2 Goal Orientation)

64. This entire exercise provides an opportunity to exercise achievement-striving behavior. Even if the student still isn't highly interested in the content of the lesson, this gives him or her a chance to get excited about setting a goal and trying to accomplish it. (R.3 Motive Matching)

65. These statements will provide esteem-building feedback to those who

made the criterion, and a focused challenge to those who need additional study. If, among the learners who would use these materials, there are some who would be discouraged rather than challenged by not making the criterion score the first time, then it would be better to avoid this kind of competition against a set standard during the learning exercise. (C.2 Challenge Setting)

66. In this example, the immediate feedback in the form of knowledge of correct results is augmented by reinforcing comments such as "Congratulations!" and "ready to smile." (S.2 Positive Consequences)

67. It can bolster confidence and help students keep expectancy for success alive if they know it's okay to get help. (C.1 Expectancy for Success)

68. Feedback that reinforces personal effort and ability as the determinants of success can be inserted in the lesson and can help the learner build internal attributions. If there is any reason to doubt that it will be effective (as when most of the learners are already highly confident in their ability to succeed), then it is better to leave this feedback out of the printed material and let the teacher present it selectively to students who need it. (C.3 Attribution Molding)

69. This is another example of immediate feedback in the form of knowledge of correct results. (S.2 Positive Consequences)

70. The way in which this sentence is stated helps sustain the learner's interest in wondering what kinds of things can be seen with a microscope. (A.2 Inquiry Arousal)

71. Keeping each lesson tied to the greater unit whole helps the student maintain contact with the greater mission of his learning and provides more of a payoff for his work on this single lesson than merely being finished with it. (R.2 Goal Orientation)

REFERENCES

Berlyne, D. E. (1965). Motivational problems raised by exploratory and epistemic behavior. In S. Koch (Ed.), *Psychology: A study of a science* (Vol. 5). New York: McGraw-Hill.

Keller, J. M. (1979). Motivation and instructional design: A theoretical perspective. *Journal of Instructional Development, 2*, 26–34.

Keller, J. M. (1983a). Motivational design of instruction. In C. M. Reigeluth (Ed.), *Instructional design theories and models: An overview of their current status*. Hillsdale, NJ: Lawrence Erlbaum Associates.

Keller, J. M. (1983b). The use of the ARCS model of motivation in teacher training. K. Shaw (Ed.), *Aspects of educational technology* (Vol. XVII). London: Kogan Page.

Keller, J. M. (1987). Motivational design. In R. McAleese & D. Unwin (Eds.), *Encyclopaedia of educational media, communications and technology*. Westport, CT: Greenwood Press.

Keller, J. M., & Dodge, B. (1982). *The ARCS model of motivational strategies for course designers and developers*. Fort Monroe, VA: Training Developments Institute.

Keller, J. M., & Kopp, T. W. (1985). A systematic model for designing motivation in instruction. Florida State University: Instructional Science and Technology Program Occasional Paper.

Kopp, T. W. (1982). Designing boredom out of instruction. *NSPI Journal, 32*, 23–27.

Kopp, T. W. (1983). *Boredom in college lecture instruction*. Unpublished doctoral dissertation, Syracuse University.

Malone, T. W. (1981). Toward a theory of intrinsically motivating instruction. *Cognitive Science, 4*, 333–369.

Maw, W. H., & Maw, E. W. (1968). Self appraisal of curiosity. *Journal of Educational Research, 61*, 462–466.

McCombs, B. L. (1984). Process and skills underlying continuing intrinsic motivation to learn: Toward a definition of motivational skills training interventions. *Educational Psychologist, 19*, 199–218.

Reigeluth, C. M. (Ed.). (1983). *Instructional design theories and models: An overview of their current status*. Hillsdale, NJ: Lawerence Erlbaum Associates.

Wlodkowski, R. J. (1981). Making sense of motivation: A systematic model to consolidate motivational constructs across theories. *Educational Psychologist, 16*, 101–110.

Wlodkowski, R. J. (1985). *Enhancing adult motivation to learn*. San Francisco: Jossey-Bass Publishers.

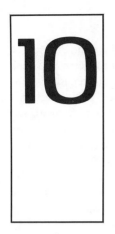

Contrasting and Complementary Approaches to Instructional Design

Glenn E. Snelbecker, Ph.D.
Temple University

INTRODUCTION

The preceding chapters have described illustrative approaches to the design of instruction, based on selected theories. The present chapter considers these alternative approaches, individually and collectively, in the context of earlier instructional theory development and emergent contemporary trends. Some suggestions are also provided for examining these theories and for exploring how they might be applied to instruction of interest to readers.

The title of this chapter indicates the author's position that readers can gain helpful information from each of these theories, even when one chooses to rely mainly on one theory. It is proposed that we might view these respective approaches to instructional design as having both contrasting and complementary features.

Some Cautions About the Specific Applications

This book provides some useful illustrative applications of the respective theories; however, readers should keep in mind at least three cautions. First, as some chapter authors already have noted, designers' approaches depend on the subject matter being addressed as well as on the respective theories being used.* Thus, one should keep in mind the nature of the subject matter commonly addressed by these theories. It would be prudent to examine carefully what kinds of subject

---

*For example, Gagné–Briggs' depends on their categories and subcategories of learning outcomes; Merrill depends on his content types and performance levels; and so on.

matter are addressed in your situation and to explore similarities and differences between your subject matter topics and those addressed in these chapters. Such comparisons should not only take into account the subject matter topics but, perhaps even more importantly, should also include the types of instructional objectives, processes, and learning tasks. The instructional objectives addressed in this book are described and classified in chapter 1. Careful examination of the chapters applying these theories will provide more details about the objectives, processes, and tasks affiliated with each theory's application.

Second, each application represents only one of many ways in which the respective theories could be used with this subject matter. It is conceivable not only that someone else using a given theory might apply it in somewhat different ways but also that the same designer might even use the theory in different ways at different times.

Third, given the central, integral role accorded to evaluation during the design process, one should remember that the respective chapters describe tentative (not final) plans and materials before undergoing customary formative evaluations and revisions. Comments offered in the present chapter will be based on the assumption that at least some of the needed modifications would be made during such formative evaluation and revision procedures.

Different Audiences, Different Expectations

Four different, but not mutually exclusive, types of potential "audiences" have been identified for instructional-design literature (Snelbecker, 1983) with each audience having somewhat different expectations about instructional theories. Briefly, the potential readers of this book can be identified as follows:

1. Researchers, who typically conduct empirical studies and/or evaluation studies on selected aspects of the theories.
2. Theorists, who particularly are interested in integrating/synthesizing findings and evolving conceptual systems for selected areas of interest (broad or narrow in scope, usually focusing on many but not all relevant variables).
3. Instructional designers (or designers), who serve as intermediaries relating the new knowledge provided by researchers and theorists to the concerns of practitioners and who provide plans for instruction.
4. Practitioners (e.g., instructors, administrators), who primarily are using instructional theories and instructional plans for some practical matters.

For purposes of the present book, we can consider the researchers and theorists in one group, and the designers and practitioners in another group. Two major areas in which expectations can be quite different are: (a) the basis for planning instruction; and (b) the practical implications resulting from such plans.

Researchers and theorists typically are especially interested in the underlying rationales and the empirical support for the particular applications of theories. They most likely will expect the chapter authors to identify the main variables associated with their instructional interventions and to have some means for measuring the effects of the instruction. What practical details are needed to implement the instructional plans and whether the selected variables necessarily address most facets of the practical context are not high-priority concerns for the researchers and theorists.

In contrast, although the designers and practitioners obviously want a sound basis for practice, their primary concern typically is with the practical aspects and implications of each instructional application. They particularly are interested in the roles and activities—for instructors and for students—that are derived from the respective theories, especially as they influence instructional/learning processes. There also are important differences with regard to the range of conditions and variables addressed by the two groups. Whereas researchers and theorists may be content to address only selected aspects of the instructional context, designers and practitioners expect that all major facets of their particular settings will be considered in the instructional plans—whether or not all aspects are explicitly addressed by the theory.

Comments in the present chapter take into account these diverse and overlapping expectations. Given the focus of this book, many comments are addressed to the designers and practitioners. Some comments emphasize the expectations of researchers and theorists, while others address the common interests of readers in general.

Select One Theory, or More?

An obvious question for any reader is this: "Is it 'better' to select one theory when designing instruction or to draw ideas from different theories?" This question has important implications for all four potential audiences previously identified! Answers to this question depend to a great extent on our purposes in considering instructional theories, with the attendant expectations we may have about theories.

For researchers and theorists, the answer is rather straightforward: In general it is best to focus on one theory when conducting research or delineating principles. Of course, there are some instances in which exploration of different points of view may be the focus of the research, and theorists sometimes attempt to integrate ideas from two or more theories. However, reviews of psychological and educational research and theory construction ventures during the past century (cf. Snelbecker, 1985) suggest that researchers and theorists are more likely to obtain coherent results when efforts are organized around a specified conceptual system.

For practitioners and designers, the question is not as readily resolved. There is considerable debate among respected authorities about the most appropriate approach. Traditionally, both applied psychologists and educators have been "advised" to rely exclusively or primarily on some preferred approach, even when it is recognized that the theory (no matter which one is chosen!) may not address all variables that are important in the practical situation. As a result, we've had numerous examples of theories that are "stretched" to address practical matters that have not even been considered within the scope of those theories. However, in recent years there has been growing support for various forms of what I've identified as "systematic eclecticism."

It is instructive to observe what has been happening with regard to theories in a parallel area of applied psychology where similar problems and trends exist. The area involves the construction and use of psychotherapy theories. During the past several years there has been growing interest in finding ways to help practitioners to select theories and techniques that could be useful in particular practical situations. For example, after commenting critically about the long-established tendency to rely on only one theory, Goldfried (1980) observed: "There is a growing discontent among therapists of varying orientations. Psychoanalytic, behavioral, and humanistically oriented clinicians are starting to raise serious questions about the limits of their respective approaches and are becoming more open to contributions from other paradigms" (p. 991). Unfortunately, thus far there have been few guidelines to assist therapists in deciding which therapy theory to select for which patient under what kinds of conditions. This led Goldfried and others to invite people with similar views (including the present author) to establish the Society for the Exploration of Psychotherapy Integration. It is noteworthy that many of the major psychotherapy researchers and theorists have joined this organization, even while maintaining their own "partisan" activities.

In a similar manner Norcross (1985) pointed to the need for more extensive consideration of ways to select and use psychotherapy theories. He quoted some remarks by Abraham Maslow to the effect that "if you only have a hammer you treat everything like a nail" (p. 757). The remark was offered as a criticism of the long-established tendency among psychotherapists to use some treatment approach with which they are familiar rather than to consider carefully whether the particular approach would be appropriate for the client's problems. Norcross observed that there are some important changes occurring in "the emerging psychotherapy zeitgeist: the systematic integration of diverse theoretical systems. Whether it goes by the label of rapprochement, convergence, eclecticism, prescriptive psychotherapy, or integrationism, this movement seeks an end to the 'ideological cold war' and 'dogma eat dogma' environment in psychotherapy"

(p. 758). He cited the book he was reviewing—*Differential Therapeutics in Psychiatry: The Art and Science of Treatment Selection,* by Frances, Clarkin, and Perry—as a good example of emerging efforts to help practitioners to view "rival approaches as complementary rather than contradictory" (p. 758).

Research on counseling psychologists' views about preferences in psychotherapy orientations has produced results similar to the findings obtained earlier with clinical psychologists: Practicing counseling psychologists (and clinical psychologists) are much more eclectic than therapy researchers and theorists. For example, Smith (1982) observed: "Each new system of therapy has faulted its predecessors on one ground or another and has claimed superiority to them" (p. 802). Citing findings from his survey of counseling psychologists, Smith concluded: "Eclecticism is clearly the preference of the largest number of psychologists. Yet, there seems to be a dissatisfaction with the term *eclecticism* per se. Concepts such as multimodal, creative synthesis, emerging eclecticism, integration, and systems theory appear to be the most descriptive of the current trend toward broad spectrum approaches to counseling and psychotherapy" (p. 808).

One other item is worth noting. While preparing the present chapter I had opportunity to read a prepublication draft of Murray's chapter (Murray, 1986), "Possibilities and Promises of Eclecticism," for Norcross's (1986) *Handbook of Eclectic Psychotherapy.* Murray acknowledges that much remains to be understood about using different therapy theories in a practical context, but he also proposes that potential benefits will be more than worth the effort.

Of course, selection and use of instructional theories does not necessarily involve the same issues and prospects found in the selection and use of therapy theories. However, research findings and guidelines about selections among instructional theories are not as extensive as the work concerning therapy and counseling theories. Thus, it would seem that these two areas (therapy and instruction) are sufficiently similar that people interested in instructional design may benefit from the work being done with regard to selection and use of therapy theories.

Each reader of this book must decide whether to focus exclusively or primarily on one theory or to derive ideas from several theories, and should consider how—if at all—ideas from different theories may be useful. It is plausible that "novices" may elect to rely mainly on one theory, inasmuch as considering several different theories can seem overwhelming. More experienced readers may find it quite comfortable to derive ideas from different theories. Novices may find the present book useful in helping them to select among theories addressed here and may even gain ideas about examining other theories as well. Comments in the present chapter consider both the contrasting and complementary features of the instructional theories applied in the previous chapters. Hopefully, these comments will prove to be useful no matter whether you choose one or more theories to guide your work.

Which Theory (Theories), and How Adequate?

No matter whether we choose to rely on one theory or whether we want to derive ideas from different theories, questions about how we should select theories typically arise. Along with selection issues, questions are also typically raised about the adequacy and appropriateness of whatever theories are selected.

Many years ago Kendler (1952) offered some advice that is still relevant today. Kendler suggested that "selection of any theoretical model, be it physiological or phenomenological, or for that matter, physical, mechanical or statistical, is in the last analysis a decision having no *truth character*" (p. 276). To an extent we might say that selection among theories involves personal and professional judgments. We could even suggest that, like "beauty," the "appropriateness" of a theory lies partly—but not entirely!—in the eyes of the beholder.

With regard to instructional theories, it is important that we clarify carefully what it is that we "expect" of the theories. Unfortunately, in education and training there has been a tendency to select theories and to adopt allegedly good innovations without fully evaluating what contributions they might provide to teaching/learning processes and outcomes. Kirst and Meister (1985) have identified a number of educational innovations that have persisted and those that have failed to last in education. Included in the "failed" group are: Individually Prescribed Instruction (IPI), new math, computer-assisted instruction, and programmed instruction. Kirst and Meister conjecture that reforms that are most likely to persist in the late 1980s and 1990s will be those that involve constituencies and that are easy to monitor while staying within cost constraints.

Considering the close affiliation between some of these "failed" innovations and instructional theory, it is worth noting some of the processes by which theories seem to have been selected in education and training during the past century (Snelbecker, 1985). For example, the philosophical views associated (correcty or incorrectly) with theorists traditionally have been important influences on teachers' and instructors' choices among theories. Some selection decisions apparently have been based primarily on the ease with which the theory enables the user to analyze locally relevant instructional components and procedures. Another prominent influence has been the belief that designated theories may be more compatible with certain instructional goals than are other theories. Other criteria for selecting theories have involved preferences for certain types of instructional activities. For example, selections of some theories apparently have been made because the particular instructors prefer group discussions and explorations of feelings; some theories have been selected because the instructors prefer to focus on thinking and problem solving, or because they choose to emphasize behaviors and demonstrable competence on specified tasks. Some theories have received favorable attention because of their "prescriptions" for teacher and student activities, while others have been warmly received because of their guidelines for organizing and addressing curricular content.

Practically all of these features are relevant for most instructional contexts. Problems in selecting theories are more likely to come from considering too few features, rather than too many, in exploring the relevance of theories for a particular instructional setting. Most practical situations typically involve a wider range of variables and conditions than can be addressed by any given theory. How can one identify theories that might be useful? One first step for readers of this book could be to explore, in depth, the purpose and the global goals for the instruction as well as the specific objectives and the conditions under which the instruction is to be available. As the purposes and characteristics expected of the instructional experiences are clarified, one then has a basis for recognizing which theories might "match up with" and be relevant for that particular situation.

The descriptions of and comments about the illustrative applications in this book can provide some useful cues about the potential relevance of each of the theories. The first chapter provides details about the subject matter and the objectives addressed in these illustrative applications. Each of the eight illustrative theory application chapters contains notes about the uses of the respective theory and lists major features of that theory. This information can help to highlight central features of each theory that may prove to be useful in a given practical situation.

Inevitably, even if many theories are "consulted," it will become obvious that some aspects of the practical situation simply are not addressed by currently available instructional theories. At that point the researcher and the theorist may simply "delimit" their area of inquiry and so advise the reader without any felt need for apology. In contrast, the designer and the practitioner must make some decisions as to how—not whether!—such additional facets must be addressed. Astute researchers and theorists will seize this opportunity to identify new variables and conditions that should be studied and incorporated in the theory. Knowledgeable designers and practitioners will draw from their previous practical experiences to generate potentially relevant means for handling the practical problems and for "filling in the gaps" not addressed by the theories.

Some Attributes to Consider Among These Approaches

Included in the chapters of this book are eight different but somewhat overlapping approaches to instructional design. In the context of the foregoing comments, here are some suggestions about attributes to consider when reviewing the applications of these theories.

First, it is recommended that you be alert to the common characteristics as well as the unique features among these theories. Obviously, there are many advantages in trying to identify the way in which each theory adds something different or provides a unique feature for the design of the instruction. (Some of these features will be enumerated in the next section of this chapter.) However, it also is important to note the commonalities among some or all of these theories. Recognition of these commonalities can facilitate your integration of ideas from different theories. The commonalities also help to define the emerging synthesis of information about instructional design referred to in the first chapter of this book.

Second, it is suggested that you note which aspects of instruction seem to be "central" for a given theory and which seem to be "peripheral." This information will help you to recognize those aspects of the practical situation for which each theory may have important contributions.

Third, it is strongly suggested that you be alert to ways in which the theories can be used to analyze practical situations. The theories can provide a systematic means for conceptualizing the practical situation and for identifying those conditions and variables that are most pertinent for effective, efficient, and enticing instruction. Moreover, the theories can help you to recognize how even quite different instructional problems may have common feaures and, possibly, common solutions.

Fourth, it should be noted that the theories can have interesting "intertwined" relationships with instructional practices. It is quite possible, indeed highly probable, that similar practical approaches can be derived from several different theories; this can occur even though the rationales for the particular practical approaches differ from one theory to another. Perhaps more obviously, the theories can differ substantially with regard to instructional techniques and practices. Thus, in reviewing the examples across these chapters, it is worth observing the extent to which different theories may "dictate" similar approaches in some cases and quite different approaches in others.

Observations About
the Eight Illustrative Approaches

In chapter 1, some general information is provided about the nature of instructional theories as they have evolved over the decades and as they exist at the present time. Also in chapter 1 is a description and discussion of the subject matter and the instructional objectives addressed by each of the theories in this book. Each of the eight subsequent chapters provides detailed illustrations, comments, and explanations, including the most important features of each theory. Without duplicating this information about the respective theories, some comments are made here about each of the approaches portrayed in this book as well as about some other contemporary theories of possible interest to readers.

Only one in the present collection of theories can be identified as clearly "behavioral" in nature: Gropper's Behavioral Approach, in chapter 3. This is a much more comprehensive use of behavioral theory than is generally identified with the programmed instruction theories of the 1960s. But it is reasonably representative of the broader, somewhat more sophisticated application of behavioral principles found today in instructional settings and clinical settings.

Note that much of the terminology in chapter 3 comes directly from behavioral learning theory (e.g., discriminations, generalizations, associations, chains) but that the topics addressed are not limited to narrowly defined, overtly observable behavior, per se. As examples, note that one of the first topics addressed in chapter 3 is the need to gain and maintain readers' "attention," and that throughout the chapter there are attempts made to aid students in understanding how the microscope works rather than merely being able to operate the microscope. Even 1960s "vintage" instructional theories with a behavioral orientation had some of these features, but Gropper's approach is broader in terms of both the topics addressed and the resources used as a basis for the instructional interventions. As is customary with behavioral approaches, there is considerable emphasis on evaluation. However, note that this includes self-evaluation as well as instructor evaluation. The behavioral theory is quite evident, as the objectives for each component are specified in measurable terms and the instructional techniques and evaluation procedures are related to each objective. The chapter includes rather explicit descriptions of ways in which behavioral concepts and principles were used to design the instructional procedures presented in the chapter.

Three of the eight theories can be described as essentially cognitive in nature—namely, Landa's Algo-Heuristic Theory (chapter 4), Scandura's Structural Learning Theory (chapter 5), and Collins's Inquiry Teaching approach (chapter 6). However, each of these three provides a somewhat different emphasis, despite their common emphasis on cognitive aspects both in the instructional context and in the theory from which their plans are derived.

Collins's approach particularly clarifies some of the instructional techniques and processes that can facilitate understanding and critical thinking by the learner. As the chapter 6 title indicates, this approach provides theory-based guidelines and techniques for a "dialogue" between instructors and students. Initially, the focus is on aiding students to understand the terminology about lenses so that higher levels of understanding can be attained. This chapter then provides numerous examples of inquiry techniques through which instructors can aid students to develop and test hypotheses (or rules) about factors influencing focal length. These examples take into account some of the problems one encounters when using inquiry instructional techniques.

Scandura's approach involves a systematic analysis of the structure of the subject matter so that it can be organized in ways that facilitate students' understanding. More specifically, the intent with Scandura's theory is to identify the "rules" students need to learn, as well as the "rules" that can guide such learning. However, it is important to recognize that Scandura's definition of "rule" is not the same as the rather casual definition found in Collins's chapter. Because rules are so important in Scandura's theory, you may want to examine carefully the brief discussion about rules in chapter 5 and also review the more extensive discussion in the 1983 companion volume (Reigeluth, 1983). Consistent with cognitive theory more generally, Scandura's approach focuses on the thought processes needed to guide behavior. Both conscious processes and "automated" (or less conscious) processes typically are involved in applying Structural Learning Theory.

Landa's Algo-Heuristic Theory is somewhat similar to Structural Learning Theory in its focus on a type of "structure," but Landa's approach places even greater emphasis on interactions with the subject matter than on the subject matter, per se. The focus is less on the hierarchical structure of the content and more on the procedural cognitive operations involved in learning and using knowledge. Although it is not so clear with the present subject matter as would be the case with some other content, Landa's approach especially attempts to discern how "experts" approach the subject matter so that "novices" can be taught similar ideas and procedures. Typically, this consists of a combination of "algorithms" (dependable, step-by-step procedures) and "heuristics" ("rules of thumb," when no set procedures are appropriate). Chapter 4 includes examples of how this can be done as well as some cautions about the difficulties of identifying these cognitive operations and of teaching them to students. One of the contributions of this theory is its central concern with clarifying both the hierarchical organization of the subject matter and the different types of cognitive operations that students need to learn.

One general idea should be noted about these three chapters: All three of these theories involve the assumption that the cognitive operations provide necessary and sufficient conditions for appropriate behavior to occur. That, of course, is consistent with cognitive psychology's central concerns but contrasts with almost a "reverse" order found in behavioral theories like that provided by Gropper.

Chapter 9 provides the only example, in this collection, of theories that have some affiliation with or compatibility with humanistic psychology. However, Keller's approach primarily focuses on "motivational" aspects and devotes little attention to other intrapersonal and interpersonal variables characteristically found as a central part of humanistic psychology theories. Figure 9.1 provides an overview of the basic categories of motivational variables in the ARCS (Attention, Relevance, Confidence, Satisfaction) Model. It is from these main components and their subsidary concepts that Keller proposes to gain and to maintain the motivation of students. Note that affective, behavioral, and cognitive aspects are addressed, but that the underlying idea is to get and keep the student involved in the instructional ideas and activities. Many of the techniques and examples in this chapter are consistent with the research findings and theory about "effective" classroom teachers. In some respects it can be said that the other theories in this collection consider how students interact with the subject matter. However, application of the ARCS Model requires that the instructional designer and practitioner continually attempt to get the student's perspective, to detect why and how the student might be motivated to learn this content.

The other three theories can be labeled "eclectic," although each of these three involves a different approach. The examples of eclectic instructional theories consist of the following: Gagné and Briggs's Task Analysis Theory (chapter 2), Merrill's Component Display Theory (chapter 7), and Reigeluth's Elaboration Theory (chapter 8). They are eclectic in at least two ways: (a) they address a wide range of issues with regard to the subject matter, rather than focusing primarily or exclusively on narrowly defined instructional objectives and techniques; (b) they use diverse resources as a basis for their instructional plans instead of deriving ideas only from some single theory or narrowly oriented approach to instruction. Obviously, there are some constraints on the range of issues addressed by each of these theories. However, these three theories are comparatively broader in perspective than many other instructional theories.

The earliest established theory (of these three) is the Task Analysis Theory of Gagné and Briggs. This theory was developed in its initial form before "instructional theory" had received much formal recognition. The Gagné and Briggs approach emphasizes classifying instructional objectives in terms of tasks involved so that an appropriate learning theory, and its relatd instructional principles and techniques, can be used to design nine types of "events of instruction." It formally accommodates (in ascending order of emphasis in this theory) teaching attitudes, motor skills, and cognitive skills, although the theory does not include some of the higher-level cognitive processes nor their interrelationships, such as are included in the three cognitive theories (chapters 4, 5, and 6). In the early uses of this theory there was some tendency to focus on behavioral objectives and to draw from behavioral learning theory; but both the topics addressed and the resources used are broader today, as is evident in the examples in chapter 2.

Merrill's Component Display Theory (chapter 7) and Reigeluth's Elaboration Theory (chapter 8) actually should be considered more as complementary theories than as competing approaches. Merrill's theory explicitly focuses on the details of instruction, and it is referred to as a "micro" theory. In contrast, Reigeluth's theory is considered a "macro" theory because it addresses broader issues in the design of instruction. Both theories are eclectic with regard to the instructional features that they can address as well as with regard to the research and theory that serve as foundations for the instructional design.

As is noted in chapter 7, the Component Display Theory should be applicable to a wide range of education and training contexts in that it addresses components of importance in virtually any instructional presentation. Component Display Theory is especially useful in making certain that there is consistency across designation of objectives, presentation of instruction, and evaluation of outcomes. This consistency can be attained by using a two-dimensional performance-content classification system, a taxonomy of presentation forms, and a set of prescriptions or guidelines for relating the classification system and the presentation forms. Thus, Component Display Theory provides more details about the presentation of instruction than do the Gagné and Briggs theory and the Reigeluth theory. The examples provided in chapter 7 illustrate how different instructional objectives can be classified and related to appropriate instructional techniques. It should be noted that although Component Display Theory does address instructional events in considerable detail, it still is possible for instructors to implement the prescriptions in many different ways. This theory mainly provides the context within which the specific instructional procedures can be planned and implemented.

As a "macro" theory, Reigeluth's Elaboration Theory (chapter 8) was developed to aid users in relating the general purposes of instruction to plans for the instruction. This theory intentionally does not specify how the instruction is to be presented. It does provide a means for examining how the aspects of the instructional activities relate to each other and to organized plans reflecting the purposes of the instruction. Guidelines derived from this theory include prescriptions for structuring and sequencing a course so that the component parts and the overall goals of the course or curriculum will be addressed in an appropriate manner. The subject matter selected for applications in this book led to a "simple-to-complex" sequence, but you should recognize that other approaches could be derived from this theory for different subject matter. Note that the individual components that are identified in chapter 8 are generally similar to those in other chapters but that Elaboration Theory emphasizes identifying the rationale and plans for relationships among component parts. Of three types of knowledge explicitly accommodated in Elaboration Theory (conceptual, procedural, theoretical), the author of chapter 8 selected a theoretical organization. As a result, the analytic procedures and the instructional interventions differ, for example, from some of the procedural features emphasized in Landa's Algo-Heuristic Theory approach (chapter 4). In examining carefully the application of Elaboration Theory (as well as the other theories), you should keep in mind the fact that the subject matter addressed partly delimits and shapes the manner in which topics have been addressed by the theory.

Concluding Observations and Comments

This book and the earlier companion volume (Reigeluth, 1983) have provided a reasonably representative sample of currently available instructional theories. The earlier volume offered descriptions of each theory. The present volume illustrates how each of these theories might be applied to the same subject matter and instructional objectives. What can we conclude about use of these theories in particular, and about applications of instructional theories more generally? Answers to such a general question should include perspectives drawn from past experiences and from emergent trends that may be relevant to the development and use of instructional theory.

Historical Perspective and Contemporary Trends. Most authors seem to agree that instructional theory has been recognized as a viable entity only since midcentury, starting with programmed instruction and other education/training ventures in the middle to late 1950s. (See more details about these historical patterns in Snelbecker, 1985, chapter 5, and Snelbecker, 1983). This "starting point" in the 1950s is identified even though it is recognized that over the centuries people have expressed views about instruction and have proposed various "education theories," and that research relevant to instruction has been conducted since at least the late nineteenth century. What did emerge at midcentury were theories (only later identified formally as instructional theories) that involve systematic efforts to clarify instructional objectives, to provide detailed descriptions of techniques and conditions that can facilitate attainment of those objectives, and to use empirical scientific methods to assess merits and to plan modifications of the theories and the instructional plans.

It also seems reasonably clear that progress in the development of instructional theories has not been consistently positive! Since the enthusiasm of the 1950s and 1960s, instructional theory has not had stable support or reception within the education and training communities, although groups have continued to develop and to use instructional theory even while such were not "popular" ventures. It is noteworthy that the work on the theories described in this book proceeded during years in which there was less enthusiasm and support as well as during times when this general enterprise was more favorably received and supported.

Since the late 1970s, there has again emerged considerable support for instructional theory development and use. The resurgence of interest and support can quite readily be linked to two general "events." One consists of the emerging uses of microcomputers in education and training. The other involves residual reactions to the numerous reports that have been raising questions about our educational establishment and have been pointing to the need to improve the quality of instruction. Let's consider these two "events" and their implications for further development and use of instructional theory. Each has the potential for fulfilling the criteria that were identified by Kirst and Meister (1985) as being necessary for success as an educational innovation, namely the existence of an identifiable support group and constituency, and means for monitoring cost-effective applications.

The emergence of more and more powerful microcomputers at continually decreasing costs has stimulated expectations about assistance that could come from technology-assisted instruction. Although many have and will raise questions about the worth of some microcomputer applications in education and training (cf. Snelbecker & Stepansky, 1985a), few will wonder if there is an identifiable, enthusiastic support group and consistuency for technology-assisted instruction. But getting technology-assisted instruction designed and presented in ways that are relevant, effective, and within reasonable cost constraints is much more difficult than most instructors and administrators have realized. Instructional theory could make major contributions by helping to identify both the characteristics needed to facilitate learning and the design-development steps required to "produce" the necessary instructional resources and systems. In ways not really possible with conventional classroom instruction, technology-assisted learning includes means for leaving "audit trails" of steps taken and progress attained (for individuals and for groups) as well as for providing guidelines for improving the instructional plans and theories.

On numerous previous occasions (e.g., Snelbecker, 1983) I've suggested that there can emerge a positive reciprocal relationship between these computer uses and the development and use of instructional theory. Just as World War I requirements established expectations and support for standardized testing, so the current needs for producing good quality technology-assisted learning can enhance expectations and support for the further development and use of instructional theory.

The second general "event" of our times that can further enhance the development and use of instructional theory is the increasing pressure for improvement in the quality of instruction available to students. Although some debates have emphasized "curricular" changes, here I will focus on the concerns being expressed—by the general public as well as by professionals in the field—about the need to improve the quality of instruction in education and training contexts. During the past several years a series of reports have identified problems and have called for reforms. For the first time, discussions about selecting textbooks now include comments that instructional theory and instructional design can be useful. Similarly, more and more discussions about the future of educational psychology have included suggestions and recommendations that instructional theory and instructional design should be a more central part of that field.

Observations About These Approaches Collectively.   What can be said, finally, about the present collection of theories as well as the broader work concerning development and use of instructional theories? The answers to this question partly can be phrased in general terms and partly will depend on each person's interest in and expectations about instructional theories. I've already identified two major groups, respectively, as (a) researchers and theorists; and (b) designers and practitioners. I'll first consider readers in general, and then the two general groups noted.

Both my comments in this chapter and the respective chapter authors' comments have provided you with guidelines about the "central" topics for each theory and, sometimes by explicit comment and other times by mere omission, those topics that either are ignored or are "peripheral" for each theory. You should recognize that no theory can possibly address all aspects of a given instructional setting and that each theory must set some priorities for topics to be addressed. Nonetheless, this collection of theories and their applications to the designated subject matter should provide you with informative and practically useful samples. From these samples plus further examination of the theories, you should be able to recognize the extent to which any given theory may be relevant and appropriate for a practical situation. Moreover, by careful examination and study of the theories presented in this book, you should also evolve some procedures and decision rules that can aid you in evaluating the potential value of other instructional theories you may encounter.

Are these the only instructional theories that are worthy of your attention? Certainly not! These eight theories do provide you with a reasonably representative sample of well-developed instructional theories. However, by no means should you consider this collection to be a comprehensive listing or an exhaustive array of currently available instructional theories. You can find, for example, additional models and theories oriented toward training contexts in such sources as Anderson and Goodson's (1980) paper. A good array of education-oriented theories can be found in the book by Joyce and Weil (1982).

How "good" are the present theories? Obviously, they were considered to be of some value, or they simply would not have been included here. As one basis for comparison, you might want to review a paper by Rosenberg (1982) entitled "The ABCs of ISD" (Instructional Systems Design). In that paper Rosenberg describes some of the fundamental features of instructional theories as they typically are applied in the design of instruction. The present collection of theories goes well beyond the minimal features ("ABCs") included in Rosenberg's paper. Many instructional-design efforts tend to be limited to clarifying objectives and evaluating students' progress, with only "intuitive" means provided for designing instructional techniques, procedures, and resources. The present collection of theories not only addresses the curriculum design issues and evaluation issues but also includes additional systematic provisions relevant to instructional techniques, procedures, and resources. In particular, the present collection of theories provides quite extensive, systematic, and detailed provisions for planning, presenting, and evaluating instructional endeavors.

Is there really a need for instructional theory if we use computers? Won't computers make all of this analysis and planning unnecessary? It is quite surprising to find such questions as these raised frequently by otherwise knowledgeable persons. Yes, computer technology and other forms of "high technology" can and should have an important role in today's and tomorrow's schools. However, we should recognize that someone or some group must make decisions about the instructional relevance of whatever uses we make of computers. Earlier (Snelbecker, 1982), I strongly emphasized that uses of computers require at least as much of the careful planning that we long have recognized as being necessary for any other instructional resources. Many authors have raised serious questions about the propriety of using computers without adequate examination of the contributions being made to the teaching/learning processes and outcomes (cf. Bonham 1983; Raben, 1983; Rossman, 1984; Snelbecker & Stepansky, 1985a). Instructional theory can constitute one means by which we can decide why and how to use various instructional resources.

Are instructional theories relevant only in military or industry training contexts? This is a question often raised by educators. Recently we (Snelbecker & Stepansky, 1985b) conducted a very extensive search of literature and a series of contacts with authors who typically had worked only in education or in training. Our intent was to conduct a functional analysis of the topics they addressed and the descriptions/prescriptions they have formulated concerning the design of effective, efficient, and enticing instruction. What was abundantly clear was that so-called "teacher effectiveness" studies, usually conducted in classrooms, and various forms of instructional-design projects, typically conducted in training contexts, had identified many of the same issues, problems, and solutions concerning instruction! More recently, in conjunction with some convention sessions on instructional design and through other meetings, I've had the opportunity to be in communication with a wide range of people concerned with instruction. They come from industry, higher education, intermediate units, early childhood education, the military, etc. From their comments it is reasonably clear that, despite differences that obviously may stem from their "local" situation, there are many matters for which communication across instructional contexts could help to clarify issues and aid in finding means for improving instruction.

Consequently, it seems clear that the theories presented in this book can be applied in a wide range of situations where people are concerned with improving the quality of instruction.

Earlier I did distinguish between the interests and expectations of researchers and theorists versus those of designers and practitioners. A few comments in closing are addressed to each of these audiences.

Researchers and theorists should learn from these chapters that far more needs to be done to expand the range of variables addressed in our currently available instructional theories. Yes, we should be pleased about the progress that has been made, especially in the few decades in which research and theory have focused on instructional topics per se. However, there is much more work to be done. Researchers and theorists should be aware of each time one of the applications of the theory in this book did not address all relevant aspects, and should use these as opportunities to improve on our current efforts.

Designers and practitioners should, of course, find numerous instances in which these chapters can provide guidelines for addressing practical problems. However, you should never overlook the limitations of the theory. A prudent approach is always to proceed with caution and to evaluate relatively modest implementations of plans before embarking on more ambitious applications. No matter whether you choose to rely on one theory or more, you should exercise discretion in selecting the ideas you plan to implement and in evaluating the results of your efforts. In a sense, these theories and our efforts (as designers or as practitioners)—no matter what rationales we have to guide them—are only as "good" as they prove to be in facilitating learning for our students, whether in education or training contexts.

REFERENCES

Anderson, G. H., & Goodson, L. A. (1980) A comparative analysis of models of instructional design. *Journal of Instructional Development, 3,* 2–16.

Bonham, G. W. (1983). Computer mania: Academe's inadequate response to the implications of the new technology. *The Chronicle of Higher Education,* (March) *1983,* 72.

Goldfried, M. R. (1980). Toward the delineation of therapeutic change principles. *American Psychologist, 35,* 991–999.

Joyce, F., & Weil, M. (1980). *Models of teaching* (2nd ed.) Englewood Cliffs, NJ: Prentice-Hall.

Kendler, H. H. (1952). What is learned?—A theoretical blind alley. *Psychological Review, 59,* 269–277.

Kirst, M. W., & Meister, G. R. (1985). Turbulence in American secondary schools: What reforms last? *Curriculum Inquiry, 15,* 169–186.

Murray, E. J. (1986). Possibilities and promises of eclecticism. In J. C. Norcross (Ed.), *Handbook of eclectic psychotherapy.* NY: Brunner/Mazel.

Norcross, J. C. (1985). For discriminating clinicians only. (Review of *Differential therapeutics in psychiatry: The art and science of treatment selection* by A. Frances, J. Clarkin, and S. Perry. *Contemporary Psychology, 30,* 757–758.

Norcross, J. C. (Ed.). (1986). *Handbook of eclectic psychotherapy.* NY: Brunner-Mazel.

Raben, J. (1983). Advent of the post-Guttenberg university. *Academe—Bulletin of the AAUP, 69,* No. 2, 21–27.

Reigeluth, C. M. (Ed.). (1983). Instructional design theories and models: An overview of their current status. Hillsdale, NJ: Lawrence Erlbaum Associates.

Rosenberg, M. J. (1982). The ABC's of ISD. *Training and Development Journal, 36,* 44–50.

Rossman, M. (1984, February). How to use the computer in science class (and how not to). *Classroom Computer Learning,* 13–18.

Smith, D. (1982). Trends in counseling and psychotherapy. *American Psychologist, 37,* 802–809.

Snelbecker, G. E. (1982). Impact of computers and electronic technology on the teaching methodologies and the learning process. *Journal of Children in Contemporary Society, 14,* 43–53.

Snelbecker, G. E. (1983). Is instructional theory alive and well? In Charles M. Reigeluth (Ed.), *Instructional design theories and models: An overview of their current status.* Hillsdale, NJ: Lawrence Erlbaum Associates.

Snelbecker, G. E. (1985). *Learning theory, instructional theory and psychoeducational design.* Lanham, MD: University Press of America. (Originally published by McGraw-Hill, 1974.)

Snelbecker, G. E., & Stepansky, D. S. (1985a). "GIGO" (Garbage In, Garbage Out)—How does it apply to computer-based instruction? Paper presented at the 26th International Meeting of the Association for the Development of Computer-Based Instructional Systems, Philadelphia, March 26. *26th ADCIS Conference Proceedings.* Bellingham, WA: ADCIS.

Snelbecker, G. E., & Stepansky, D. S. (1985b). Implications of instructional design for classroom teachers? Paper presented at the Annual Meeting of the American Educational Research Association, Chicago, April 1.

Author Index

Subject Index